SOCIAL STUDIES TEACHER'S SURVIVAL KIT

SOCIAL STUDIES TEACHER'S SURVIVAL KIT

Ready-to-Use Activities for Teaching Specific Skills in Grades 7–12

Ronald L. Partin

and

Martha T. Lovett

THE CENTER FOR APPLIED
RESEARCH IN EDUCATION
West Nyack, New York 10995

THE CENTER FOR APPLIED
RESEARCH IN EDUCATION

West Nyack, N.Y.

10 9

Library of Congress Cataloging-in-Publication Data

Partin, Ronald L.
Social studies teacher's survival kit: ready-to-use activities for teaching specific skills in grades 7-12 / Ronald L. Partin and Martha T. Lovett.
p. cm.
ISBN 0-87628-782-8
1. Social sciences—Study and teaching (Secondary)—United States. 2. Activity programs in education—United States. 3. Creative activities and seat work. I. Lovett, Martha T. II. Title.
H62.5.U5P36 1989
300'.7'1273—dc19 88-29957
CIP

ISBN 0-87628-782-8

THE CENTER FOR APPLIED RESEARCH IN EDUCATION
West Nyack, NY 10994

On the World Wide Web at http://www.phdirect.com

Printed in the United States of America

ABOUT THE AUTHORS

RONALD L. PARTIN, Ph.D., is Professor of Educational Foundations and Inquiry and Coordinator of the Guidance and Counseling Program at Bowling Green State University. As a counselor educator, he has taught courses in counseling, educational consultation, group dynamics, and learning psychology. A former high school teacher and coach, Dr. Partin has taught social studies for eight years.

Dr. Partin has presented over two hundred workshops and seminars to schools throughout Ohio. In addition to numerous journal articles, Dr. Partin has coauthored P.R.I.D.E., a training program on effective classroom management, which has been completed by over thirty thousand teachers nationwide.

MARTHA T. LOVETT received her Ph.D. in Educational Administration and Supervision from Bowling Green State University. She is currently Director of Graduate Programs at Converse College in Spartanburg, South Carolina. Her teaching experience includes teaching social studies at both the junior high and senior high levels.

In addition to presenting many workshops throughout Ohio, Wisconsin, Michigan, and Virginia, and to being a member of several professional organizations, Dr. Lovett has recently been elected to *Who's Who in American Education* for 1988.

ABOUT THIS BOOK

As a secondary social studies teacher, you want to offer your students a variety of stimulating teaching activities. However, because of the paucity of ready-made materials at this level, you may have had to design your own or to gradually accumulate ideas from other teachers and from professional publications. These are very time-consuming and haphazard approaches.

The *Social Studies Teacher's Survival Kit* provides you with over 110 learning activities that encourage active student participation and involvement in the subject. The book's focus is on skill and attitude development, rather than on knowledge accumulation. These activities, for grades 7–12, are intended to communicate that the social studies are relevant to students' daily lives and can be interesting and even fun. Each teaching strategy aims to stimulate your students' appreciation and to bring home their involvement in their immediate world.

Here you will find a variety of ready-to-use teaching ideas, homework suggestions, long-term assignments, and projects. The content is not tied to any particular text but enhances the broader skills usually included in all secondary social studies courses.

The teaching activities in this book are organized into seven sections:

- American History
- World History
- American Government
- Consumer Economics
- Sociology
- Psychology
- Geography

The activities within each chapter are arranged in order of increasing difficulty with suggested grade levels. Of course, the appropriateness of any activity must be based on the capabilities and needs of your students. Moreover, most activities can be modified to fit your particular objectives and class situation, making them simple to adapt.

Each section also includes a variety of reproducible activity sheets and handouts to accompany the teaching activities. These include questionnaires, interview forms, graphs, crossword puzzles, maps, and simulation games. Suggestions for relevant field trips, resource persons, and addresses of organizations worth writing to are included at the end of each chapter.

A special feature of the book is the appendixes that include current addresses of major distributors of social studies films, as well as those of foreign embassies. You will also find answer keys to all the activity sheets.

The *Social Studies Teacher's Survival Kit* can be used in a variety of ways. Many of the activities are designed as long-term assignments that can be completed either individually or in teams, while others require total class involvement in producing a final product such as a newspaper. Several activities can be quickly inserted into your lessons if you have extra time available. Others are suitable as enrichment activities for more advanced students. Some projects require the students to interact with parents, senior citizens, local officials, peers, or community leaders, giving them an even greater sense of how social studies is part of the everyday world they live in.

We invite you to use the *Social Studies Teacher's Survival Kit* to make social studies both inviting and fun for yourself and your students. Enjoy it!

Ronald L. Partin
Martha T. Lovett

CONTENTS

Chapter 4
CONSUMER ECONOMICS • 120

Chapter 5
SOCIOLOGY • 148

Chapter 6
PSYCHOLOGY • 182

Chapter 7
GEOGRAPHY • 236

SOCIAL STUDIES TEACHER'S SURVIVAL KIT

Chapter 1

AMERICAN HISTORY

History can be fun! It can also be relevant to students' daily lives. Research on learning has shown that 80 percent of the dates, names, places, and other facts memorized are completely forgotten one year later. The lasting impact of studying American history comes not from the facts memorized but from the skills and attitudes developed.

The activities included in this section have as a common goal to make American history come alive, to convince students that every day they are living a part of the history of their country. Many of these activities encourage students to see the effect historical events have had on their own lives.

Projects such as collecting oral history or working on family trees help bridge the gap between generations and help students see their parents and grandparents from a different perspective. When students explore the historical changes of their neighborhood or school, past events are given personal meaning. They see that they are a part of that heritage.

Through activities such as "On-the-Spot Reporting," the "Who Am I?" game, or "Publishing a Newspaper," students hone their skills of historical inquiry and critical thinking.

The maxim that students "learn by doing" was first proposed by Aristotle and later reiterated by John Dewey. There is no reason that American history should remain a passive experience dominated by lectures and worksheets. The variety of activities in this chapter will both motivate and challenge your students.

(1-1) "WHO AM I?" GAME

Objectives:
- To review reading assignments
- To develop an interest in historical persons

Grade Level: 7–8

Time Required: 15–40 minutes

Materials Needed: None

Description:

1. After giving some examples, have students develop lists of clues for persons who have been studied in class or through reading. Usually 5 to 6 clues per subject are sufficient. For example:

   "Who am I?"

   "I graduated from West Point."

   "I was a general in the Civil War."

   "I completed my *Memoirs* of the Civil War four days before I died."

   "I was elected president of the United States in 1868."

   (Answer: U.S. Grant)

2. The class can be broken into 2 or more teams. Alternating turns, a team receives a clue. If they answer correctly based on the first clue, the team receives 10 points; after the second, 8 points, and so on. You may want to keep the clues on file for future classes.

(1-2) PERSONAL TIMELINES

Objectives:
- To introduce the concept of the timeline
- To increase the teacher's knowledge of students' personal lives
- To reinforce the concept of selection of data in historical reporting

Grade Level: 7–8

Time Required: 30 minutes

Materials Needed: None

Description:

1. Have students draw a line on a 2–3 foot roll of paper (or several sheets taped together). They should mark the line at equal intervals: 1 or 1½ inches equals one year. The students then indicate above the line the major personal events that have occurred during their lives. They might include

births of siblings, major trips, accidents, most important accomplishments, and so on. (See the sample.)

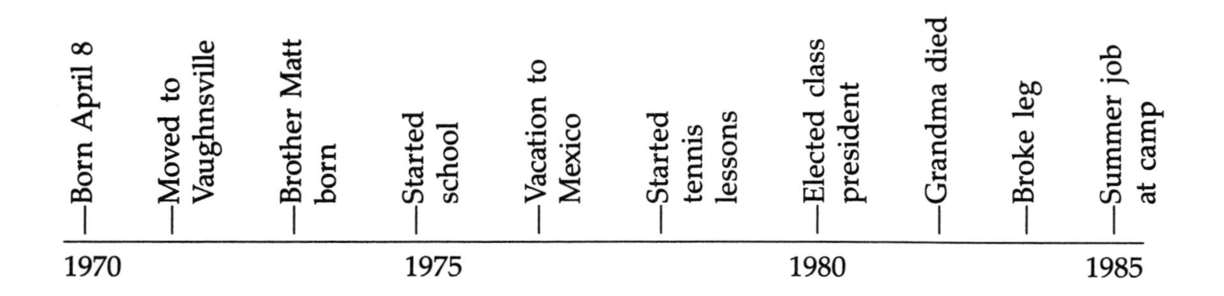

2. On top of the line, students should indicate the major world events that have occurred during their lifetime. You might choose to demonstrate the process by drawing your own timeline on a chalkboard.

(1-3) ON-THE-SPOT REPORTING

Objectives:
- To stimulate an interest in historical events
- To encourage objectivity

Grade Level: 7–9

Time Required: 2–10 minutes in each class

Materials Needed: None

Description:

1. Using the format of an "on-the-spot" television reporter, have students report on specific historical events as though they were there. Of course, they must study the details of the event before they can offer a complete and objective report. Working in groups, they might even interview eyewitnesses. The more enthusiastic students might choose to videotape their "reports," perhaps in period costumes. Reports might be of any historical event, such as battles, assassinations, introduction of new inventions, or major trials.
2. If you do not want to use class time for presentation of these reports, they can be written as dispatches from the field.

(1-4) BUGGY BUMPER STICKERS

Objective:
- To identify the major issues of a specific era to encourage creativity
- To encourage creativity

Grade Level: 7–11

Time Required: 40–60 minutes

Materials Needed: Variety of bumper stickers

Description:

1. Bring to class several bumper stickers that reflect people's opinions about current political and social issues (nuclear disarmament, abortion, drug abuse, presidential campaigns, and so on).
2. As homework, students might be assigned to record interesting bumper stickers related to local or national issues. They might even make facsimiles of the more interesting ones. Hang these around the room or assign a group of students to make a bulletin board display of them.
3. A group discussion can focus on the role and meaning of people displaying bumper stickers. The following questions might be considered:
   a. Why have bumper stickers become so popular?
   b. What can you learn about a car's owner from bumper stickers?
   c. In what ways might bumper stickers be of value to society or to the individual?
   d. Can they be harmful?
   e. What were the early historical equivalents of today's bumper stickers?
4. Slogans have been popular throughout American history. A few such as "California or Bust" may have appeared on buggies or wagons. Others may have been limited to newspapers and posters. Cite examples of slogans that might have appeared on bumper stickers had they been in vogue.

   For example: "Remember the *Maine*"
   "No Taxation Without Representation"
   "Fifty-four Forty or Fight"
   "Remember the Alamo"
   "Tippecanoe and Tyler Too"

   Solicit other examples from the class.

5. Assign the class to design buggy bumper stickers that may have been displayed during earlier eras of American history. These should accurately reflect the attitudes of an earlier group on some historical issue. Examples might include the following:

   Opposition to the whiskey tax
   Loyalists' support for the Crown
   Antifederal sentiment
   Muckraking
   Alien and Sedition Acts
   Antitrust movement
   The purchase of Alaska
   Carpetbaggers
   The McKinley Tariff
   Battleship diplomacy
   Free schools
   Labor organizing
   Woman's suffrage
   The gold standard
   Prohibition
   Trust-busting

(1-5) PRESIDENTS CROSSWORD PUZZLE

Objective: • To review and reinforce facts about the U.S. presidents

Grade Level: 7–12

Time Required: One period

Materials Needed: Copies of "Presidents Crossword Puzzle"

Description:

Distribute copies of the crossword puzzle for students to complete during class.

Name ______________________ Date ______________________

PRESIDENTS CROSSWORD PUZZLE

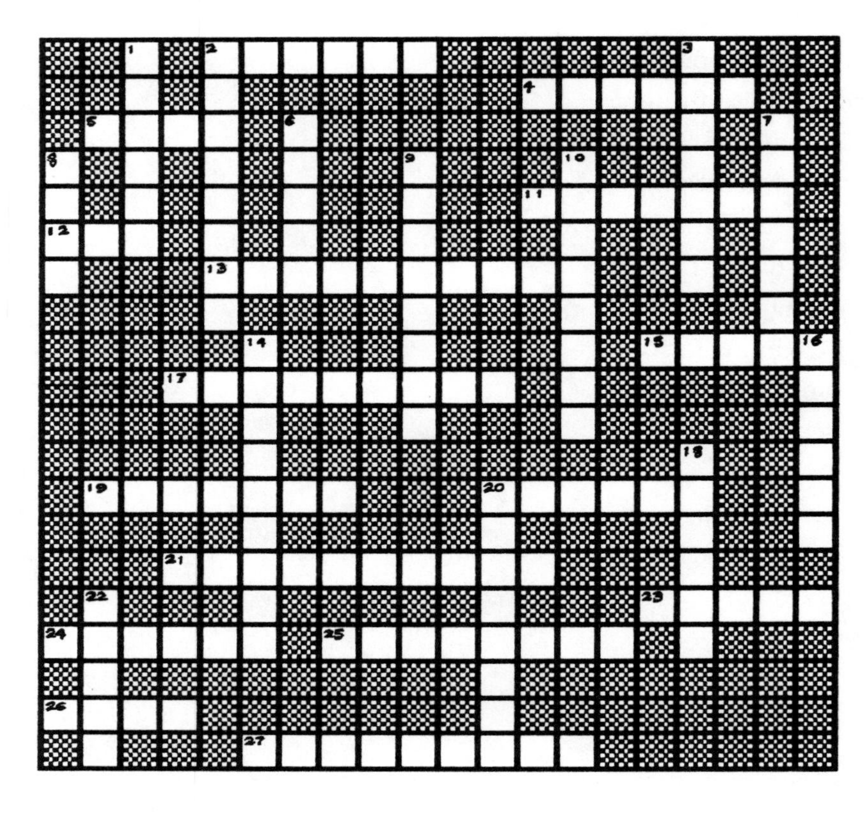

ACROSS

2. Guaranteed independence of western hemisphere from European interference
4. Former movie actor
5. Presided over Mexican War
11. "Old Hickory"
12. Longest-serving president (initials)
13. World War II general
15. Met Lee at Appomattox
17. Elected two nonconsecutive terms
19. President during Bay of Pigs invasion
20. A peanut farmer
21. "First in the hearts of his countrymen"
23. Husband of "Lemonade Lucy"
24. League of Nations promoter
25. Shot by Guiteau
26. Never elected president or vice-president
27. "The Rough Rider"

DOWN

1. Food administrator in World War I
2. Pulled into Spanish-American War
3. "The Father of the Constitution"
6. Father and son presidents
7. "The Great Emancipator"
8. Later, a chief justice
9. Only president to never marry
10. "Old Tippecanoe"
14. Sponsored the Louisiana Purchase
16. "Old Zack"
18. Fired MacArthur
20. "Silent Cal"
22. Only president to resign

(1-6) LOCAL HISTORY

Objectives:
- To develop the skills of historical research
- To use primary documents in reaching conclusions
- To personalize history
- To recognize the relationship of local and national events

Grade Level: 7–12

Time Required: Variable, depending on the depth of the project

Materials Needed: None

Description:

1. By studying the history of their own community, students can gain a greater appreciation of the interrelationship of historical events. A variety of primary sources are available for study, one of the rare opportunities for most students to utilize original resources in their study of history.
2. Local history can be studied through individual or group projects, interviews, guest speakers, or field trips. You may choose to study only one facet of the community's past, such as ethnic composition, commercial development, population shifts, its role in the Civil War, or its prominent citizens. An alternative would be to diffuse various aspects of local history study throughout the entire year.

Resources Available:

Cemeteries	Published local histories
Businesses	Older residents
City directories	Land office maps and deeds
Church records	Newspaper records
Census records	Local histories

Optional Activities:

1. Invite someone from a local business to describe the history of the company.
2. Interview the area's oldest residents for their recollections.
3. Graph the population growth of your community.

4. Plot the properties and the proportions of various ethnic groups if those data are available.
5. Ask a local genealogist to discuss the early families of your community. Some may be ancestors of your students.
6. Collect early photographs of the community and develop a display for your school or in another public building.
7. Draw a map of the community as it appeared in earlier records. If you can locate the information, it will be most valuable to compare the community's growth with several maps, for example, 1860, 1900, 1930, and the present.
8. Study the decline or transition of neighborhoods within the community.
9. Develop biographies of prominent or interesting people. Require that a variety of resources be used to gather the information. Have individual students look up the person's death, marriage, or other records at the courthouse.
10. Invite the county recorder or other government official to visit the class to describe the types of historical records maintained by that office.
11. Have a student investigate the geology of the local area by interviewing the county engineer, a geology professor, or a science teacher. Using their report on the major geological features of the area, have students identify the influence of those geological features on the development of the region.
12. Study the effect of the Depression on your community through newspapers, official employment records, or interviews.
13. Assign students to discover when telephone and electricity were first available to the community. When was the first road paved? The first school or church built? Who owned the first car or television? When was the last horse-drawn milk wagon used? Or streetcar? Or the last blacksmith?
14. If an early city directory or telephone directory can be found, have students report on the businesses listed. What occupations were represented?
15. Study the Indian tribes that originally inhabited your region.
16. Map the major arteries of migration to your community.
17. Take a field trip to any local archaeological excavations that might be available.

Helpful Resources:

Dymond, David P. *Writing Local History: A Practical Guide.* London: Bedford Square Press; Brookfield, VT: Distributed by Renouf, 1981.

Jolly, Brad. *Videotaping Local History.* Nashville, TN: American Association for State and Local History, 1982.

(1-7) PUBLISHING A NEWSPAPER

Objectives:
- To stimulate an interest in history
- To build research skills
- To enhance team-building skills

Grade Level: 7–12

Time Required: 3–6 weeks

Materials Needed: None

Description:

1. Have the class write and publish a newspaper covering the local and national news of a selected year. To provide sufficient material for inclusion, focus on the events of a two- to four-month period during the chosen year. Divide the tasks among students, preferably in teams. Roles needed would include editor, sketch artist, advertising department, reporters, layout, and copy editors.
2. Have students research the events of that time period through books, journals, and old newspapers at the library. They should choose a name for the newspaper. Studying an authentic paper of that era would help in determining the authentic writing style and layout to be used. Be sure to include not only descriptions of major national events but also local news. Other potential news items might include the following:

Sports results	Fads and fashions
Current music	Plays
Recent books published	New inventions patented
New products marketed	Natural disasters and accidents
Weather	Local births and deaths

3. Seek help from a typing class in editing the final version. Some schools have print shops that might cooperate with the project. If none is available, mimeograph and distribute copies of the final edition.

Helpful Resources:

Old newspapers and magazines; local museums; courthouse records for births, deaths, crimes, trials, land sales; and so on.

(1-8) HISTORY OF LOCAL SCHOOLS

Objectives:
- To use primary resources for historical research
- To enhance interviewing skills

Grade level: 7–12

Time Required: 3–5 weeks

Materials Needed: Copies of "A History of Our Local Schools" outline; copies of "Student Interview Form"

Description:

1. As a group project, investigate the history of education in your community. Students should be encouraged to examine local documents related to the school system's development. Encourage students to gain a full picture of early schools. Details such as school hours, lunches, sports teams, and school social life will give them a comparison with their own experiences.
2. Different groups might be assigned to other tasks such as the following:
   a. Making a map locating each school building in the area's history
   b. Locating pictures of each school building
   c. Writing an accurate description of school life at the time of the opening of the first school in the area
   d. Interviewing retired teachers and administrators about their school experiences
   e. Searching early newspapers for articles related to your schools
3. Distribute copies of "A History of Our Local Schools" outline and "Student Interview Form."

A HISTORY OF OUR LOCAL SCHOOLS

I. First Schools
   A. The first free schools
      1. Date
      2. Location
      3. Founders
      4. Early school life
   B. The first high school
      1. Date
      2. Location
      3. Building
      4. Teachers
      5. Administration
      6. The curriculum
      7. School life

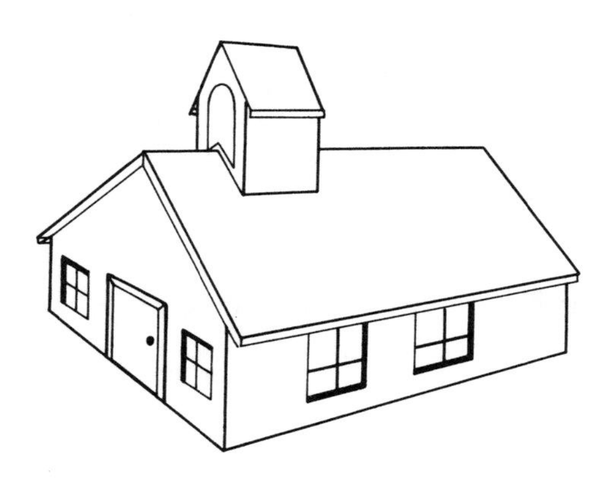

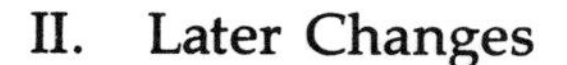

II. Later Changes
   A. Growth of schools
      1. New buildings
      2. Curriculum changes
      3. Enrollment data
      4. Significant local events (consolidations, fires, and so on)
   B. The faculty
      1. Roster of all who taught here
      2. Significant or interesting faculty
      3. Major events (strikes, unionization, and so on)
   C. The administration
      1. Roster of all administrators
      2. Major contributions
      3. Interesting anecdotes
   D. The students
      1. Prominent alumni
      2. Personal experiences
      3. Social life
      4. Extracurricular opportunities
   E. Our school today
      1. Buildings
      2. Faculty
      3. Administration
      4. School life
      5. Changes in school rules and privileges

STUDENT INTERVIEW FORM

Interviewer's Name ______________________________ Date__________

____

Name of person interviewed ______________________________

When did you first attend school here? ______________________

Which buildings did you attend? ___________________________

What is your earliest memory of school here?

Who were your teachers?

Describe a typical school day:

How do you think school life differed then as compared to today?

What was your school social life like? What did you do for fun?

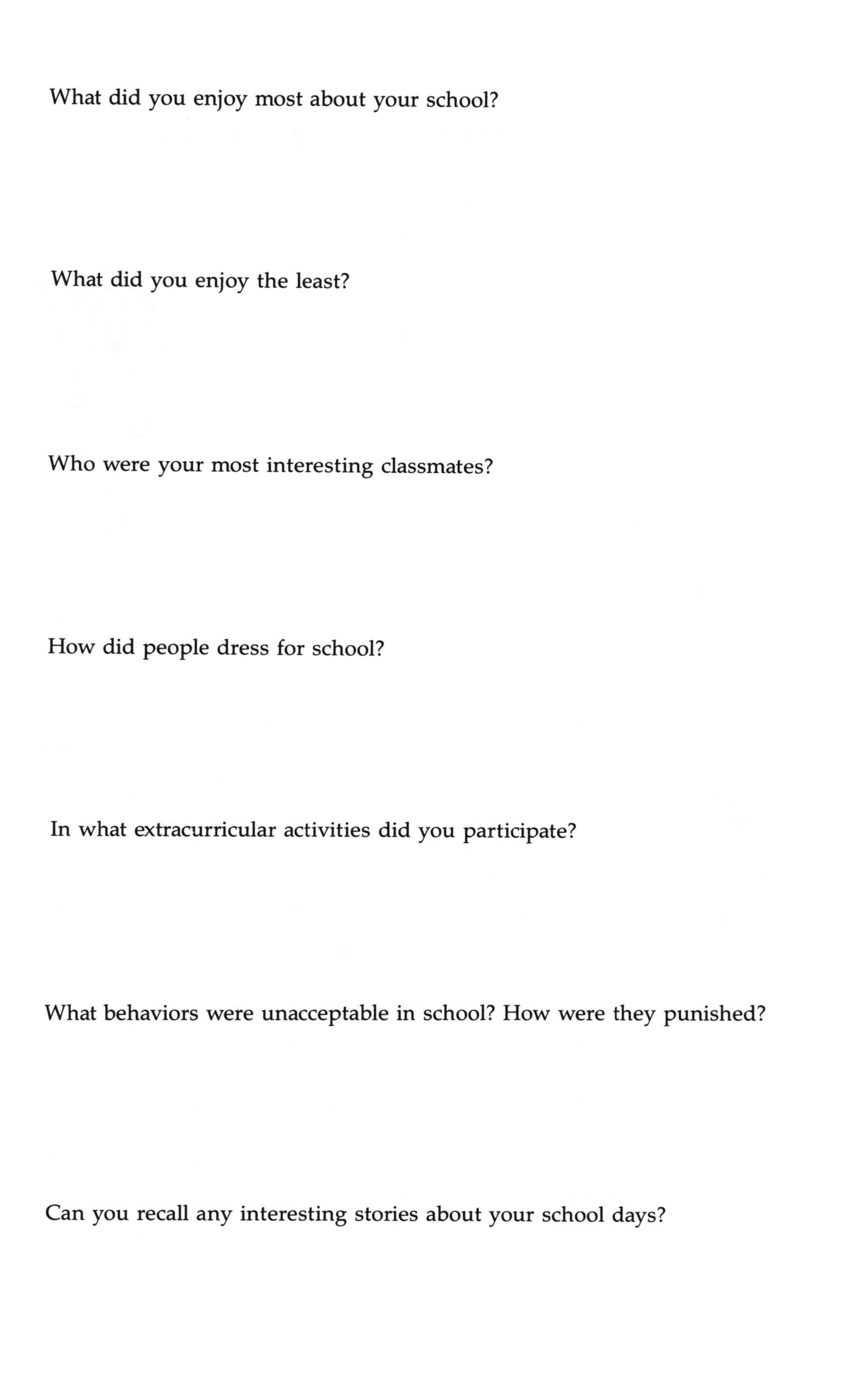

What did you enjoy most about your school?

What did you enjoy the least?

Who were your most interesting classmates?

How did people dress for school?

In what extracurricular activities did you participate?

What behaviors were unacceptable in school? How were they punished?

Can you recall any interesting stories about your school days?

(1-9) PRESS CONFERENCE INTERVIEWS

Objectives:
- To develop empathy for other people, especially those experiencing different conditions
- To encourage in-depth study of a historical character or event
- To develop listening skills

Grade Level: 7–12

Time Required: 1–2 weeks out-of-class preparation; 10–15 minutes per interview in class

Materials Needed: None

Description:

1. The press conference or interview is a valuable journalistic tool for gathering information about an event or a personality. To prepare for their interviews, all students are assigned or select roles of specific historical characters. It may be a well-known individual, such as Benjamin Franklin or Andrew Jackson, or a generalized role, such as a Confederate soldier or a worker involved in the Haymarket Affair.
2. The students prepare for the interview by studying the details of the era under consideration, including whatever eyewitness accounts may be available in the library. Encourage students to develop a sense of what it was like to be their assigned individuals and to formulate their "stories" based on accurate historical data.
3. The potential roles for interviews might include the following:

   Prisoner at the Civil War prison, Andersonville

   Tory during the American Revolution

   Two white southerners in 1850: one proslavery and one antislavery

   Cherokee Indian on the Trail of Tears

   Middle-class businessman experiencing the stock market crash in 1929

   Rider on the Pony Express

   Circuit-rider preacher

   Teacher in a one-room schoolhouse

   Passenger on the *Mayflower*

   Indian at the Battle of Wounded Knee

Flapper in the 1920s
Speakeasy owner and a prohibition official
Naval officer at Manila during the Spanish American War
Irish immigrant in the 1850s
Passenger on an early railroad
U.S. soldier in the Battle of the Bulge
Astronaut on a trip to the moon
Vietnam War draft evader in Canada
Representative to the Continental Congress
Whig
Early nineteenth-century doctor
Witness to the Boston Massacre
Temperance leader
Worker on the Panama Canal
South Carolina "nullifier" in 1832
Child working in a New England mill during the 1810s
"Forty-niner" California gold miner
John Brown follower at Harpers Ferry
Reconstruction Era carpetbagger
Labor union organizer in 1900
WPA laborer
Hooverville occupant during the Depression
Supporter of the Marshall Plan

4. The interviews might be scheduled periodically over several weeks, allowing 10–15 minutes for each. Two or 3 individuals might be interviewed together in a "Meet the Press" format. The entire class, an assigned committee, or the teacher could assume the task of asking questions designed to explore the historical event. While their answers should be based on valid research into the topic, students should be encouraged to project the feelings and attitudes that they believe to be consistent with their role.

(1-10) STUDYING A LOCAL HISTORICAL BUILDING

Objectives:
- To personalize history through local resources
- To develop skills of historical research
- To gain experience in using primary resources

Grade Level: 7–12

Time Required: 3–7 weeks

Materials Needed: Copies of "Architectural Survey Interview Guide"

Description:

1. Select a building that is of architectural or historical significance. It may be an older building, such as a library, jail, barn, school, church, or post office. The role of the building in the development of the community, its designer, or its noteworthy architectural style can be considered in choosing a building to study.

2. The entire class may study one building, with various teams researching different aspects of the building's history, or groups can be assigned to pursue a building's history through each of the various resources listed below.

3. Group assignments can be carried out as long-term assignments or as part of a class field trip. By having the project featured in the local newspaper, you may invite assistance from local residents. Using the "Architectural Survey Interview Guide," assign students to interview architects, occupants, owners, public officials, and others connected with the history of the selected building.

4. The following are the data to collect:
   a. *Type of architectural style.* Local architects and books such as those listed on the following page will help in identifying the particular type of architecture represented by your selected building.
   b. *Has the building been modified?* Were major modifications made to the building? What was the purpose of such changes? To add more room? Change the function of the building? Did such changes reflect a different architectural style? What restoration attempts have been made?
   c. *Who occupied the building?* Discover as much as you can about the people who owned and used the building. What was their role in local history?
   d. *How did historical events affect the building?* Did the Depression force the building to be sold? Was it used for different purposes during wartime?

5. To present the research, the class can put together a documented record of the building, including not only the written narrative but also photographs, copies of relevant documents, and sketches, where available. The report might be presented to the local library or historical society. The local newspapers may even do a feature article on the building, based on the class's research.

Resources Available:

Architects	Local libraries
City records	Newspapers
Local histories	Historical societies
Current occupants	Building owners
Tax records	Local residents

Helpful Resources:

Ball, V. K. *Architective and Interior Design: Europe and America.* New York: Wiley, 1980.

Blumenson, J. G. *Identifying American Architecture: A Pictorial Guide to Styles and Terms, 1960–1945.* Nashville, TN: 1978.

Diamonstein, B. *Buildings Reborn: New Uses, Old Places.* New York: Harper and Row, 1978.

Poppeliers, John C. *What Style Is It?: A Guide to American Architecture.* Washington, DC: Preservation Press, 1983.

Wiffen, M. *American Architecture Since 1780—A Guide to Styles.* Cambridge: M.I.T. Press, 1969.

ARCHITECTURAL SURVEY INTERVIEW GUIDE

Name of Interviewer ______________________ Date of Interview__________

Name of Resource Person ______________________________

Address of Building ______________________________

____

Year of construction ______________ Original owner ______________

Current owner ______________ Current occupant(s) ______________

Previous owners of this property ______________________________

Do you know of any existing photographs of this building?

Who has occupied this building previously?

What interesting events have occurred in this building?

What additions or changes have been made to this building?

What architectural style is this building?

(1-11) MAKING HISTORY COME ALIVE THROUGH ORAL HISTORY

Objectives:
- To increase students' interest in history
- To develop interviewing skills
- To stimulate students' curiosity about their personal heritage

Grade Level: 9–12

Time Required: Variable: can be a one-night assignment or woven through the entire course

Materials Needed: None

Description:

1. An oral history project can be as large or as small as you wish. It might be simply interviewing parents or grandparents about their early work experiences, or as broad as the extremely successful Foxfire Project, undertaken by a rural Georgia English teacher.
2. It is best to begin small. Select a topic or allow the students to do so. Oral history projects can focus on any topic or event related to the twentieth century. The purpose is to allow students to capitalize on the living resources in their community. Relatives, neighbors, senior citizens, and public officials are usually quite willing to share their early experience with adolescents. For many, it may be a rare opportunity to seriously talk with a person of another generation.
3. The following are some topic ideas:

    Physical changes in the neighborhood and the community
    School life
    Living through the Depression
    World War I or II from the eyes of veterans
    World War I or II on the home front
    Early movies and music
    Fads and fashions of the 1920s, 1930s, and so on
    Prohibition experiences
    Entertainment before television
    Changes in local transportation
    Community moralities
    Life in the home: appliances, chores, and so on

Lost handicraft skills (for example, soap making, horseshoeing)
Old-time farming
Life without electricity
Local disasters
Major crimes
Childhood heroes and heroines
Vietnam War experiences

4. Before sending students out to do live interviews, teach them interviewing skills. Let them practice interviewing you or each other first.
5. Have the class develop a list of questions to structure their interviews. It may be possible to have some resource person such as a retired citizen visit the school to be interviewed by the whole class or in small groups.
6. Out-of-school interviews will be reported more accurately if tape-recorded and then transcribed by students. This will take more time but yields greater accuracy.
7. It is generally best to have the oral history culminate in some type of product: a booklet, a written report, perhaps even a videotape. These may be used in future history classes or contributed to a local historical society, library, or museum.

(1-12) VALUES AND ADVERTISING

Objectives:

- To recognize the values of a society as reflected in its product advertisements
- To identify changes in the advertising approaches used by sellers
- To recognize instances of sexual and racial stereotyping as used in advertising

Grade Level: 10–12

Time Required: 2 hours

Materials Needed: Copies of "Advertisement Analysis Form"

Description:

1. Collect several popular magazines representing one or more decades from the 1920s through the 1980s. They may be all from one decade or, preferably, a few from each.

2. Using copies of the "Advertisement Analysis Form," have pairs of students examine and analyze the advertisements that appear in each magazine. This might be done as homework or in class. During the next class, students will report on their findings. Use the following questions to guide your discussion:
    a. For each decade, how were women portrayed? Were they in work roles? What kind?
    b. What sex role stereotypes were reinforced in the advertising? Were any of the stereotypes challenged?
    c. How were cigarettes promoted? What proportion of smokers depicted in the ads were women? What age did the smokers appear to be?
    d. What appeals did the advertisers employ in their ads? For status? Security? Sex appeal? Patriotism? Celebrity testimonials?
    e. How were minorities depicted in the advertisements?

Name ______________________ Date ______________________

ADVERTISEMENT ANALYSIS FORM

Magazine ______________________ Date of issue ______________

1. What products are advertised in this magazine?

2. How many men appear in the advertisements? ______ How many women? ______

3. In what work roles are men depicted?

4. In what work roles are women depicted?

5. To what needs do the advertisers seem to appeal?

6. Do minorities appear in any of the advertisements in the magazine?

   a. How many?

   b. In what roles?

   c. For what products?

(1-13) GENEALOGICAL RESEARCH IN THE HISTORY CLASS*

Objectives:
- To develop a personal interest in history
- To enhance students' awareness of their cultural and ethnic heritage
- To develop problem-solving skills

Grade Level: 10–12

Time Required: 3–15 weeks

Materials Needed: Copies of "Research Log," "Ancestral Chart," and "Family Worksheet"

Description:

A few principles that must be learned to trace a family tree are relatively simple but inviolable, for they clearly determine the difference between success and failure.

Goals: The cardinal rule for successful genealogical research is to proceed from the known to the unknown. There are 4 requirements one must meet for each ancestor before going back to the previous generations:

1. *Name.* Locating facts about an individual is extremely difficult if the name is not known. (Imagine trying to find someone's telephone number in a telephone directory if the name is unknown.) Be sure to emphasize that it is not uncommon to find the same family name spelled differently, often by the same person. Several persons of the same name may exist in the same area.
2. *Location.* Searching for an ancestor would be much like hunting for the proverbial needle in a haystack if the hunt is not confined to some general geographical area. Certainly the more specific the place, the more defined and manageable the search.
3. *Time.* It is helpful to know that Allen Davis lived in Knox County, Tennessee, but to narrow the search further, a general time period should be identified.

---

* Adapted from R. L. Partin. "Genealogy Skills in the Social Studies Class," *Social Studies Review* 17:1 (Fall 1977).

4. *Source.* Name, place, and time are essential ingredients in establishing a lineage. However, valid genealogical research always specifies the course of each fact or piece of data collected.

Recording Discovered Information. Most genealogists or family history researchers have discovered the hard way the price of inadequate recording of information. The key to successful genealogical research is a systematic plan for recording and preserving discovered information.

Although genealogists adapt their own systems of preserving and cataloging information, three basic forms are necessary. Multiple copies of each of the following forms should be given to each student. (The ideal size is 8½" X 11" with holes punched for binding in a large three-ring notebook.)

1. "*Research Log.*" The purpose of the log is to record the date, source, and findings of each search, whether successful or unsuccessful. Duplicated effort can be eliminated, and systematic coverage of all relevant sources is assured through a research log. The log should be kept at the front of each genealogical notebook for quick reference.

   Neatness and accuracy in all records are vital. A carelessly written *6* can easily be read as *0* or a *7* as a *1*. Neatly typed records are the ideal; next best are records printed in ink.
2. "*Ancestral Chart.*" A family tree traced just a few generations back will yield hundreds of names. Twenty generations would yield over a million grandparents. To keep track of the relationships, a numbering system has been developed that pinpoints where an individual name fits on the family tree. Note that the person doing the research enters her name on the line numbered 1. Her father is number 2 and the mother is number 3. The paternal grandfather is assigned number 4 and his wife (the paternal grandmother) is number 5. Observe that the number assigned any individual's father is double his own number. The mother's number is double his own number plus one. As new names are added to the family tree, a preassigned number awaits them. The "Ancestral Chart" included here has room for four generations. To continue on to the fifth generation, a new chart is renumbered such that the name of the family member of the fourth generation is recorded in the lefthand blank. For example, number 11 is written on the lefthand blank, and the number 1 is changed to 11, and the rest of the chart is renumbered accordingly.
3. "*Family Worksheet.*" The basic unit of genealogical research is the family, that is, a father, a mother, and their children. The "Family Worksheet" is used to record the discovered biographical information about any family member. There are several simple guidelines to follow in completing a worksheet:

   a. Specify the source of the information recorded on each "Family Worksheet"
   b. Record information from only one source on each worksheet. Do not mix information from several sources on one worksheet, even if it is

about the same family. This is important for later evaluation of the information.

c. Record the father's assigned number from the "Ancestral Chart" on the top of the "Family Worksheet." Worksheets should be arranged in the notebook according to the father's numbers.

d. Include any additional information located, even if there is not a blank specifically labeled for that event. Each little bit of information can become a valuable clue later.

Successful family histories are more than a network of names and dates. Ancestors become real when pictures, birth certificates, death certificates, news clippings, and other documents are used to paint a detailed picture of the ancestor's life. Students should be encouraged to include copies of personal documents in their notebooks.

Exploring Resources. Most cities and many countries have genealogical societies—organizations of family history researchers who schedule meetings and workshops on various research topics. If not, the local historical society likely has at least one member who is interested and experienced in genealogical research. Invite such members to class to share their skills. Most are quite enthusiastic about their hobby and will provide many hints on local resources available.

The courthouse is a gold mine for the student genealogist. Land records, death certificates, wills and probate records, birth records, marriage certificates, and various legal proceedings provide a plethora of information and experience in using primary resources. Guest speakers from the city or county courthouse can enhance students' awareness of what records are available and how to use them. Certainly students whose family have lived in the same county for several generations have a definite advantage; however, distance is not the insurmountable barrier it first appears. If students know what county records they need, they can write for the information. Indeed, 80 percent of the genealogical research done by amateur genealogists is by mail. Certainly the ability to write a clear and concise letter is a skill essential for successful genealogical research. (See *The How-to Book for Genealogical Research* by George Everton, Sr., listed below, for hints on how to write genealogical letters.)

Perhaps the most widely used genealogical resource is the census record. Every decade since 1790, the federal government has conducted a census. All surviving census records from 1790 to 1890 are open to the public and are available on microfilm in many libraries. (Most of the 1890 records were destroyed by fire; the 1900 records are open to research under restricted conditions.) Since 1850 each person residing in a household was listed by name, along with other biographical information such as place of birth and age. Many of the census records are available in printed form. The federal government will conduct a limited research of census records and provide, for a small fee, a copy of the census record for the individual family requested.

All states have depositories of birth, death, and other records. For a few dollars, the student can obtain copies of certificates for births or deaths that have occurred since around 1900. The exact dates, cost, and archive address for each state are listed in *The Handy Book for Genealogists* by George Everton.

If a paperback resource such as Doane's *Searching for Your Ancestors* is not used, lecturettes or handouts on the various resources each student should consider might be used. In addition to court and census records, students should be aware of the potential value of each of the following:

1. Newspapers—Obituaries contain much genealogical information. Local events that may have affected the lives of ancestors also provide valuable clues.
2. Church records—Marriage, baptismal, christening, and burial, and other religious activities were generally well documented. Many of the records prior to 1900 have been published.
3. Published family histories—Thousands of family histories have been published. Some of your students may have a printed family history for their family. Caution must be advised because errors are common; thus, the records should be validated through independent research, if possible. The printed family history can provide valuable hints for further research.
4. Cemetery records—Much genealogical information is recorded on the gravestones of a cemetery.

Student Autobiography. An important part of each student's family history is his autobiography. Students often regard this as one of the most rewarding experiences; for many, it is the first time they have fully reflected on their lives. Who are they at this point? What are the major events that have affected their lives thus far? By encouraging the student to emphasize his achievements, interests, and ambitions, teachers may enhance the individual's self-concept. Students should be encouraged to describe their lives in detail; ten to twenty typewritten pages is easily obtainable from most high school students. It is helpful to provide an outline or list of topic areas, including at least the following:

Birth data
Residences
Childhood friends
Vacations
Clubs and sports
Hobbies
Awards and achievements
School experiences, classes, teachers
Religious background
Employment or volunteer work
Future plans and ambitions

Grading. Do not grade students on how far back they can trace their family history. Some students will have easy access to documents, or perhaps someone in their family has already completed some of their family history. Others, such as first- or second-generation immigrants, may have a difficult time identifying more than three or four generations. The emphasis should be on the quality of the search and the validity of the logic. Specific criteria for evaluation might include the following:

1. All available sources should have been searched. For example, at least two letters of inquiry should be written, with copies included in the notebook. The "Research Log" should include a record of all searches and their results.
2. Each item of information should have its source clearly indicated on the worksheet.
3. Each worksheet should be appropriately numbered according to the number of that family's father.
4. The "Ancestral Chart" should include all direct ancestors identified on the "Family Worksheets."
5. Are the assumptions and conclusions logical? For example, if the information given on a family tree indicates that a child was born in 1890 and that his father was born in 1883, it is reasonable to assume that an error in recording information or an error in logic has occurred.
6. Additional assignments can be associated with the family tree, expanding on some aspect of the individual's family history. For example, a project could describe how one or more economic events affected the family history (the Irish potato famine, the development of assembly-line factories, or the Great Depression).

Helpful Resources:

Doane, Gilbert H. *Searching for Your Ancestors*. New York: Bantam, 1974.

Everton, George B., Sr., ed. *The Handy Book for Genealogists*. Logan, UT: Everton Publishers, 1981.

Everton, George B., Sr., ed. *The How-to Book for Genealogists*. Logan, UT: Everton Publishers, 1971.

The Genealogical Helper published bimonthly by Everton Publishers, Logan, UT.

Preece, Floren Stocks, and Preece, Philiss Pastore. *The Sure Guide to Genealogy Research: The Preece System*. Mendon, UT: Genealogy Club of America, 1969.

An extensive list of genealogical publications and worksheets is available from Everton Publishers, P.O. Box 358, Logan, UT 84321.

RESEARCH LOG

Search Number	Date of Speech	Source	Number of Worksheets

ANCESTRAL CHART

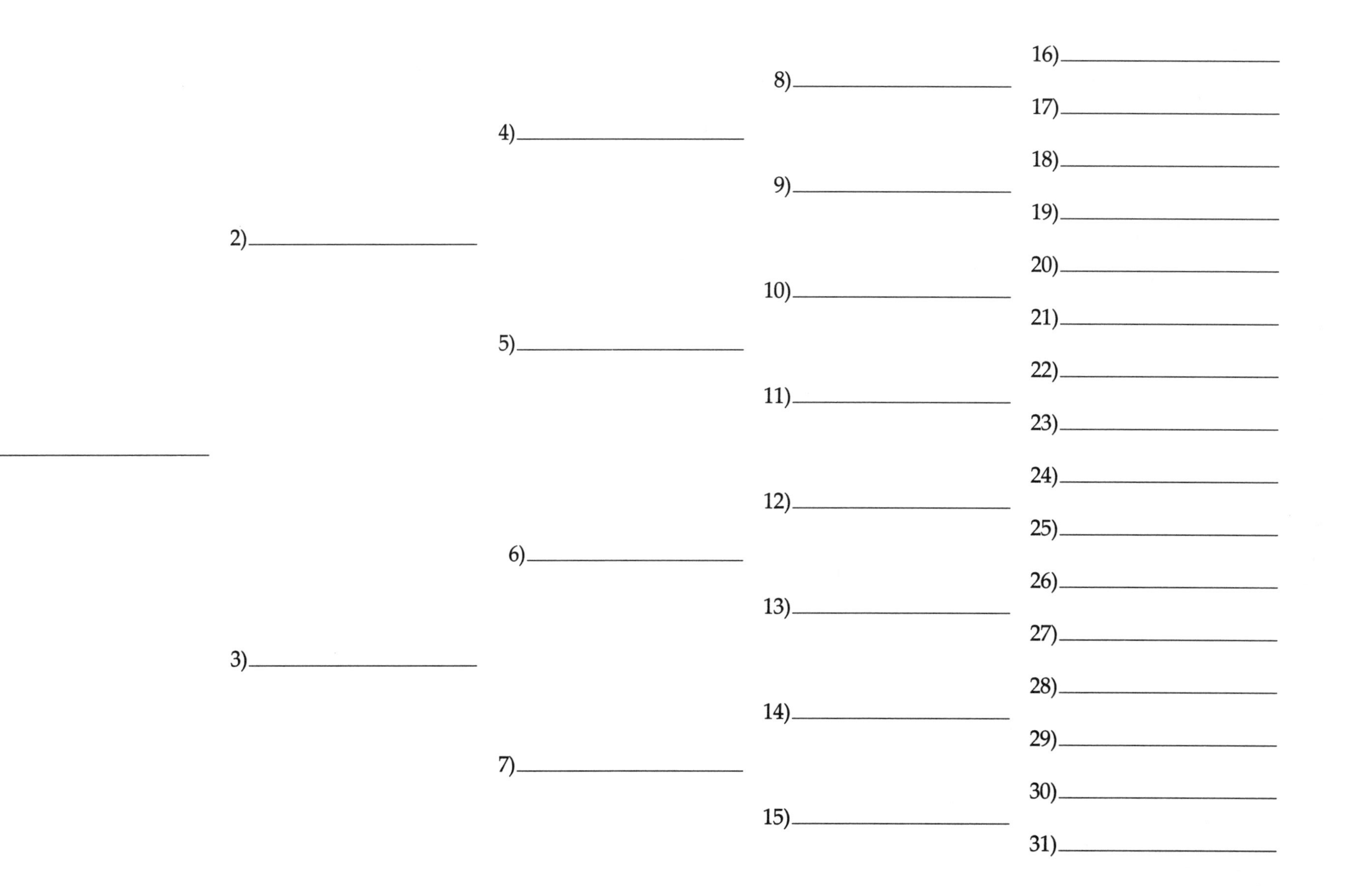

FAMILY WORKSHEET

Husband's Name: ______________________________ Family Number: __________

	MO	DAY	YR	Place	Comments
Born					
Married					
Died					

SOURCE:

Places of residence: ______________________________

Occupation: ______________ Religion: ______________

Mother: ______________ Father: ______________

Wife's Maiden Name: ______________________________

	MO	DAY	YR	Place	Comments
Born					
Married					
Died					

Places of residence: ______________________________

Occupation: ______________ Religion: ______________

Mother: ______________ Father: ______________

Use only one source per family worksheet.

Children's full names		MO	DAY	YR	Place	Other data
1. ______________ Spouse:	Born					
	Married					
	Died					
2. ______________ Spouse:	Born					
	Married					
	Died					
3. ______________ Spouse:	Born					
	Married					
	Died					
4. ______________ Spouse:	Born					
	Married					
	Died					
5. ______________ Spouse:	Born					
	Married					
	Died					
6. ______________ Spouse:	Born					
	Married					
	Died					
7. ______________ Spouse:	Born					
	Married					
	Died					

(1-14) IMMIGRATION: GRAPH INTERPRETATION

Objective: • To interpret data from a histogram

Grade Level: 7–12

Time Required: 15–20 minutes

Materials Needed: Copies of "Immigration: 1820 to 1984"

Description:

1. Distribute copies of "Immigration: 1820 to 1984." Students may complete the questions in class or as homework. It might also be used as a quiz.
2. You might use the following questions to process the activity:
   a. Why was there such a burst of immigration during the first two decades of this century? From where did these people come? How were they received?
   b. Why did immigration decline so much during the decade of the 1930s?
   c. What are the economic effects of high immigration?
   d. What immigration issues face our country today?
   e. Do we still welcome the "huddled masses yearning to be free"?
   f. What would be the likely effects of unregulated, open immigration?
   g. What criteria should be used to restrict immigration to the United States?

Name ______________________ Date ______________________

IMMIGRATION: 1820 TO 1984

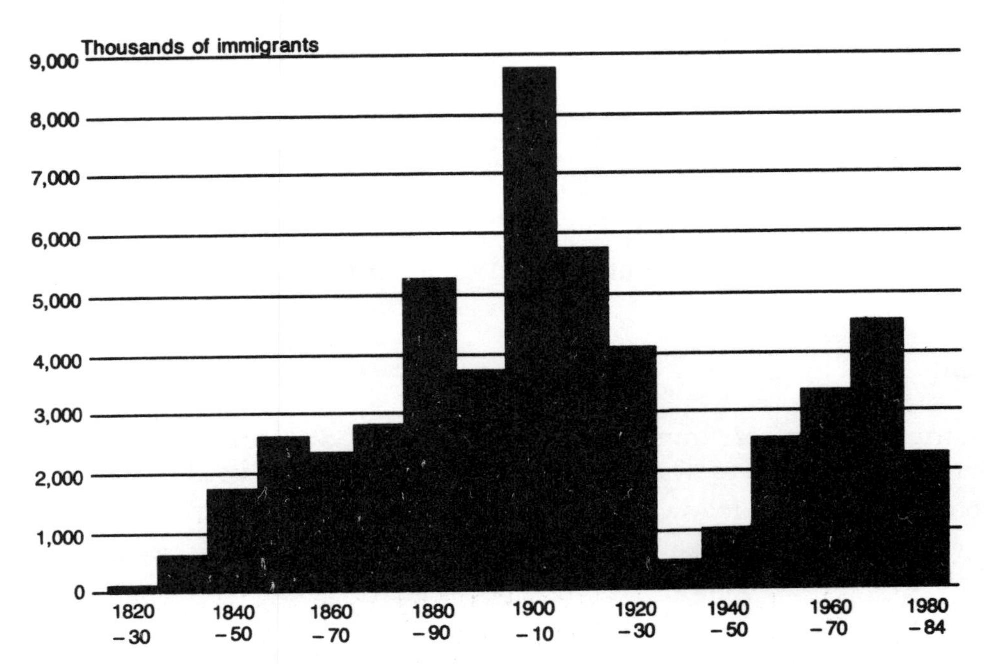

Source: *U.S. Statistical Abstract* (1986).

Using the above graph, answer the following questions:

1. In what decade was immigration the highest? ______________________
2. In which decades have less than two million people immigrated to the United States? ______________________
3. Approximately how many people immigrated to the United States between 1920 and 1930? ______________________
4. Was the flow of immigration higher in the 1920s or the 1970s? ______________________
5. In how many decades has the number of immigrants exceeded five million? __________
6. In which decade did the number of immigrants first exceed two million? __________
7. Was the number of immigrants coming to the United States higher in the 1960s or the 1970s? ______________________

ADDITIONAL PROJECTS

1. *A Taste of History.* After studying the foods of the period, students may prepare a meal based on the diet of that specific era. As much as possible, they should follow authentic cooking procedures, using raw, natural ingredients.

Helpful Resources:

Old cookbooks, grandparents, home economics teacher, and so on.

2. *The Music of History.* Have students investigate the music popular during a particular period of American history. They might bring recordings to class, or musically talented students may sing or play selections for the class.

Helpful Resources:

Chase, Gilbert. *American's Music.* 2nd rev. ed. New York: McGraw-Hill, 1966.

Hitchcock, H. Wiley. *Music in the United States: A Historical Introduction.* Englewood Cliffs, NJ: Prentice-Hall, 1969.

Kingman, Daniel. *American Music: A Panorama.* New York: Schirmer Books, 1979.

Lowens, Irving. *Music in America and American Music.* Brooklyn, NY: Institute for Studies in American Music, 1978.

3. *Costumes.* Students may research the fashions of a given era or changes in styles, such as police uniforms, over time. They might present their findings through sketches, or the more ambitious by actually sewing and modeling costumes.

Helpful Resources:

DeMarly, Diana. *Fashion for Men: An Illustrated History.* New York: Holmes and Meier, 1985.

Cassin-Scott, Jack. *The Illustrated Encyclopedia of Costume and Fashion 1550–1920.* New York: Sterling Publishing, 1986.

Copeland, Peter F. *Working Dress in Colonial and Revolutionary America.* Westport, CT: Greenwood Press, 1977.

Laver, James. *Costume and Fashion: A Concise History.* New York: Oxford University Press, 1983.

Torrens, Deborah. *Fashion Illustrated: A Review of Women's Dress, 1920–1950.* New York: Hawthorn Books, 1975.

4. *Political Cartoons.* Well-done cartoons often demonstrate deep insight into an issue. After studying examples of political cartoons from magazines and newspapers, students may draw cartoons related to past or current events. As they are shown, have the class give their interpretations of each cartoon. Perceptive cartoons dealing with current local issues might even be submitted to local or school newspapers for publication.
5. *Letter Writing.* Have students assume they are living in a particular historical era (for example, antebellum South, Chicago during the Roaring Twenties) or have witnessed a specific historical event (the Scopes trial, a wagon train ride over the Oregon Trail, or the Haymarket Affair). In a letter to a friend or relative, students should describe the experience as a firsthand account. Before writing, they should gather information at the library on the event being reported. They may exchange their letters and read each others'. You might post some or all on the bulletin board to be read, or read a few to the whole class.
6. *The History of Ships.* As an individual or a small-group project, have students research the changes in sailing vessels from the 1400s to the twentieth century. Their in-class report might include drawings of the various vessels, highlighting the improvements. It may be worthwhile to invite someone with a knowledge of sailing to discuss the basic principles of sailing with the class.
7. *Maps.* The two maps of the United States that follow can be used for a variety of projects or activities. Keep a supply of copies on hand for the students.

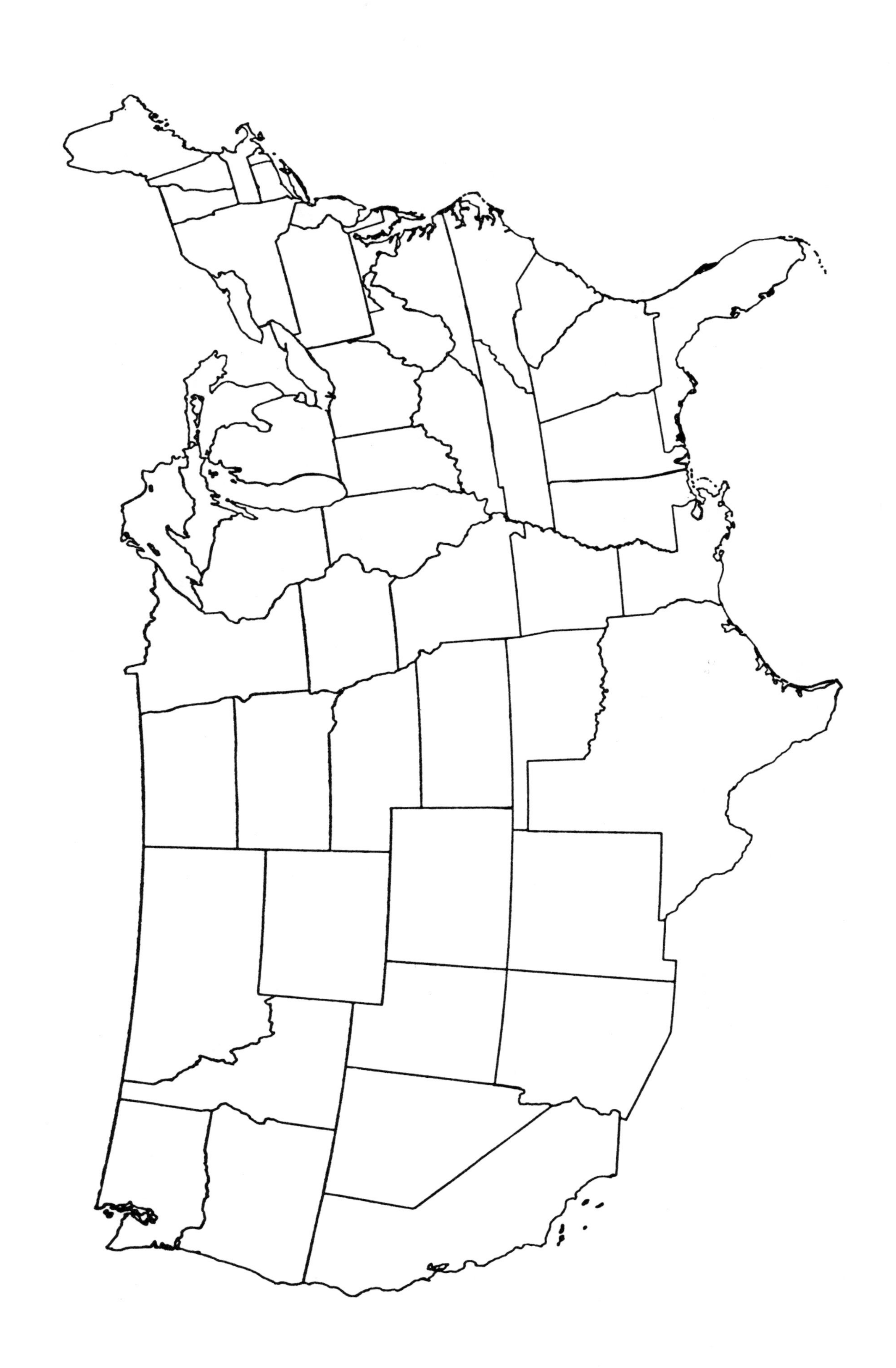

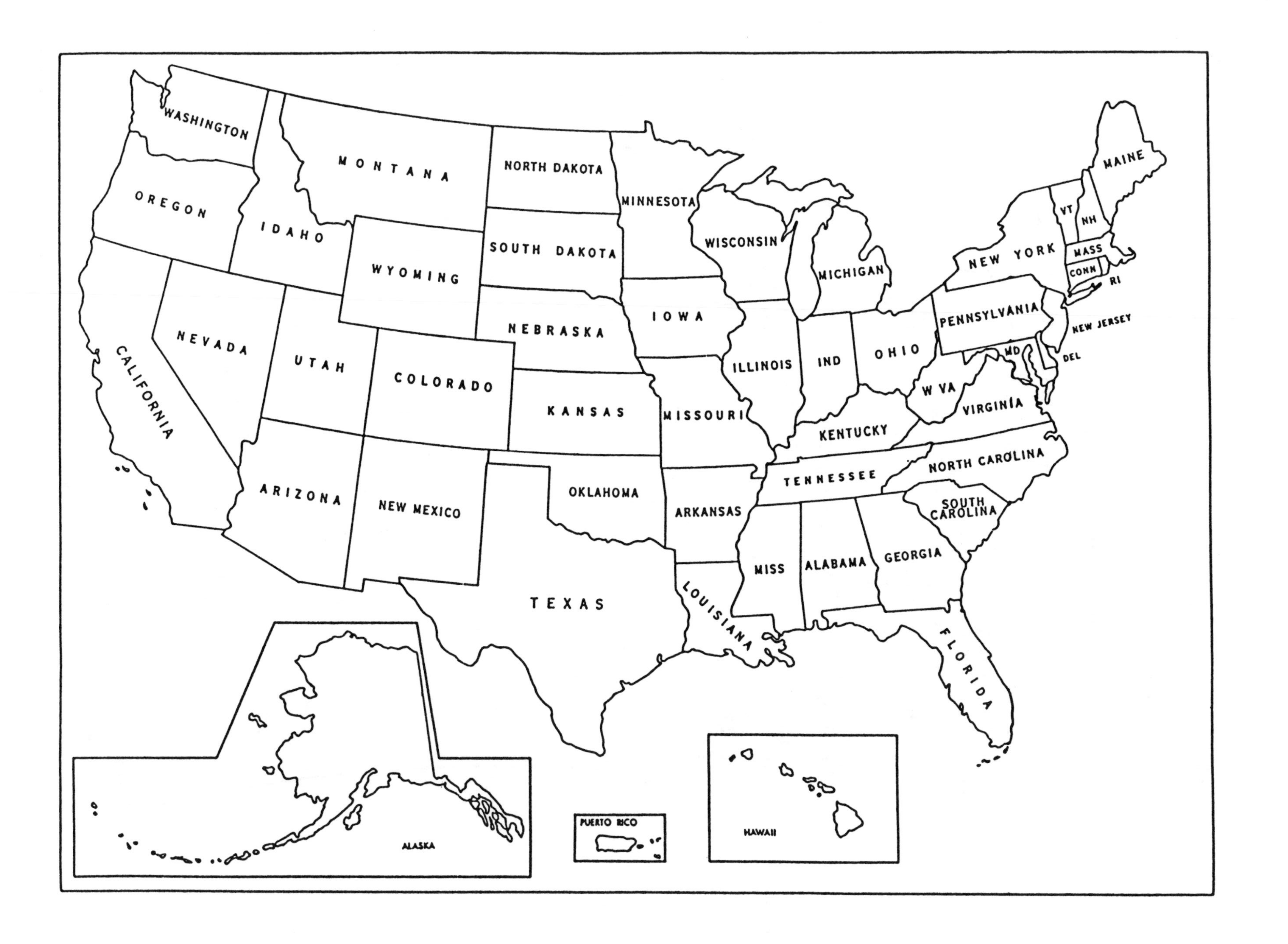
WASHINGTON
OREGON
CALIFORNIA
IDAHO
NEVADA
MONTANA
WYOMING
UTAH
ARIZONA
COLORADO
NEW MEXICO
NORTH DAKOTA
SOUTH DAKOTA
NEBRASKA
KANSAS
OKLAHOMA
TEXAS
MINNESOTA
IOWA
MISSOURI
ARKANSAS
LOUISIANA
WISCONSIN
ILLINOIS
MICHIGAN
IND
OHIO
KENTUCKY
TENNESSEE
MISS
ALABAMA
GEORGIA
FLORIDA
SOUTH CAROLINA
NORTH CAROLINA
VIRGINIA
W VA
PENNSYLVANIA
MD
DEL
NEW JERSEY
NEW YORK
CONN
RI
MASS
VT
NH
MAINE
ALASKA
PUERTO RICO
HAWAII

DEBATE TOPICS

Resolved:

The United States was justified in entering into the war with Mexico.

Slavery would have ended in the South even without the Civil War.

It is not necessary to read much since television provides the information we need.

An amendment to the Constitution requiring a balanced budget should be passed.

Mandatory national service for all youth should be instituted.

The spoils system is a necessary part of a democracy.

The United States should withdraw from the United Nations.

The electoral college should be replaced with direct election of the president of the United States.

The United States was justified in its Vietnam intervention.

The presidential term of office should be extended to six years.

Families should be used in frontline military combat roles.

POSSIBLE RESOURCE PERSONS

Antique auto collectors

Antique collectors

Art dealer on American art trends

Bankers

Candlestick maker

Cartographers on mapmaking

Clergy on religious change

Dance studio instructor on varieties of early dance

Economist to discuss the "business cycle"—inflation, recession, depression

Entrepreneur on the problems of starting a business

Farmer for understanding contemporary agricultural programs

Folk-dance clubs for demonstrations

Folk music performers

Genealogists

Ham radio operator to demonstrate the use of Morse code

Immigrant

Immigration official

Investigative reporter from a newspaper or television station

Judges

Local historians
Model railroad builder
Owners of antique farm machinery
Peace Corps or Vista volunteer
Person who attended a one-room schoolhouse
Political campaign workers
Railroad buffs
Sheriff or police chief on the changes in crime in your area
Stamp or coin collectors
State representative or senator
Stockbrokers
Union official to discuss positive role of unionism on America's industrial development
War veterans
Weaver to demonstrate spinning and weaving processes
Woodworker to demonstrate early hand tools

FIELD TRIP IDEAS

Archeaological excavations
Archives
Art museum
Bank
Cemetery
Courthouse
Farm
Folk art festival
Genealogical library
Genealogical society meeting
Historical museums
Historical play
Horse-drawn sleigh ride
Local historical district
Local manufacturing plant
Nearby battlefields
One-room schoolhouse
Steam locomotive trip
Town meeting
Walking tour of historical architecture

ORGANIZATIONS WORTH WRITING

American Historical Association
400 A Street, SE
Washington, DC 20003

Association on American Indian Affairs
95 Madison Avenue
New York, NY 10016

Bureau of Indian Affairs
U.S. Department of the Interior
1951 Constitution Avenue, NW
Washington, DC 20245

Center for History of the American Indian
Newberry Library
60 West Walton Street
Chicago, IL 60610

CIA Public Affairs Office
Washington, DC 20505

ERIC Clearinghouse for Social Studies/Social Science Education
855 Broadway
Boulder, CO 80302

Historical Association
Patron: Her Majesty the Queen
59a Kensington Park Road
London SE11 4JH, England

Lincoln Filene Center
Tufts University
Medford, MA 02155

National Archives and Records Service
General Services Administration
Eighth Street and Pennsylvania Avenue, NW
Washington, DC 20408

National Council for the Social Studies
3501 Newark Street, NW
Washington, DC 20016

Chapter 2

WORLD HISTORY

History is our story. When we go to bed tonight, our day has become the past. World history is simply a more grand sweep of all the nights and all the mornings since our earliest ancestors made their way into written records by recording a sale of wheat.

It is an exciting story—much of which is unknown. Our written accounts are severely limited. They make up approximately "one minute out of a day of human life." Yet our "one minute" has carried us from the lush papyrus reeds of the Nile to the silent, barren craters of the moon. Our world history is a powerful, dramatic saga of our time on the earth.

The activities that follow are planned to engage, to excite, to stimulate the thoughts of students as together we seek to understand our world's history.

(2-1) CHAIN OF CHANGE

Objective: • To realize that change produces a ripple effect

Grade Level: 7–9

Time Required: Ongoing project for the duration of the course

Materials Needed: Paper, scissors

Description:

1. Place one of the following posters on the wall as each time period of world history is studied:

Prehistoric
Early civilizations
Middle ages
Renaissance
Rise of states
Explorations
Colonization
Industrial Revolution
Modern world

2. Have students make a chain of events and hook other chains of events each event produces as the study of world history progresses. For example:
   a. *Prehistoric*
      Domestication of animals (What chain of events did it produce?)
      Domestication of plants (led to)?
      Invention of pottery (led to)?
   b. *Industrial Revolution*
      Spinning jenny (caused what)?
      Cotton gin
3. Discuss the following: The rate of change keeps accelerating. It took more than fifty thousand years to change from a hunting and gathering society to an agricultural one.
   It took approximately five thousand years after the onset of agriculture for the first civilization to develop. With each succeeding century (except for the Dark Ages), changes accelerated. The eighteenth century produced more changes than all the past history of the world. The nineteenth and twentieth centuries speeded up the process even more. Not only does change beget change, it also affects the rate of change. A possible culminating activity for the end of the school year would be to predict the changes the computer will bring (or space travel, and so on).

(2-2) BE A HISTORIAN

Objective: • To have students distinguish between historical fact and interpretation of historical fact

Grade Level: 7–12

Time Required: 1–2 class periods

Materials Needed: Cord (18 inches); magazines; paper; markers; pins or stapler or glue

Description:

1. Students should locate pictures in magazines to represent events in their lives (or draw them). Students attach their pictures to their 18-inch string. If time allows, let the students "tell" their stories.
2. Help students understand that they had to make a choice of what to include due to limitations of string—as do historians. Inquire as to the choice of pictures used. Would someone else (friend, mother, teacher) have told "their" story differently? Emphasize that the choice of historical events influences what we read as history.
3. Ask if other authors chose the same event, would they interpret it the same? Historians need to interpret fact. Share the following example:

   > Throughout the history of the ancient Middle East, Sumerian cities were conquered by desert nomads [historical fact]. As the population of the nomads increased, their needs became greater, and they began to push closer and closer to the city-states [historical interpretation].

   The first sentence is a statement of fact because it can be verified by looking at available evidence about the Sumerians. Sumerian cities were invaded by nomads. The second sentence is an interpretation because it states the historian's opinion of why the invasion occurred. It cannot be objectively verified. We can never know for certain why the nomads invaded cities. Therefore, while it is the historians' role to report historical events, it is sometimes necessary for them to interpret the events.

(2-3) IN THE BEGINNING— THERE WAS THE WORLD

Objective:
- To provide and reinforce information about the earth's beginnings

Grade Level: 7–12

Time Required: 30–40 minutes in class, or as homework

Materials Needed: Copies of "In the Beginning Wordsearch"

Description:

1. The wordsearch encourages study of the physical beginning of the earth. It may be used as a high-interest follow-up to a lecture or to the study of the

origin of the universe. It may be assigned as homework or may be completed individually or in pairs during class.

2. You might ask to have individuals or the class design their own word graphs using other topics you are studying. Some of these may be reproduced and completed by the rest of the class. You might want to save some of the more outstanding examples for future use.

Name ____________________ Date ____________________

IN THE BEGINNING WORDSEARCH

Read the following account of our earth's creation. Then locate each underlined word in the wordsearch and circle it. Words can be found horizontally, vertically, and diagonally.

G N N N S U X Z B G M E G P
H E P O T W Y P F H I A U H
I B Q R U S H A E L S R N E
S U G F T Y D Y C K J T I N
T L O A S C B B D N N H V O
R A T I L D E I P R P O E M
N E C M N A Y L L Q O L R E
Q S T A T E X L A R E G S N
P U X M A N C I N M T V E A
S T A R S I G O E S U W X N
O Y S H K J H N T S O Z I A
V A Z I L Y T I S R E V I D
W L K J G S T E N A C B C B
D E V E L O P M E N T S E D

The exact story of the origin of man, the earth, and our universe is unknown. The real story is shrouded in mystery. There is evidence to suggest that at the beginning there was a large, dense mass of gas. This gas consisted of hydrogen, the simplest of the 92 chemical elements known to occur in a natural state. This original mass of gas underwent an evolution into galaxies, stars, and planets. The historical developments that led from the initial state to the complexities of the present universe were produced by phenomena that modern physics seeks to understand. It appears that the almost incredible diversity of the galaxies, nebulae, stars, planets, and other objects present in our universe originated in a very simple state. Our homeland, the earth, probably made its appearance about three and one-half billion years ago.

(2-4) A THUMB, A THUMB—MY KINGDOM FOR A THUMB

Objectives:
- To recognize the advantage people have over animals in changing their environment due largely to a small anatomical feature—the thumb
- To gain insight into the adaptation required to adjust to a physical impairment

Grade Level: 7–12

Time Required: First 5 minutes and last 10 minutes of class

Materials Needed: Two strips of adhesive tape per student

Description:

1. As students enter the classroom, tape their thumbs against the palms of their hands so they cannot be used. It may speed up matters to use a few volunteers to help with the taping.
2. Continue teaching the regular lesson as planned without special attention to the taped thumbs. Do try to incorporate some activities such as opening their books, writing, sharpening pencils, and so on.
3. If the curriculum includes a segment on evolution, this may be used to aid students in understanding why people became primary toolmakers.
4. During the last 10 minutes of the class, ask the class what it was like to work without thumbs.

(2-5) SAY WHAT?

Objectives:
- To understand the need for measuring time
- To understand the difficulty early people had in measuring time

Grade Level: 7–9

Time Required: One class period

Materials Needed: Two decks of Calendar Fact cards

Description:

1. Print the calendar facts on 5″ × 7″ note cards. Two sets of the Calendar Facts cards will be needed. The cards will last longer if you laminate the sheets before you cut the cards apart. Cut out the cards to make 2 complete decks. Shuffle the decks and randomly number the backs of the cards 1 to 20.
2. Hang the 2 decks in numerical order with the numbers showing. They can be held in place with tape or thumbtacks.
3. Divide the class into 2 teams. Have the teams place their desks on opposite sides of the room.
4. Have a scorekeeper. The teacher is the moderator.
5. Students must participate in the order in which they are seated. Flip a coin to determine which team begins.
6. The first participant calls out a number. The teacher turns the corresponding card from the first deck and reads aloud the fact printed on it. The student then tries to find a match by calling a number on the other set of cards.
7. The teacher reads the second card aloud. If it matches the first card, the team receives a point and the team member continues. If there is no match, the teacher returns both questions face down to their places on the board. The second team selects.
8. At the end of the designated playing time, the team with the most points wins.

CALENDAR FACTS

1. Early primitive people marked time by phases of the moon because it was easier to see than the yearly movements of the sun.
2. A lunar month is 29 days, 12 hours, 44 minutes, and 2.8 seconds.
3. Early biblical people rounded the lunar month to 30 days.
4. The Greeks and Romans used 29½ days in their lunar calendar.
5. Early Egyptians created a solar calendar in 4236 B.C. in order to know when the Nile would flood.
6. The original Egyptian calendar with 12 months—30 days a month—360 days a year was unable to predict the flooding of the Nile due to 5¼ days not accounted for.
7. The Egyptians put their original calendar of 360 days back into the phase of the Nile by ending each year with 5 days of religious holidays.
8. In 238 B.C., King Ptolemy III disobeyed the priests, ruling that the calendar could not be changed and decreed that one day should be added every four years. The present-day solar calendar began.
9. In 46 B.C. when Julius Caesar assumed Roman leadership, he adopted the Egyptian calendar and named the months.
10. The original Roman Julian calendar had six 30-day months and six 31-day months, which gave them a 366-day year. Because February was considered an unlucky month, one day was removed from it.
11. The reason July and August both have 31 days is that Augustus Caesar wanted his month to have as many days as Julius Caesar's July.
12. By adding another day to August, it was necessary to take another day from February, so now it has 28 days.
13. Julius Caesar settled on a solar year of 365 days and 6 hours, which was used until 1582, when Pope Gregory changed it again.
14. The Mayans in Mexico created a solar calendar around 500 A.D. of 18 months—20 days in a month in order to predict the seasons for their crop planting.
15. The Julian calendar was revised by Pope Gregory XIII in 1582. It is our present calendar.
16. It was necessary for Pope Gregory to revise the Julian calendar in order to subtract 11 minutes and 14 seconds from the year.
17. In order to make his correction, Pope Gregory had to shorten 1582 by ten days. October 4 became October 15.
18. Christmas is celebrated on December 25, according to the Gregorian calendar. There are some Christians who celebrate the holiday 12 days later because they still follow the Julian calendar.
19. The Chinese continued to use the lunar calendar until 1912.
20. The leap day in the year 2000 will be omitted to account for the slight difference that accumulates every year.

(2-6) TIC-TAC-FOE

Objectives:
- To review facts of the Middle Ages
- To develop a positive attitude toward studying history

Grade Level: 9–12

Time Required: 40–60 minutes

Materials Needed: A "TIC-TAC-FOE" transparency made from the master

Description:

1. Prepare the "TIC-TAC-FOE" board and display it where the whole class can see it.
2. Divide the class into two teams; one is X, the other is O.
3. Each team must choose a space and answer the question designated for the selected space. Suggested questions are included below. You or your students may make up more.
4. When a student answers correctly, the team gets an X or an O. Three Xs or Os in a row wins.

Politics

1. What was the name of the system of protection, devised in medieval Europe, when nobles were given land in exchange for military service? (Feudalism)
2. What was the treaty that divided Europe after Charlemagne's reign in 843 and became the basis for modern France, Germany, and Italy? (Treaty of Verdun)
3. Who was elected King of France in 987? (Hugh Capet)
4. The agreement between a lord and his vassal was solemnized at a formal ceremony called__________. (Investiture)
5. What was the most powerful force in the Middle Ages? (The church)
6. What emperor fell into a stream of water en route to a crusade and drowned because of the weight of his armor? (Frederick Barbarossa)
7. The vast power of the church is well illustrated in Henry IV's pilgrimage in 1077 to plead for the pope's forgiveness. Where did he make his pilgrimage? (Canossa)
8. How could a serf obtain his freedom? (Run away to town for a year and a day)

9. What event led Clovis to become a Christian? (He saw an image of a cross in the sky.)
10. Often the king appointed churchmen who were educated to help him run the affairs of the government. They were known as ____________. (Bishops)

Religion

1. What was the official language of the Roman Catholic Church? (Latin)
2. Buying and selling of church offices was called ____________. (Simony)
3. The church's prohibition against charging interest when money was lent was known as ____________. (Usury)
4. A special court set up to try people for heresy was called the ____________. (Inquisition)
5. Denial of the sacraments to those who disagreed with church teachings was called ____________. (Excommunication)
6. A philosophical system using reason and logic to support Christian beliefs was called ____________. (Scholasticism)
7. Who wrote *Summa theologica?* (Thomas Aquinas)
8. A person who opposed the church's teachings was called a ____________. (Heretic)
9. Monks who dedicated their lives to service and poverty were called ____________. (Franciscans)
10. The practice of giving one-tenth of one's income to the church is called ____________. (Tithing)

People

1. In 797 the first woman to be sole ruler of the Eastern Roman Empire came to the throne. Name her. (Irene)
2. Pope Leo III in Rome refused to recognize a woman as Roman emperor and in 800 on Christmas Day crowned whom? (Charlemagne)
3. Name the Scandinavian invaders of Europe and North America. (Vikings)
4. Name the monk who set up a school for children of Frankish nobles. (Alcuin)
5. The people from Asia who invaded Europe in the ninth century were ____________. (Magyars)
6. A wandering poet who entertained at castles was a ____________. (Troubadour)
7. Joan of Arc claimed that heavenly voices had told her to lead French armies against whom? (English)
8. What was Joan of Arc's nickname? (Maid of Orleans)
9. Who was Mohammed's successor? (Caliph)
10. What are the pope's assistants called? (Cardinals)

Social

1. What was an estate called that was given for military service? (Fief)
2. What was the code of conduct for knights called? (Chivalry)
3. What was the annual fee paid by a vassal to his lord? (Relief)
4. During the Middle Ages, people did not use last names. They were often known by their ______________. (Occupation or trade)
5. What style of architecture was characterized by rounded arches and very thick walls? (Romanesque)
6. What style of architecture was characterized by tall, pointed arches and large windows? (Gothic)
7. The people who believed they could change worthless metal into gold were called ______________. (Alchemists)
8. A peasant who was tied to a manor was a ______________. (Serf)
9. A person who learned a trade from a master craftsman was ______________. (An apprentice)
10. What were trade organizations called that were made up of craftsmen in order to control quality and price? (Guilds)

Dates

1. When did Rome fall? (476 A.D.)
2. When did Charles Martel defeat the Muslims? (732 A.D.)
3. What was the span of the Middle Ages? (500 A.D.— 1500 A.D.)
4. When did the Normans conquer England? (1066)
5. When was the Magna Carta signed? (1215)
6. When were the Muslims driven out of Spain? (1492)
7. When was the first crusade? (1095)
8. When did Constantinople fall? (1453)
9. When was Charlemagne crowned? (800 A.D.)
10. When did Gutenberg invent moveable-type? (1450)

Geography

1. The place in France where Charles Martel, leading the Christians, defeated the Muslims was ______________. (Tours)
2. The holy city central to the cause of the Crusaders was ______________. (Jerusalem)
3. The place in which the pope first called for a crusade was ______________. (Clermont, France)
4. Marco Polo traveled to what country? (China)
5. The capital of the Byzantine Empire was ______________. (Constantinople)
6. What was the richest city of the Muslim world? (Baghdad)

7. Where was the Hanseatic League organized? (Northern Europe)
8. Where did the Angles, Saxons, and Jutes settle? (British Isles)
9. The land located in Rome belonging to the church and housing the pope is ____________. (Papal States or Vatican)

Wars

1. A feudal warrior was known as a ____________. (Knight)
2. A war launched to end Muslim control of the Holy Land was the ____________. (Crusades)
3. What famous king and queen were able to raise an army to drive the Muslims out of Spain? (Ferdinand and Isabella)
4. Joan of Arc became famous during which war? (Hundred Years War)
5. What battle forced King John to sign the Magna Carta? (Runnymede)
6. The major fortification of the Middle Ages was the ____________. (Castle)
7. In order to become a knight, a young boy had to go through what two stages? (Page and squire)
8. A mythical king who led his knights in deeds of valor was ____________. (King Arthur)
9. How many crusades were there? (Four)
10. What illness destroyed more people than all of the wars of the Middle Ages? (Black Death or bubonic plague)

Barbarians

1. What Frankish King converted to Christianity? (Clovis)
2. One of the Germanic tribes had a name that has become the root of a word to describe needless destruction. Who were they? (Vandals)
3. What tribe expanded into a kingdom eventually to become the nation of France? (Franks)
4. What tribe occupied northern Italy? (Lombards)
5. What tribe occupied central Europe? (Saxons)
6. What were the barbaric tribes called who invaded Europe from Scandinavia? (Vikings)
7. Charles Martel, the Franks' leader, had a son who was the father of Charlemagne. His name was ____________. (Pepin)
8. Who was the Viking who probably came to North America? (Leif Ericson)
9. Which barbarian tribe crossed the Danube and asked Rome for protection? (Visigoths)
10. What ferocious non-Germanic barbarian tribe swept across Siberia? (Huns)

Arabs

1. What is the meeting place where Arabs pray? (Mosque)
2. What is the Arab's holiest city, the birthplace of Mohammed? (Mecca)
3. A slender tower on a mosque is a ____________. (Minaret)
4. What is the holy book of Islam? (Koran)
5. What is the name of the meteorite that has become a sacred shrine in Mecca? (Kaaba)
6. The Islamic holy month of fasting is ____________. (Ramadan)
7. Mohammed's journey from Mecca to Medina is called ____________. (Hejira)
8. The birthdate of the Islamic religion is ____________. (622)
9. The person who calls the faithful to prayer five times a day is known as ____________. (Muezzin)
10. Muslims who settled in Spain were known as ____________. (Moors)

TIC - TAC - FOE

Middle Ages

POLITICS	**RELIGION**	**PEOPLE**
SOCIAL	**DATES**	**GEOGRAPHY**
WARS	**BARBARIANS**	**ARABS**

(2-7) RENAISSANCE OF LITERATURE

Objective:
- To recognize the names of authors who not only told the story of the Renaissance but who also changed the literary form they used

Grade Level: 7–12

Time Required: 30 minutes

Materials Needed: Copies of the activity sheet, "Renaissance of Literature"

Description:

This activity sheet may be completed individually as homework or in teams in class.

Name ______________________________ Date ______________________________

RENAISSANCE OF LITERATURE

Fill in the blanks with the name of a Renaissance author. The following ten authors not only gave us insight into the Renaissance but changed the literary form they used to tell their story:

Bacon	Chaucer	Spenser
Calvin	Dante	Machiavelli
Cervantes	Jonson	Petrarch
		Shakespeare

R E B I R T H

1. Wrote *Don Quixote.* __ **E** __ __ __ __ __ __ __

2. Wrote Elizabethan drama. __ __ **N** __ __ __

3. Wrote *The Divine Comedy.* __ **A** __ __ __

4. Theologian who developed a unique style of prose. __ __ __ __ **I** __

5. Wrote *Faerie Queene.* __ __ __ __ **S** __ __

6. Became master playwright of Elizabethan period. __ __ __ __ __ **S** __ __ __ __ __

7. Espoused that the "end justified the means." __ __ __ __ __ **A** __ __ __ __ __

8. Wrote *New Atlantis.* __ __ __ __ **N**

9. Wrote *The Canterbury Tales.* __ __ __ __ **C** __ __

10. Known as the father of Italian prose. __ **E** __ __ __ __ __ __

(2-8) PROGRAM THE COMPUTER

Objective: • To identify the chronological order to historical events

Grade Level: 7–12

Time Required: 2 class periods

Materials Needed: Copies of "pretend" computer cards, reference books

Description:

1. Instruct students to assume they are programming a computer with a sequence of events. You might draw a flow chart on the board to demonstrate the chronological sequence of steps represented in a computer program.
2. Duplicate copies of the following pages of "pretend" computer cards, containing different historical events. Cut the sheets apart to form decks of "computer" cards.
3. Distribute the decks of cards to pairs or triads of students. Challenge them to arrange the cards in the appropriate sequence.
4. Have the groups arrange their sequences on tables or tape them to a wall. As you process the activity, explore the following questions:
   a. Which events were most difficult to place? Why?
   b. Which events were most incorrectly placed?
   c. Even if you did not know the exact dates, how did you use logic to discover the approximate sequence of events?

"PRETEND" COMPUTER CARDS

A great light illuminates the sky when Gautama Buddha is born. The ill become well.	Records of sales transactions are first written.
Hammurabi of Babylon draws up a code of law.	The pyramids are built.
The plow is invented.	The Phoenicians sail the Mediterranean.
The Ice Age ends.	King Solomon, the Hebrew king, builds a temple.

"PRETEND" COMPUTER CARDS

Nebuchadnezzar II of Babylon builds a beautiful hanging garden to remind his homesick wife of her homeland.	Athenians practice the world's first democracy.
The Greeks capture Troy with the ruse of a wooden horse.	Rome is founded by the twins, Romulus and Remus, who according to legend have been raised by a she-wolf.
The Greeks begin the Olympic games.	Hannibal, the Carthagenian, marches over the Alps with elephants to surprise the Italians in battle.
The Cretans build a civilization that includes such luxuries as bathrooms with copper plumbing, majestic stairways, distinctive murals, pottery, and jewelry.	Carthage is completely destroyed, and salt is spread over the ruins.

(2-9) THE CHALLENGE OF CHANGE

Objectives:
- To understand the concept of pace of change
- To differentiate between revolution and evolution

Grade Level: 9–12

Time Required: 40–60 minutes

Materials Needed: Beatles' recording of "Revolution"; magazines; glue; paper

Description:

1. Discuss a change that occurred in your life. After sharing several changes, that is, changing schools, moving, loss of a parent, and so on, have the students make a collage depicting the change and the feelings it evoked.
2. Discuss the following: Was the change fast or slow?
   How did it affect your life?
   What challenges did it present?
   What adjustments did it require?
   Which type of change (fast or slow) is harder to adjust to?
3. Play the Beatles' recording of "Revolution."
4. After listening, use the word *evolution* for slow change, *revolution* for a fast change. Discuss the following:
   What is a political revolution?
   What is a social revolution?
   What is an industrial revolution?
   What is an intellectual revolution?
5. Lead into feelings and challenges facing the people who lived in the times of these events.

(2-10) DIVISION OF LABOR

Objectives:
- To illustrate the advantages and disadvantages of changes brought by the Industrial Revolution
- To comprehend the role division of labor played in history

Grade Level: 7–12

Time Required: 1–2 class periods

Materials Needed: Colored paper, scissors, colored markers

Description:

1. Start a greeting card business to produce valentines, birthday cards, congratulatory cards, sympathy cards, and other greeting cards in two different production styles.
2. Choose 1 to 3 students to design and complete 5 cards on an individual basis, completing each card before starting another.
3. Set up 2 assembly lines to "mass-produce" cards. This method of production should include the following:
   Design
   Cutting
   Coloring
   Printing
   Pasting
   Quality control
   Placing cards in envelopes
4. Assign students to perform each task. Allow 40–60 minutes for production.
5. Discuss the quality of cards produced in two different ways (job satisfaction, boredom, cost, and so on): (1) Relate to the Industrial Revolution, its ensuing achievements and problems and (2) In what types of tasks is division of labor least productive?

(2-11) CAN YOU PREDICT?

Objective: • To analyze the relationship between two world events

Grade Level: 7–12

Time Required: 2 class periods

Materials Needed: Course textbook

Description:

1. Divide the class into groups of 4. After studying the period of explorations, have each group record what they predict the next chapter of the textbook will say and give the reason for their decisions.
2. Have each group share ideas with the rest of the class. On the second day, have groups read the next chapter to evaluate their predictions. If some predictions did not occur, discuss why they did not happen.

(2-12) BIOGRAPHICAL RUMMY

Objectives:
- To reinforce the historical information students possess
- To personalize the lives of famous figures in history

Grade Level: 7–12

Time Required: Could be used throughout the course; possibly 3 class periods

Materials Needed: 3″ × 5″ cards

Description:

1. Assign each student one of the names listed below or names suggested by students or the teacher. Each student is given 2 cards. The name of the historical personage is printed on the card and labeled A. It is the teacher's choice of whether or not to decorate the card as rummy cards.
2. The first card, labeled A, gives a time period for the historical figure and a brief description of the accomplishment or time period (which the student must research). The second card, labeled B, contains some little-known fact about the life of the historical figure (see the examples below). Students must use research to discover this information.
3. Cards can be duplicated and divided into decks. Students can then choose other students to play "Biographical Rummy." Students are dealt 6 cards, with the remaining cards left in a bank. Students take turns asking for an A "Cleopatra" or B "Cleopatra" from another student, then discard. Once a pair is completed, it is removed from the hand and placed face down in front of the player. When all cards are depleted from a hand, the player calls, "Rummy." The score is determined by adding a point for each pair laid down and subtracting a point for each card left in the hand.

A CLEOPATRA 69–30 B.C. Queen of Egypt Last ruler of the dynasty founded by Ptolemy A	A JULIUS CAESAR 100–44 B.C. A great general and dictator of Rome A	A KARL MARX 1818–1883 German economist expelled to England because of writings A
B CLEOPATRA Was once married to her brother B	B JULIUS CAESAR Had two illegitimate children by Cleopatra B	B KARL MARX Thought the workers' revolution would be in England B

BIOGRAPHICAL RUMMY

Alexander I Czar of Russia
Alexander the Great
Archimedes
Aristotle
Augustus Caesar
Julius Caesar
Francis Bacon
Cleopatra
Alexander Graham Bell
John Bunyan
John Calvin
Jacques Cartier
Edmund Cartwright
Catherine the Great
Catherine of Aragon
Henry Cavendish
Miguel de Cervantes
Neville Chamberlain
Charlemagne
Geoffrey Chaucer
Chiang Kai-shek
Chou En-lai
Winston Churchill
Claudius
Clovis
Christopher Columbus
Confucius
Copernicus
Coronado
Hernando Cortez
Crassus
Oliver Cromwell
Vasco da Gama
Dante
Darius
Charles Darwin
Leonardo da Vinci
Daniel Defoe
Charles de Gaulle
Demosthenes
Benito Juarez
Nikita Khrushchev
Ponce de León
Louis XV
Thomas Mann
Charles Martel
Cardinal Mazarin
Molière
René Descartes
Hernando de Soto
Bartholomew Diaz
Benjamin Disraeli
Francis Drake
Albert Einstein
El Greco
Elizabeth I, England
Elizabeth II, England
Erasmus
Leif Ericson
Francis I, France
Francis Ferdinand
Francis Joseph, Austria
Francisco Franco
Frederick Barbarossa
Frederick the Great
Mohandas Gandhi
Garibaldi
Genghis Khan
George III, England
William Gilbert
William Gladstone
Goethe
Johannes Gutenberg
Emperor Hadrian
Hammurabi
Henry the Navigator
Herodotus
Paul von Hindenburg
Hippocrates
Adolf Hitler
Homer
Horace
John Huss
Isabella of Spain
Ivan the Terrible
Jesus Christ
Joan of Arc
John, King of England
Emperor Justinian
Kublai Khan
David Livingstone
Machiavelli
Mao Tse-tung
Karl Marx
Metternich
Thomas More
Wolfgang Mozart
Benito Mussolini
Napoleon Bonaparte

continued

Louis Napoleon
Gamal Nasser
Nebuchadnezzar
Jawaharlal Nehru
Horatio Nelson
Isaac Newton
Alfred Nobel
Louis Pasteur
Paul the Apostle
Pepin the Short
Henri Petain
Peter the Great, Russia
Petrarch
Philip of Macedon
Philip II, King of Spain

Francisco Pizarro
Marco Polo
Rasputin
Richard the Lion-Hearted
Cardinal Richelieu
Robespierre
Jean-Jacques Rousseau
José de San Martin
William Shakespeare
Socrates
Henry Stanley
George Stephenson
Jonathan Swift
Charles de Talleyrand
Leon Trotsky

Moise Tshombe
Voltaire
William II (Kaiser)
William the Conqueror
William III of Holland
Samuel Johnson
Jomo Kenyatta
Nikolai Lenin
Louis XIV
Ferdinand Magellan
Marie Antoinette
Mary Stuart, Queen of Scots
Mohammed

(2-13) WHAT IF?

Objectives:
- To understand the impact of historical events on one's life
- To appreciate the influence of people and places on historical events

Grade Level: 10–12

Time Required: One period

Materials Needed: Biographical A cards from "Biographical Rummy" game

Description:

1. Ask questions to lead students to see that history is *people.* Throughout the thousands of years of human life on this earth, every person has been different in some respects from someone else.
2. A second element of the past is *time.* Time does not pass. It remains constant. It exists while people and events pass by. Therefore, if people or events could be different, time might be different.
3. The third element of the living past is *place.* People live and do things in certain places that they could not or would not if they were somewhere else. Although the earth is our stage because of geography, we have not one but many stages. Our stage could determine our history.
4. For a project, allow those students who would like to and are capable of higher levels of thinking to draw 2 cards from the deck. Ask them to think about how the historical figure's life might have been different if she had lived in the other person's time and place. Write a brief essay on each biographical figure, depicting what might have happened to the person and how history might have been different if time spans and place were exchanged.

(2-14) WORLD MOSAIC

Objective:
- To become aware of the names of countries of the modern world

Grade Level: 7–12

Time Required: One period

Materials Needed: Colored pencils, markers, crayons; paper; student atlas

Description:

1. Have each student choose a country.
2. Locate it on a world map or globe.
3. Use the shape of the country or its name to create a design.
4. Put it together to form a mosaic that emphasizes the beauty of each individual country "coming together" to form our world.

(2-15) EARLY CIVILIZATION

Objective: • To reinforce facts about early civilization

Grade Level: 7–12

Time Required: One period

Materials Needed: Copies of "Early Civilization Crossword Puzzle"

Description:

The crossword puzzle may be completed individually or in pairs in class.

Name ______________________________ Date ______________________________

EARLY CIVILIZATION CROSSWORD PUZZLE

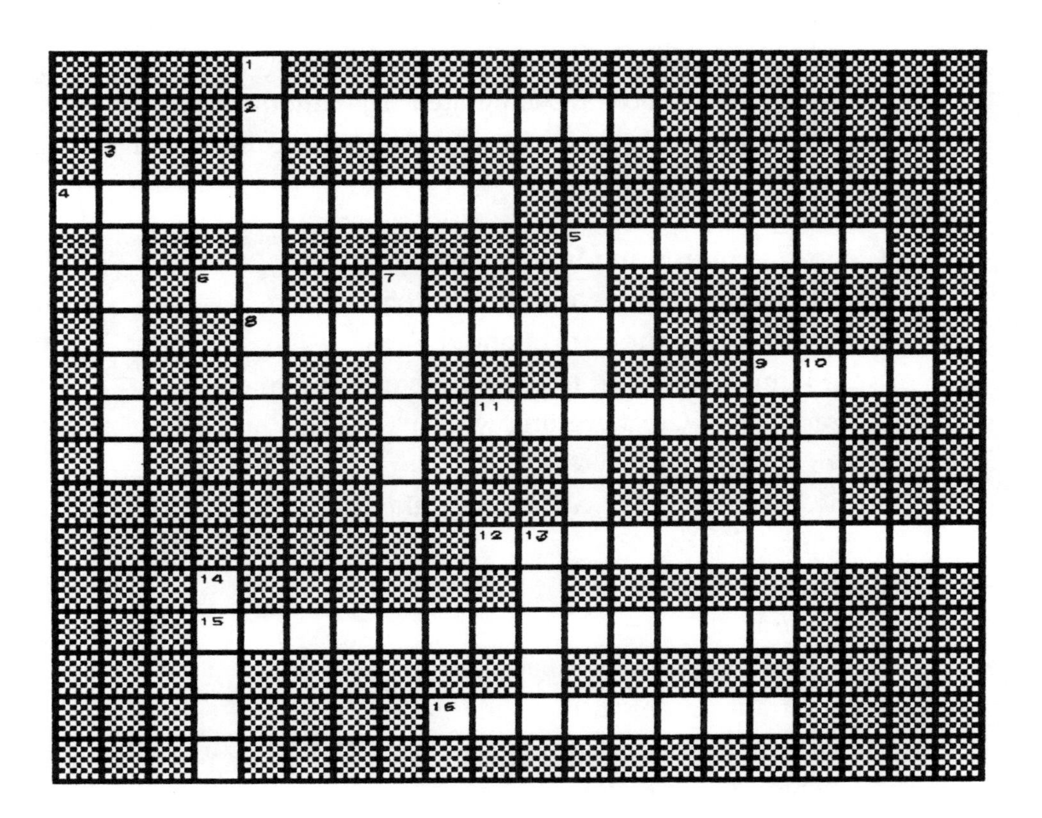

ACROSS

2. Codified Sumerian Laws
4. 1,000 years
5. Ancient writing paper
6. Egyptian Sun God
8. System of writing using wedge-shaped characters
9. "All Egypt is a gift of the ____________."
11. Cuneiform was used by this civilization
12. Civilization along the Tigris and Euphrates
15. Unlocked by the Rosetta Stone
16. Product of human workmanship

DOWN

1. Where alphabet was developed
3. Temple used by Sumerians
5. Elaborate tombs built by Egyptians
7. Ancient name for Greek world
10. Indus River civilization today
13. Land of King Tut
14. Site of Hwang Ho River

ADDITIONAL PROJECTS

1. Invite:
   - Speakers from local industries to discuss problems of world trade
   - International students to describe their country
   - Senior citizens who have emigrated from another country
   - Music or art teachers or chefs to share the culture and food of other countries
2. Dramatize:
   - Cleopatra confronting Julius Caesar
   - Joan of Arc pleading with French politicians
   - Louis XV facing the Parliament of Paris
   - King John acquiescing to the nobles at Runnymede
   - Alexander the Great arguing with his father, Philip of Macedon
3. Draw or make:
   - A medieval manor or castle or a cathedral
   - A Roman house
   - A pyramid
   - A ziggurat
   - The hanging gardens of Babylon
   - Asiatic trade routes in the Middle Ages
4. Pretend to be:
   - Any character in history
   - A child factory worker in 1820
   - A resident of London in 1831
   - An Athenian girl or boy at the age of 16
5. Write:
   - A report on a particular day in history
   - A report comparing Hammurabi's Code of Law with our Bill of Rights
   - To embassies in Washington, D.C., of other countries
   - An interview with a historical person
6. Play a game:
   - From a particular period in history
   - Still being played today in another country
7. Plan an international day that incorporates all the above.
8. Think about what our world would be like if we:
   - Spoke one language
   - Had one religion

Had no religion

Were all one race

Had the same amount of money

9. Contact one of the following organizations to locate international pen pals for your students:

   International Institute of Minnesota
   1690 Como Avenue
   St. Paul, MN 55108
   Telephone: 612-647-0191

   Student Letter Exchange
   910 4th Street SE
   Austin, MN 55912

   International Friendship League Inc.
   55 Mount Vernon Street
   Boston, MA 02108
   617-523-4273

POSSIBLE RESOURCE PERSONS

Archaeologists

Anthropologists

Collector of ancient coins

Embassy representatives

Exchange students

Folk dance groups

History professors

Immigrants

International businesspeople

International cooks or chefs

Language teachers

Musicians from other cultures

Naturalized citizens

Peace Corps volunteers

Theological historian

Travel agents

Veterans

World travelers

FIELD TRIP IDEAS

Art museums
Ethnic concerts
Ethnic neighborhoods
Folk dance performances
Food fairs
Historical museum
International festivals
International film shows
Mosque, synagogue, church
Theatrical performances
Travelogue lectures

ORGANIZATIONS WORTH WRITING

African-American Institute
833 United Nations Plaza
New York, NY 10017

Service Bureau
American Classical League
Miami University
Oxford, OH 45056

American Universities Field
Staff, Inc.
Institute of World Affairs
Twin Lakes
Salisbury, CT 06068

Asia Society
725 Park Avenue
New York, NY 10021

Center for International Education
U.S. Department of Education
400 Maryland Avenue, SW
Washington, DC 20202

Center for International Programs
and Comparative Studies
State Education Department
99 Washington Avenue
Albany, NY 12210

Food and Agriculture Organization
of the United Nations
Via delle Terme di Caracalla—00100
Rome, Italy

Foreign Policy Association
205 Lexington Avenue
New York, NY 10016

Global Perspectives in
Education, Inc.
National Office
218 East 185th Street
New York, NY 10003

Institute for World Order
1140 Avenue of the Americas
New York, NY 10036

InterCulture Associates
Box 22
Thompson, CT 06277

League of Friendship
P.O. Box 509
Mount Vernon, OH 43050

Middle East Institute
1761 N Street, NW
Washington, DC 20036

National Committee on United States-China Relations
777 United Nations Plaza
New York, NY 10017

NYSTROM
3333 Elston Avenue
Chicago, IL 60618

Olympic Airways
Suite 1189
250 S.E. 1st Street
Miami, FL 33131

One World Trust
24 Palace Chambers
Bridge Street
London SW1A 2JT, England

Organization of American States
Nineteenth and Constitution Avenue, NW
Washington, DC 20006

Overseas Development Council
1717 Massachusetts Avenue, NW
Washington, DC 20036

UNESCO Press
Commercial Services Division
7 Place de Fontenoy
75700 Paris, France

United Nations Association of the United States of America
345 East 46th Street
New York, NY 10017

United States Committee for UNICEF
331 East 38th Street
New York, NY 10015

University of Denver
Center for Teaching International Relations
Denver, CO 80208

World Council for Curriculum and Instruction
School of Education
Indiana University
Bloomington, IN 47405

World Future Society
4916 St. Elmo Avenue
Bethesda, MD 20814-5089

World Policy Institute
777 United Nations Plaza
New York, NY 10017

Chapter 3

AMERICAN GOVERNMENT

In 1789 George Washington described the government of the United States as "an experiment entrusted to the American people." His words proved to be prophetic, for our government has evolved, as has our history, from the hopes, dreams, and values of the citizenry.

The heart of American government lies in the Constitution, a living document that has changed as the conditions of our country have forced it to change.

It is essential for students to grasp and understand this "social experiment" that we are a part of—if it is to endure. Activities for this chapter are planned to allow students to question, to explore, and to value the most distinctive feature of our country: its government.

(3-1) THE JUDICIAL SYSTEM

Objective: • To comprehend the federal court system

Grade Level: 7–9

Time Required: 25–30 minutes, or as homework

Materials Needed: Copies of "Judicial System" chart and the activity sheet entitled "Judicial System"

Description:

1. Distribute the "Judicial System" activity sheet and the "Judicial System" chart to be completed as homework or in class.
2. Have the class review the answers in groups of 3.

Optional Activities:

1. Invite judges to discuss their court with the class. Encourage the class to prepare a list of questions before the visit.
2. Have the class follow a judicial proceeding of national or local interest. Each day discuss the progress of the trial.

Judicial System

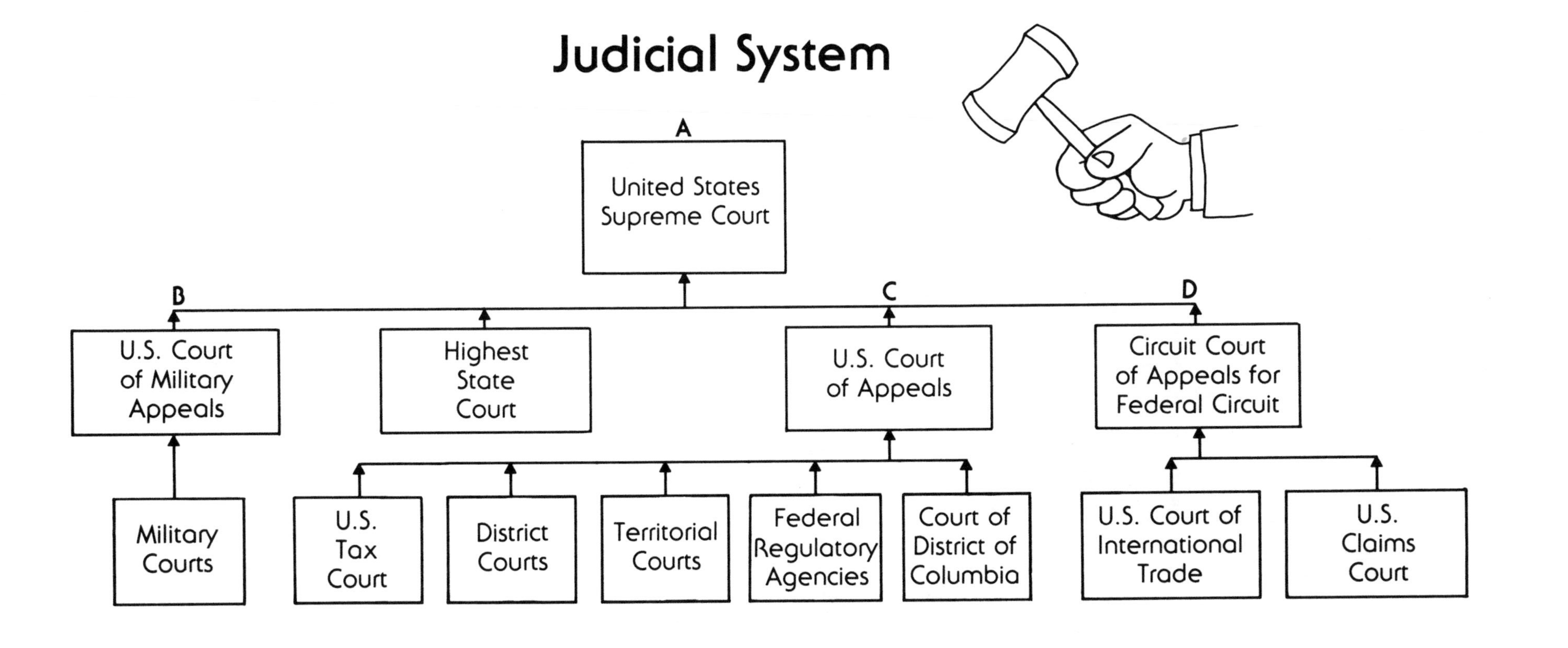

Name ______________________ Date ______________________

JUDICIAL SYSTEM

Look at the "Judicial System" chart to help you answer the following questions:

1. Name the highest court in the United States.

____

2. Name the two courts that hear cases involving military personnel.

____

3. From what state court can appeals go to the Supreme Court?

____

4. What court hears appeals from tax courts and district courts?

____

5. To what court do people living in Washington, D.C., appeal?

____

6. Which court was not established by Congress?

____

7. Which court would handle an appeal from someone living in Puerto Rico?

____

8. The Supreme Court hears cases involving states and cases involving diplomats. However, the most cases it hears are appeals that come from what courts?

____

9. Name the appeals courts.

____

____

____

10. A case involving a trade agreement with the United States would go to which court?

____

(3-2) IT'S AGAINST THE LAW*

Objectives:
- To examine humorous laws to determine what conditions in society might have led to their enactment
- To understand that laws develop in response to particular individual or societal needs and thus change as needs change
- To understand the social value of particular laws

Grade Level: 7–9

Time Required: 40–60 minutes

Materials Needed: Seven copies of the "Loony Laws" handout

Description:

1. Divide the class into 7 groups and give each group a copy of the handout. Assign 3 of the laws listed on the handout to each group. Ask the group to read their laws and figure out why each might have been passed. Ask them to consider what conditions in society they think might have led people to write such a law and what conditions today might force society to keep, rescind, amend, or ignore the law. Give the groups 15 minutes to complete their analyses.
2. Ask each group to select a group reporter and have that person present the group's ideas to the class.
3. Conclude the activity with a brief general discussion of how laws evolve as the needs of individuals and societies change. In the future, what laws that now seem very sensible might appear foolish?

Optional Activities:

1. Have the class members write down a rule or law that they must follow at home, in school, or in the community and that seems to be a silly one. Ask the students to present their rule to the class, explaining why it is silly. Challenge other students to provide valid reasons for the enactment and enforcement of these rules and laws.
2. Which laws today may be viewed as silly 100 years from now?

---

*Adapted from *Words Into Action: A Classroom Guide to Children's Citizenship Education*, by Joseph D'Amico and others (Research for Better Schools, 1980), pp. 35–36. Activity developed by John True, Huron Junior High School, Northglenn, CO 80233. Used with permission.

LOONY LAWS

1. In Nicholas County, West Virginia, no minister shall tell a funny story from the pulpit.
2. Beanshooters are forbidden by law in Arkansas.
3. In Compton, California, dancing cheek to cheek is prohibited.
4. It is illegal to hunt or shoot camels in Arizona.
5. In Los Angeles, a customer of a meat market is prohibited by city ordinance from poking a turkey to see if it is tender.
6. In Lake Charles, Louisiana, a law makes it illegal to let a rain puddle remain in your front yard for more than twelve hours.
7. In Springfield, Massachusetts, it is against the law to ride on the roof of your automobile.
8. In Hanford, California, people may not interfere with children jumping over water puddles.
9. It is against the law in Pueblo, Colorado, to raise or permit a dandelion to grow within the city limits.
10. It is against the law to slap a man on the back in Georgia.
11. In Walden, New York, it is illegal to give a drink of water to anyone unless you have a permit.
12. It is against the law in Illinois for a conductor to collect fares without his hat on.
13. In Bradford, Connecticut, it is against the law to appear on the street unless covered from shoulder to knee.
14. In Vermont it is illegal to whistle underwater.
15. All taxicabs must carry a broom and shovel in the District of Columbia.
16. In Fort Madison, Iowa, a law requires the fire department to practice fifteen minutes before attending a fire.
17. In Key West, Florida, turtle racing is prohibited.
18. It is against the law to gargle in public in Louisiana.
19. In Rochester, Michigan, anyone bathing in public must first have his suit inspected by a police officer.
20. In Kentucky, it is illegal to sleep in a restaurant.
21. Rochester, New York, firemen must wear neckties on duty.

(3-3) PAPER DOLLS

Objectives:
- To increase awareness of sex role stereotyping
- To recognize the changes in our laws as a result of societal reappraisal of sex-role limitations

Grade Level 7–9

Time Required: 40–50 minutes

Materials Needed: Copies of "Robert and Roberta" paper dolls and "Interchangeable Clothes and Accessories"

Description:

1. Each student gets a male paper doll and a female paper doll. Have the group cut them out. If you choose to laminate the sheets, the dolls can be saved for use in future classes.
2. Each student should select clothes and dress both Robert and Roberta.
3. Tally on the board the clothes and accessories allocated to Robert and to Roberta.
4. Discuss the following questions:
   a. What influenced which costumes and accessories you placed on each doll?
   b. What did you say to yourself as you were making your selections?
   c. Are more careers open to women that used to be considered exclusively male positions? Give examples.
   d. Have the career options for men likewise broadened?
   e. Are there still professions that are closed to either males or females?
   f. What problems are created by gender discrimination in career opportunities? What advantages does it bring? Will a woman ever be president of the United States? Why? When?

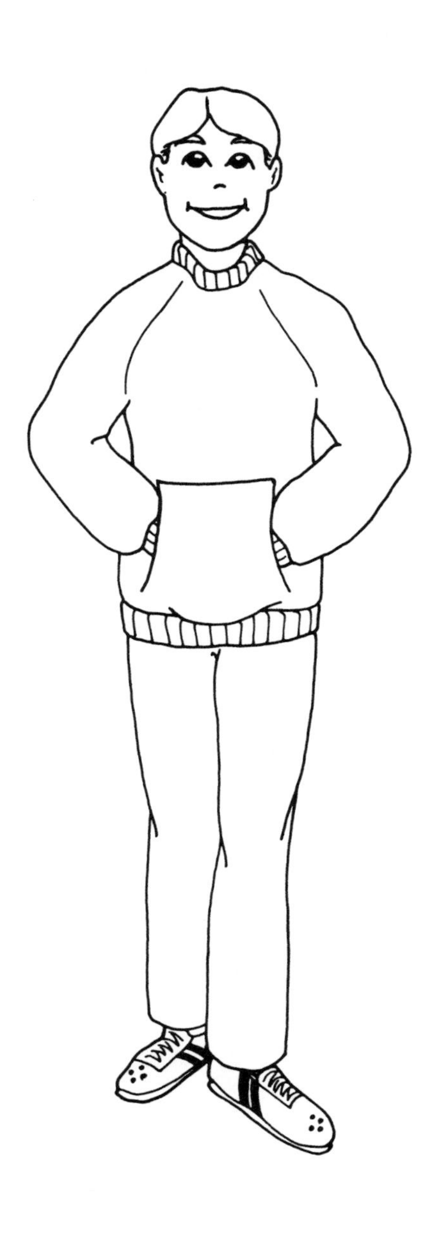

Robert

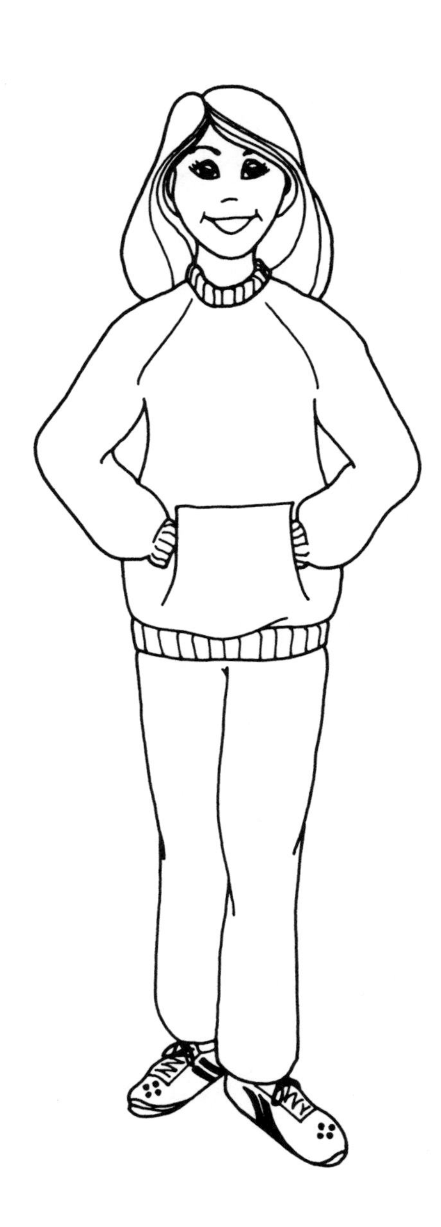

Roberta

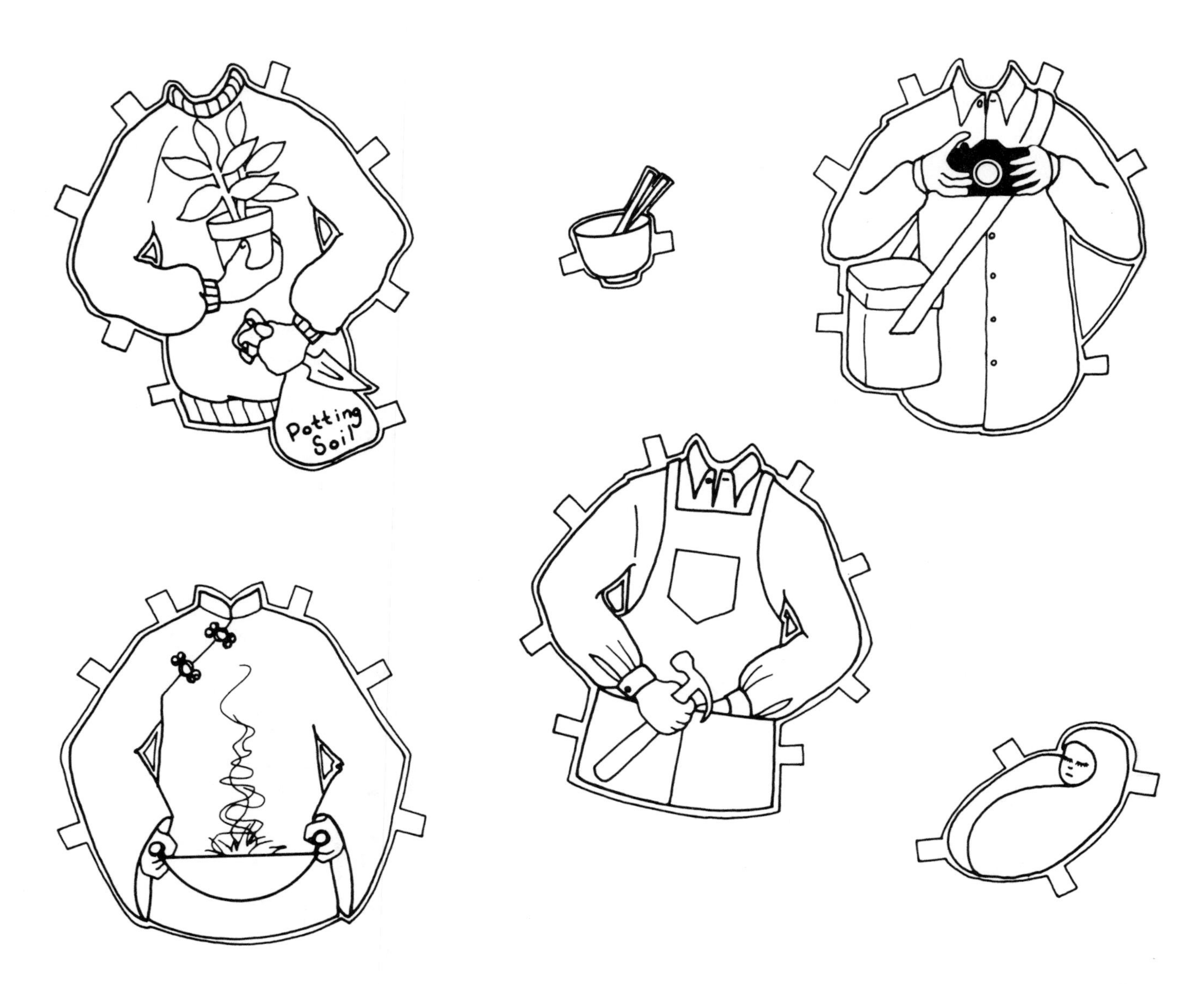

Interchangeable Clothes & Accessories

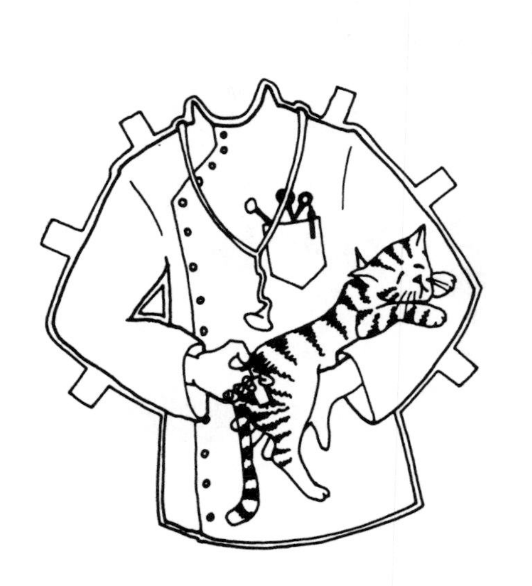

(3-4) TIGER, TEACHER, GUN

Objectives:
- To experience decision making
- To recognize the factors that influence group decision making

Grade Level: 7–9

Time Required: 30–40 minutes

Materials Needed: None

Description:

1. Divide the class into two teams. If the class is larger than 20 students, have 2 sections of 2 teams.
2. Appoint a scorekeeper and a referee for each team.
3. Each team should meet in a corner of the room. Allow them 5 minutes to select a name for their group. The scorekeeper writes the group names on the board.
4. Explain that they will soon have a chance to participate in a game called "Tiger, Teacher, Gun." It is similar to the game of "Paper, Rock, Scissors" that many played as children. The rules of "Tiger, Teacher, Gun" are as follows:

   Tiger wins over teacher.

   Teacher wins over gun.

   Gun wins over tiger.
5. Each team then decides (without the other team hearing) if it will be a teacher, a gun, or a tiger. Everyone on the team must be the same.
6. Have the teams gather in 2 lines facing each other, 15 feet apart. When the referee says "go," the two teams will walk toward each other performing the action of the role they have chosen.

   Tigers all growl and crawl or walk bent over.

   Teachers walk upright with a purposeful stride.

   Guns shoot, "Bang! Bang!"
7. The referee declares a winner, and the scorekeeper puts a point under the team name. If the entire team does not do the same action, a point is awarded to the opposing team.
8. Teams again decide on their action. The first team to reach 5 points wins.

9. Explain that the purpose of the activity was to experience group decision making. Discuss the following questions:
   a. How did you decide on a team name?
   b. Did everyone make suggestions? Why? Why not?
   c. How were game decisions made?
   d. Were you penalized for not doing the same?
   e. Why did it happen?
   f. How did you feel when someone said, "I told you so!"
   g. Did you have a leader?
   h. How was the leader chosen?
   i. Did anyone else want to be the leader?
   j. Does a group need a leader?
   k. What qualities do you want in a leader?
   l. What are the advantages and disadvantages of voting to make decisions?
   m. What are the advantages and disadvantages of an authority figure making the decision?
   n. What are the advantages and disadvantages of consulting with each team member?
   o. Can you relate this exercise to society?

(3-5) WHO'S THE BOSS?

Objective: • To recognize the need for government

Grade Level: 7–12

Time Required: 40–50 minutes

Materials Needed: None

Description:

1. The teacher writes on the board: "This is a government class. For the next 10 minutes, we shall explore government."
2. Make no further comments. Answer no questions. At the end of 10 minutes (or shorter, if the class becomes chaotic), continue.
3. Give explicit directions as to:
   Where they should sit
   Lesson assignment—book, pages, and so on

Student distribution of books (or other materials to be used)

Reading assignment

Materials should:

a. *Define* government as an institution that makes and enforces laws at federal, state, and local levels.

b. *Describe* its function to maintain social order, provide public service, provide security, and to make binding decisions.

4. Discuss by stating that they had a good example at the beginning of class of what happens when there is no direction, no authority, no one to make decisions, and so on. (Let class express feelings.)

Optional Activity:

For those students who are interested, suggest that they read about situations in which people tried to live without government. Two examples are *Lord of the Flies* by William Golding and *Earth Abides* by George R. Stewart.

(3-6) THE WAY IT IS

Objective: • To recognize the three branches of our government and the responsibilities of each

Grade Level 7–12

Time Required: 45 minutes

Materials Needed: Cardboard, yarn, markers

Description:

1. Divide the class into 3 groups.
2. Designate each as executive, judicial, or legislative.
3. Have each group make placards that depict a responsibility of its group after researching its special responsibilities.
4. Choose one member of the group to represent it. Have the 3 students stand at the front of the class as group members take turns reading the responsibilities of each branch of government as the placard is placed around the neck of the "branch" of government.
5. Hang the placards on the wall.

RESPONSIBILITIES

Judicial	Legislative	Executive
—May declare a law unconstitutional —May rule executive orders unconstitutional	—May override the president's veto —May impeach and remove the president from office —Sets salaries of federal judges —May refuse to ratify a treaty —May override Supreme Court by proposing constitutional amendment —May refuse to confirm appointments	—Appoints federal judges —Recommends legislation —Calls special session of Congress —May veto bills —May grant reprieves and pardons

(3-7) FAIL SAFE

Objective: • To understand how the power of each branch has been controlled by a system of checks and balances

Grade Level: 7–12

Time Required: 30–40 minutes

Materials Needed: "Checks and Balances" transparency; three pieces of yarn; straight pins; newsprint; markers

Description:

1. Assign one group as checks and balances of *executive*. Attach yarn from the wrist of *executive branch* to a student designated as *judicial* and to a student designated as *legislature*. Choose those checks and balances from the following transparency that the *executive* has over the other two branches. Attach each of them to the yarn that connects the branch of government.

2. Assign a second group as checks and balances of *judicial*. Follow directions of first group in attaching yarn to the wrist of student portraying *judicial* to wrist of executive and to legislature.
3. Assign third group as checks and balances of *legislature*. Follow the same directions of pinning checks and balances of *legislature* on executive and judicial.
4. When completed group stands in front of the class, the jury selected by the teacher decides if the right choice has been made.

CHECKS AND BALANCES

May override the president's veto

May impeach and remove the president from office

May declare a law unconstitutional

Sets salaries of federal judges

Appoints federal judges

Recommends legislation

May refuse to ratify a treaty

Calls special sessions of Congress

May ratify constitutional amendment

May veto bills

May grant reprieves and pardons

May rule executive orders unconstitutional

(3-8) TOSS OF A COIN

Objective: • To emphasize that a democracy lives or dies by the way its citizens balance rights and responsibilities

Grade Level: 7–12

Time Required: 30–40 minutes

Materials Needed: A "Jefferson" nickel for every class member; copies of "Bill of Rights" handout

Description:

1. What are on the two sides of this coin? (Jefferson, Monticello)
2. Tell the students that Jefferson's face represents our rights as written in the Bill of Rights.
3. Have students read Bill of Rights.
4. Turn the coin over to the Monticello side.
5. Tell the students that Jefferson's home represents the responsibilities that go with our rights.
6. Make a list of our responsibilities on the board.
7. Conclude with the thought that just as the Jefferson coin cannot be separated, neither can rights and responsibilities. (Don't forget to collect nickels!)

Discuss the following:

Freedom of speech carries a responsibility not to libel or slander.

Right to bear arms carries the responsibility to use weapons wisely.

Right to jury trial means citizens should serve on a jury.

Free elections mean we have a responsibility to vote.

Right to our property carries the responsibility to respect others' property, and so on.

Right to practice religion of choice means others may choose another religion or no religion.

BILL OF RIGHTS

First Amendment

Guarantees freedom of religion, speech, press, and the right to petition government.

Second Amendment

Guarantees the right to a state militia and to bear arms.

Third Amendment

Prohibits the quartering of soldiers in homes in peacetime.

Fourth Amendment

Prohibits unreasonable searches and seizures.

Fifth Amendment

Requires grand jury indictment for serious crimes. Bans double jeopardy. Prohibits having to testify against oneself. Guarantees no loss of life, liberty, or property without due process of law.

Sixth Amendment

Guarantees the right to speedy, impartial public trial in criminal cases with counsel, and the right to cross-examine witnesses.

Seventh Amendment

Guarantees the right to jury trial in civil suits involving $20 or more.

Eighth Amendment

Prohibits excessive bail or fines or cruel and unusual punishment.

Ninth Amendment

Rights not listed in other amendments are not necessarily involved.

Tenth Amendment

Asserts that powers not delegated to the national government or denied to the states are reserved to the states.

(3-9) SHOULD MEN HAVE THE RIGHT TO VOTE?*

Objectives:
- To explain the meaning of equality under the law
- To list the implications of a power monopoly by one sex

Grade Level: 7–12

Time Required: 40–50 minutes

Materials Needed: Copies of "Why We Oppose Votes for Men" handout

Description:

1. Use this activity in the study of woman's suffrage and the Nineteenth Amendment. The activity incorporates reverse discrimination to stimulate discussion and insight.
2. Break the class into groups of 4 or 5.
3. Distribute copies of the "Why We Oppose Votes for Men" handout. Instruct the groups to consider a society in which only women are allowed to vote, occupy political office, and possess positions of economic power. Write the following questions on the board for the groups to consider:
   a. How would things be changed if this society existed?
   b. Would men be discriminated against in such a society?
   c. What would such a society lose? Gain?
4. Have the entire class consider the following questions:
   a. Why does Alice Duer Miller's argument seem so effective?
   b. Is sex role stereotyping as severe now as the sex stereotyping depicted in Miller's argument?
   c. How much has sex stereotyping decreased since the passage of the Nineteenth Amendment?

Optional Activities:

1. Assign students to investigate the lives and influence of the women who fought for suffrage. Include Carrie Chapman Catt, Emma Goldman, Mary McDowell, Susan B. Anthony, Anna Howard Shaw, Alva Vanderbilt Belmont, and Lucretia Mott. The correspondence of these women is particulary revealing.
2. Assign students to write a letter to one of the above women describing the plight of women today.

---

*Adapted from *Law in U.S. History: A Teacher Resource Manual*, edited by Melinda R. Smith (New Mexico Law-Related Education Project, 1981), pp. 193–194. Used with permission.

WHY WE OPPOSE VOTES FOR MEN

1. BECAUSE MAN'S PLACE IS IN THE ARMY.

2. BECAUSE NO REALLY MANLY MAN WANTS TO SETTLE ANY QUESTION OTHERWISE THAN BY FIGHTING.

3. BECAUSE IF MEN SHOULD ADOPT PEACEABLE METHODS, WOMEN WILL NO LONGER LOOK UP TO THEM.

4. BECAUSE MEN WILL LOSE THEIR CHARM IF THEY STEP OUT OF THEIR NATURAL SPHERE AND INTEREST THEMSELVES IN OTHER MATTERS THAN FEATS OF ARMS, UNIFORMS, AND DRUMS.

5. BECAUSE MEN ARE TOO EMOTIONAL TO VOTE. THEIR CONDUCT AT BASEBALL GAMES AND POLITICAL CONVENTIONS SHOWS THIS, WHILE THEIR INNATE TENDENCY TO APPEAL TO FORCE RENDERS THEM PARTICULARLY UNFIT FOR THE TASK OF GOVERNMENT.

Alice Duer Miller, 1915

(3-10) THE HEART

Objective: • To become aware that our Constitution is a living document changing with the times and is at the heart of our political system

Grade Level: 7–12

Time Required: 30–40 minutes

Materials Needed: Copies of "Flow Chart for Amending the Constitution"

Directions:

1. Inform the class that in over 200 years of history, the Constitution (except the Bill of Rights with its 10 amendments) has changed only 16 times. However, our founding fathers built in a mechanism so that it could be changed, if necessary.
2. Have interested students choose one of the amendments and tell what conditions in the country produced the change.
3. Have the class discuss what changes they think should be made in the Constitution. For example:
   a. Permit prayer in school
   b. Forbid abortion
   c. Federal budget should be balanced
   d. Other
4. Have the class choose a change.
5. Look up Article V of the Constitution that tells how an amendment may be adopted. Distribute copies of the flow chart.
6. Role-play the adoption.

Flow Chart for Amending the Constitution

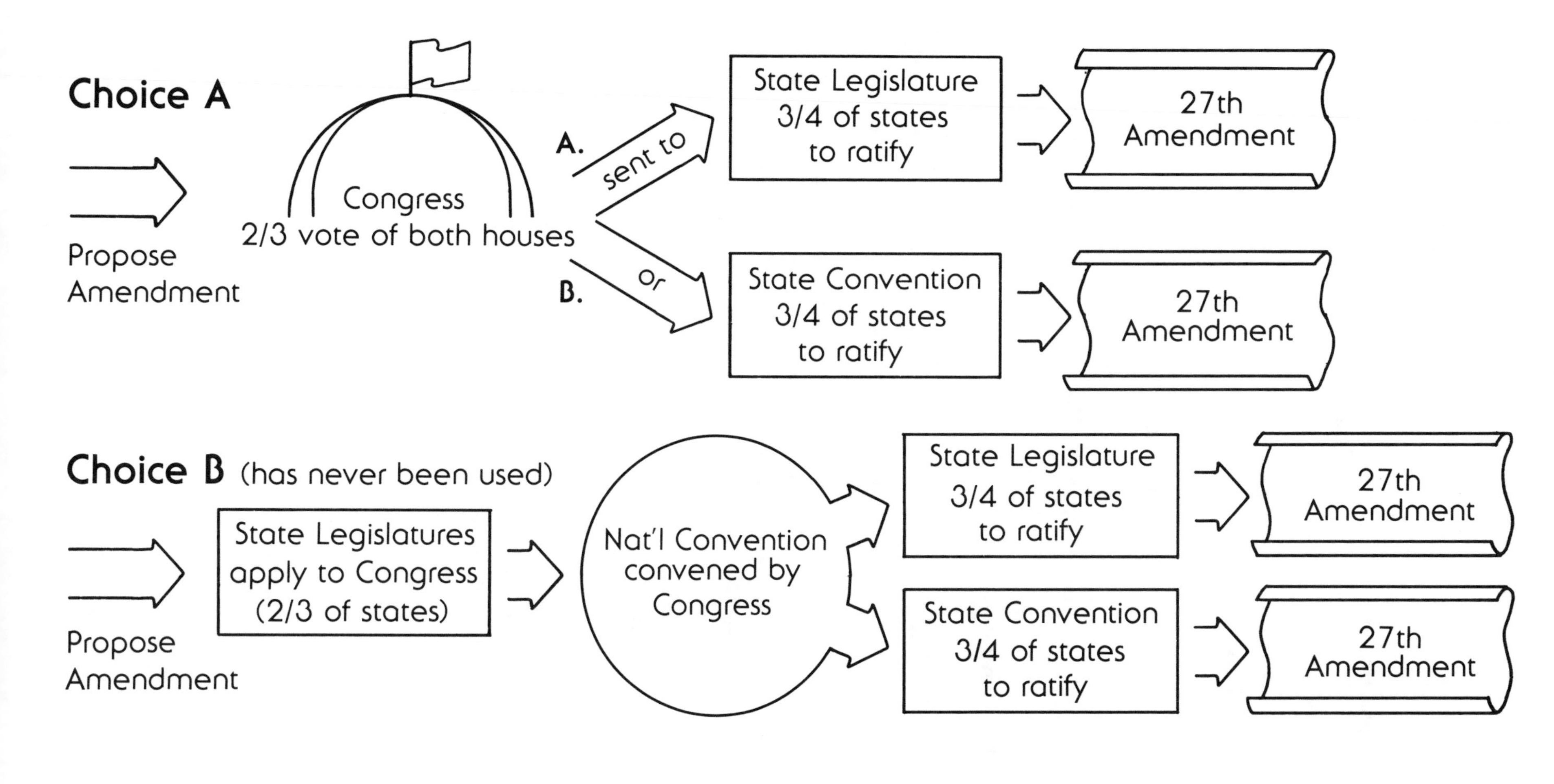

(3-11) CONSTITUTION CROSSWORD PUZZLE

Objective: • To reinforce knowledge of the Constitution

Grade Level: 7–12

Time Required: One period

Materials Needed: Copies of "Constitution Crossword Puzzle"

Description:

Distribute copies of the crossword puzzle for students to complete during class.

Name ______________________ Date ______________________

CONSTITUTION CROSSWORD PUZZLE

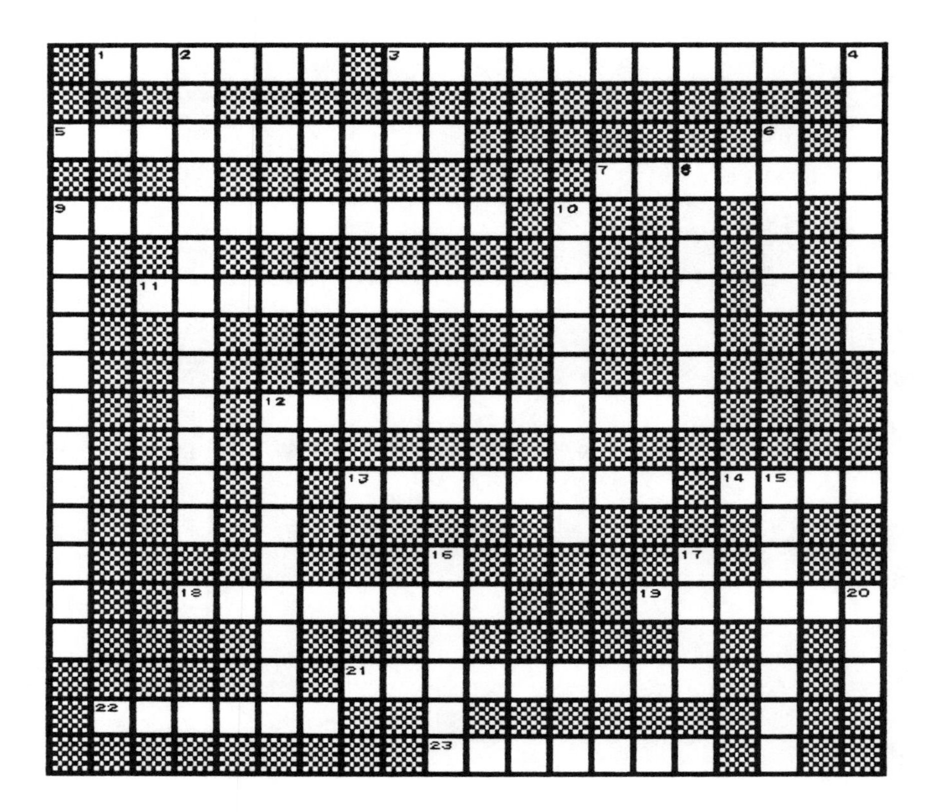

ACROSS

1. 16th Amendment tax
3. City of signing
5. Additions
7. President Pro ______ of Senate
9. Indictment of official by House
11. Law-making branch
12. Began by 18th Amendment
13. Powers belonging to people or states
14. Return of bill by president
18. Supreme Court power
19. Bill of ______
21. ______ College
22. Minimum age for senator
23. Abolished by 13th Amendment

DOWN

2. Articles of ______, the predecessor of Constitution
4. 1st Amendment's right
6. Granted vote by 19th Amendment
8. "Father of the Constitution"
9. ______ Hall
10. Enforcement branch
12. The chief executive
15. Minimum voting age
16. Writ of ______ Corpus
17. Beginning of a law
20. Senator's term

(3-12) DO YOU KNOW?

Objective: • To investigate the services provided by government

Grade Level: 7–12

Time Required: Assigned 2 weeks prior to first class period presentation

Materials Needed: Copies of "Do You Know?" handout

Description:

1. Students may work alone or with a partner. Their task is to answer the question, describe the steps necessary to obtain an answer, and identify the level of government (federal, state, local) providing the service.
2. Finished product will be presented in two forms, a written and an oral report. The written report includes a journal of time and steps involved in obtaining an answer and any pertinent data collected.
3. In the oral presentation, students are to answer the question and give the level of government providing the service.

DO YOU KNOW?

Directions:

The government provides many services. You are to investigate one of the following services to determine the steps necessary to attain it. Is the service provided by local, state, or federal government? Present your findings in writing and orally to the rest of the class. Your written report should include a record of the time and steps taken to gather the information and any pertinent data collected.

How to:

Get an appointment to Annapolis.
Apply for social security benefits if the father dies.
Apply for federally approved low-income housing.
File a complaint of sexual harassment.
File a consumer complaint.
Obtain a fishing license.
Obtain a marriage license.
Get back an impounded car.
Register a complaint against a landlord.
Obtain a divorce.
Obtain a moped license.
Obtain welfare.
Obtain a passport.
Get food stamps.
Get a patent for a new invention.
Enlist in the armed forces.
Find out the minimum wage.
Find out safety standards for cars.
Get someone committed to a mental institution.
Get help for drug addiction.
Obtain the minimum standards for funeral homes.
Sell a car and transfer the title.
Visit a jail.
Get a library card.
Obtain a beggar's license.
Adopt a baby.
Obtain a birth certificate.
Obtain a social security number.
Live with someone other than parents.
Register a dog.
Find out the rules regarding building a swimming pool.

(3-13) MISTER PRESIDENT

Objectives:
- To gather information from a chart
- To become familiar with the names of the presidents of the United States

Grade Level: 7–12

Time Required: 15–30 minutes

Materials Needed: Copies of "Mister President" and "Presidents of the United States" handouts

Description:

1. Distribute copies of the handouts to the class.
2. This activity may be completed as homework or in class, individually or in pairs.
3. As an enrichment activity, assign the following questions to the class or offer as an extra credit option to individuals:
   Which president was impeached? (Andrew Johnson)
   What caused his impeachment? (Handling of Reconstruction)
   Was he acquitted or convicted? (Acquitted)
   Why did one president resign? (Richard Nixon over Watergate)
   Why can a president serve only two terms? (Constitutional amendment)
   Should we change that?
   What would be the advantages of a six-year term?

Name ______________________ Date ______________________

MISTER PRESIDENT

Use the "Presidents of the United States" chart to answer the following questions:

1. Who was the youngest president when taking office?

____

2. Who was the oldest president when taking office?

____

3. How many Democrats have served as president?

____

4. How many Republicans have served as president?

____

5. Who was the only president to be impeached?

____

6. Who was the only president to resign?

____

7. Who served two terms but not consecutively?

____

8. Who was president for the longest time period?

____

9. Who was president when the United States entered World War II?

____

10. Who was the last Whig president?

____

BONUS: Name the presidents in your lifetime. ______________________

____

PRESIDENTS OF THE UNITED STATES

Name	Term of Office	Party	Age on Taking Office
George Washington	1789–1797	Federalist	57
John Adams	1797–1801	Federalist	61
Thomas Jefferson	1801–1809	Dem. Rep.	57
James Madison	1809–1817	Dem. Rep.	57
James Monroe	1817–1825	Dem. Rep.	58
John Quincy Adams	1825–1829	Dem. Rep.	57
Andrew Jackson	1829–1837	Democrat	61
Martin Van Buren	1837–1841	Democrat	54
William H. Harrison	1841–1841	Whig	68
John Tyler	1841–1845	Whig	51
James K. Polk	1845–1849	Democrat	49
Zachary Taylor	1849–1850	Whig	64
Millard Fillmore	1850–1853	Whig	50
Franklin Pierce	1853–1857	Democrat	48
James Buchanan	1857–1861	Democrat	65
Abraham Lincoln	1861–1865	Republican	52
Andrew Johnson*	1865–1869	Democrat	56
Ulysses S. Grant	1869–1877	Republican	46
Rutherford B. Hayes	1877–1881	Republican	54
James A. Garfield	1881–1881	Republican	49
Chester A. Arthur	1881–1885	Republican	50
Grover Cleveland	1885–1889	Democrat	47
Benjamin Harrison	1889–1893	Republican	55
Grover Cleveland	1893–1897	Democrat	55
William McKinley	1897–1901	Republican	54
Theodore Roosevelt	1901–1909	Republican	42
William H. Taft	1909–1913	Republican	51
Woodrow Wilson	1913–1921	Democrat	56
Warren G. Harding	1921–1923	Republican	55
Calvin Coolidge	1923–1929	Republican	51
Herbert Hoover	1929–1933	Republican	54
Franklin D. Roosevelt	1933–1945	Democrat	51
Harry S. Truman	1945–1953	Democrat	60
Dwight D. Eisenhower	1953–1961	Republican	62
John F. Kennedy	1961–1963	Democrat	43
Lyndon B. Johnson	1963–1969	Democrat	55
Richard M. Nixon**	1969–1974	Republican	56
Gerald R. Ford	1974–1977	Republican	61
Jimmy Carter	1977–1981	Democrat	52
Ronald Reagan	1981–1989	Republican	69
George Bush	1989–	Republican	62

*impeached, but not convicted
**resigned

(3-14) READ A CARTOON

Objective: • To interpret a political cartoon

Grade Level: 7–12

Time Required: 15 minutes

Materials Needed: Political cartoon transparency

Description:

1. Political cartoons have been used since the 1700s to communicate the essence of the American political system to the public.
2. Have the students interpret the cartoon transparency in terms of the Bill of Rights. (For example, "Responsibility is for the birds.")
   a. Who do the birds represent?
   b. Why did the cartoonist choose birds to represent people?
   c. What are the implications of political cartoons?

Optional Activities:

1. Have students draw cartoons illustrating the inseparable dimension of rights and responsibilities inherent in our political system, or bring in cartoons from local newspapers.
2. Have students bring in political cartoons. Students should show them to the class and offer their interpretation of their meanings.

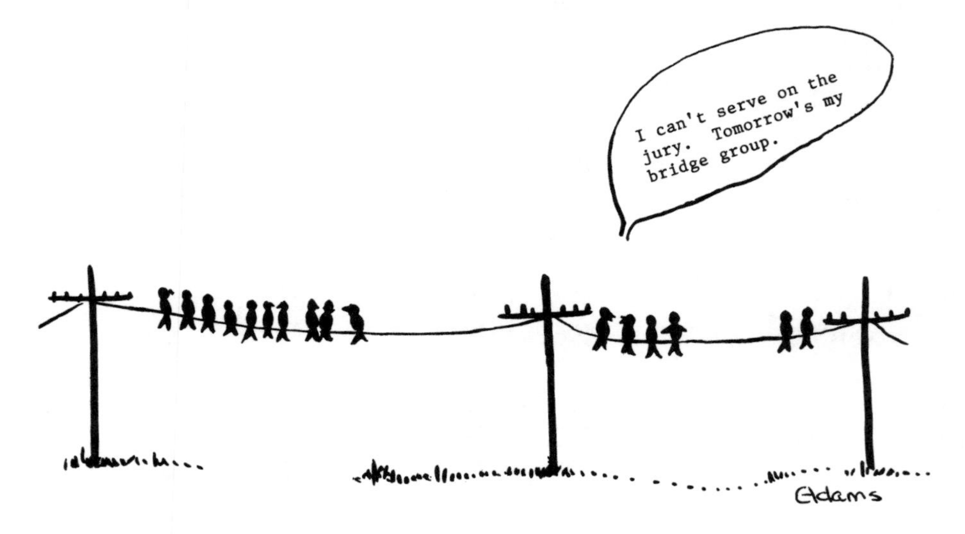

(3-15) IMMIGRATION

Objectives:
- To interpret data from a bar graph
- To recognize the patterns of immigration in American history

Grade Level: 7–12

Time Required: 25–35 minutes in class or one night as homework

Materials: Copies of "U.S. Immigration by Country of Origin" and "Immigration" handouts

Description:

1. This activity may be used as homework or completed in class.
2. Distribute the "U.S. Immigration by Country of Origin" and "Immigration" handouts. Allow approximately 15 minutes for students to answer the questions about interpretation of the graph.
3. Either collect and evaluate or review the answers in class.
4. Discuss the patterns of immigration that are represented in the graph. What are their projections for future patterns of immigration?

U.S. IMMIGRATION BY COUNTRY OF ORIGIN

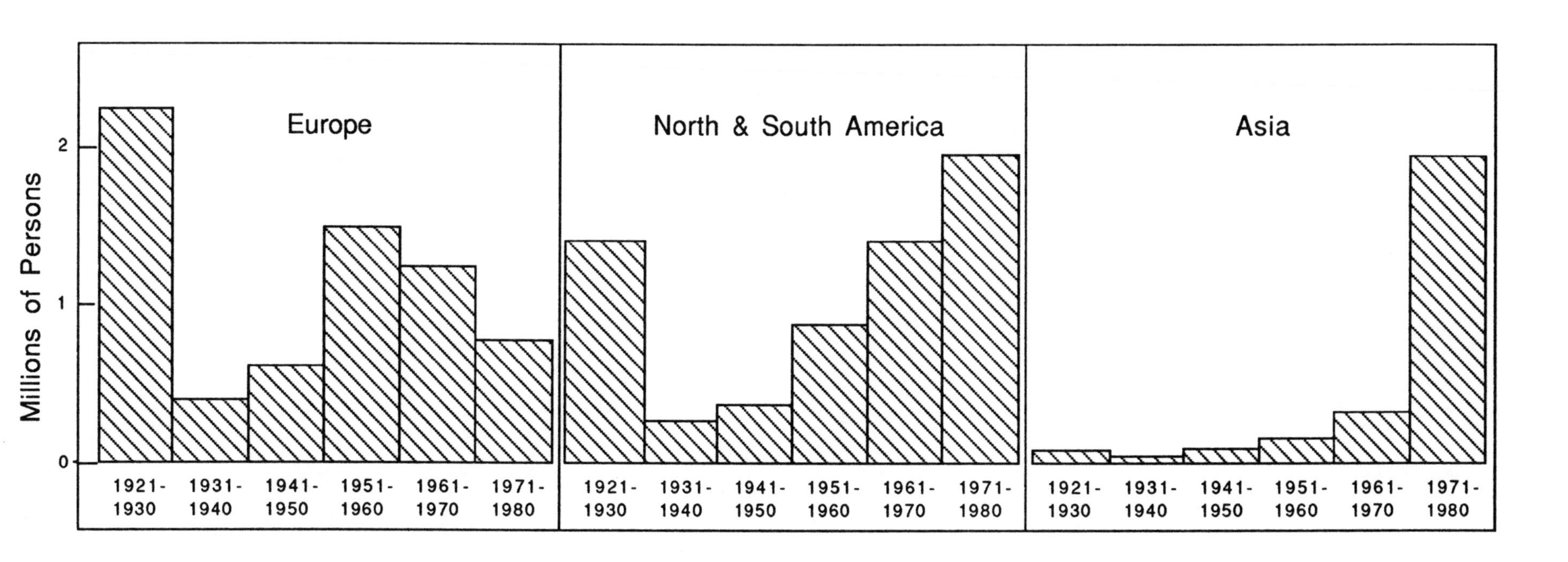

Source: Bureau of Immigration and Naturalization

Name ______________________ Date ______________________

IMMIGRATION

The United States is a country of immigrants—50 million in the last 100 years! Since 1787, restrictions placed on who may enter the country and from where have changed considerably.

Use the "U.S. Immigration by Country of Origin" handout to answer the following questions:

1. From what continent did the largest number of immigrants come during 1921–1930?

____

2. What is the estimated number of immigrants from question 1?

____

3. From what continent did the smallest number of immigrants come between 1921 and 1970?

____

4. What is the estimated number of immigrants from question 3?

____

5. What time period produced the largest number of immigrants from Europe?

____

6. Can you think of any reasons for so many people to come during the time period from question 5?

____

7. What time period produced the smallest number of immigrants?

____

8. How many people came from Europe between 1951 and 1960?

____

9. How many persons immigrated to the United States from Asia between 1971 and 1980?

____

10. Why the sudden rise in Asian immigration?

____

(3-16) WASHINGTON WEEK

Objective: • To involve the students in current events

Grade Level: 7–12

Time Required: 45 minutes

Materials Needed: List of assignments

Description:

1. Assign a specific person, place, or topic to each student.
2. Each week have the student share with the class how that person or place has made news for that week.

Suggestions:

President of U.S.	President's spouse	Hollywood
Lebanon	West Berlin	The pope
Syria	London	Gorbachev
Jesse Jackson	Foreign trade	The education system
Howard Baker	California	Nutrition
Labor unions	NAACP	Your governor
AIDS	El Salvador	Philippines
South Africa	Oil	Nuclear power
City council	Airlines	Auto industry
Canada	British prime minister	

(3-17) POPULATION

Objectives: • To read data from tables
• To acquire knowledge of the composition of the U.S. population

Grade Level: 7–12

Time Required: 20–30 minutes, or one night as homework.

Materials Needed: Copies of "U.S. Population" and "Population Questions" handouts

Description:

1. Distribute the 2 handouts in class and allow students 15 minutes to complete the questions. You might choose to have them complete the task in pairs.
2. Discuss the answers. Encourage the class to draw hypotheses on the future composition of the U.S. population.

U.S. POPULATION

By Race

	Number (millions)			Percent		
	1960	1970	1980	1960	1970	1980
White	158.8	177.7	188.4	88.6%	87.5%	83.1%
Black	18.8	22.6	26.4	10.5	11.1	11.7
American Indian	.5	.8	1.4	.3	.4	.6
Asian	1.1	2.1	10.3	.6	1.0	4.6
Total	179.3	263.2	226.5	100%	100%	100%

Source: Bureau of the Census

By Age

	Percent of Population		
Age (in yrs.)	1960	1970	1980
under 5	11.3%	8.4%	7.2%
5–9	10.4	9.8	7.4
10–19	16.9	19.6	17.3
20–29	12.1	14.7	18.0
30–39	13.7	11.1	14.0
40–49	12.6	12.0	10.0
50–59	10.0	10.0	10.3
60 and over	13.2	14.0	15.8
Median age	29.5	28.0	30.0

Source: Bureau of the Census

Name ______________________ Date ______________________

POPULATION QUESTIONS

Use the "U.S. Population" chart to help you answer the following questions:

1. During which year did whites make up the largest percentage of the U.S. population?

   ____

2. Which census showed the greater number of Asians in the U.S.?

   ____

3. How many Asians from question 2?

   ____

4. What do you think accounted for that dramatic increase in the Asian population in the U.S.?

   ____

   ____

5. What percent of the U.S. population was nonwhite in 1970? ______________________
6. What was the total population of the U.S. in 1960? ______________________
7. Which age group made up the largest percentage of the population in 1960? ____________
8. What group formed the smallest percentage in 1980? ______________________
9. Which age group showed the largest percentage increase between 1960 and 1980? ________
10. What percent of the population was between 30 and 39 years of age in 1970? ____________

(3-18) GET OUT THE VOTE

Objective: • To understand the vote of political parties, campaign methods, election rules, and voting procedures in the democratic process

Grade Level: 7–12

Time Required: Ongoing project

Materials Needed: Markers, posters

Description:

1. Divide the class into Republicans, Democrats, and Independents according to choice.
2. Choose a representative from Republicans and Democrats to be candidates for office.
3. Have fund-raisers; hold political rallies, with speeches, food, balloons, literature, hoopla.
4. Send representatives to League of Women Voters' "Meet the Candidates." Report to the class.
5. Debate the platforms.
6. Conduct a mock school election.
7. Emphasize that political parties are the result of our country's history and circumstances rather than planning by our Founding Fathers. Our Constitution does not mention political parties. Therefore, it is essential to examine the political history of our country in order to understand today's political parties.
8. Have the students research the history of political parties.

Optional Activities:

1. Write a constitution for the class.
2. Invite local business executives to give a talk on the various ways government regulates and also aids their businesses.
3. Invite naturalized citizens to describe how they became citizens.
4. Invite a judge to address the class about the court's obligation to protect the innocent (Miranda Decision, and so on)
5. Write a report on your Congressional representative or senator.
6. Keep a bulletin board of current events.

(3-19) SPACE STATION

Objectives:
- To recognize the need for laws
- To appreciate the difficulty in writing effective and fair laws
- To practice skills of consensus decision making

Grade Level: 7–12

Time Required: 40–50 minutes

Materials Needed: Newsprint

Description:

1. Divide the class into groups of 4.
2. Read the following instructions to the class:

   > You have been chosen as a citizen in space for the next NASA launch. You are invited to submit 5 rules for NASA to consider for all those people who are going up on the next space launch. Remember that your space station will remain in space for 10 years. Record your rules on the sheets of newsprint provided.

3. Invite the groups to share their sets of rules with the rest of the class. Have each group hang their list of rules on the wall as they describe their choices.
4. Attempt to have the class come to a consensus on 5 rules.
5. Discuss the decision-making process groups used in attempting to find agreement.
6. Process the insights gained into the rule-making process. Can any lessons be extrapolated to the making of school rules? Federal laws?

(3-20) COURT OF LAST RESORT

Objective:
- To understand the function of the Supreme Court

Grade Level: 7–12

Time Required: Two class periods

Materials Needed: Pencil; nameplates for the justices; copies of "Does the Fourth Amendment Belong in School?" handout

Description:

1. Choose students to portray the following roles:
   a. Nine justices
   b. Nine clerks for the justices
   c. One attorney (for petitioner)
   d. One attorney (for respondent)
   e. Two petitioners
   f. Two respondents
2. Point out that two types of cases come to the Supreme Court: First, *original jurisdiction*: cases involving representation of a foreign government or certain cases involving a state; and second, *appellate jurisdiction*: cases appealed from lower courts.
3. Distribute the handout and facilitate the role playing.
4. Additional resources addressing constitutional rights of students, and the *T.L.O.* case in particular, include the following:

Clayman, Robert. "Once an Adult, Always an Adult," *Update on Law-Related Education*, American Bar Association (Fall 1983).

Force, Robert, and Baum, Daniel Jay. *Introduction to Law* and *Student Rights and Responsibilities*, Cincinnati, OH: Southeastern Publishing, 1982.

Naylor, David. "Teaching about Student Rights and Responsibilities," *Update on Law-Related Education* (Fall 1979).

Riekes, Linda, and Ackerly, Sally Mahe. *Courts and Trials, Law in Action Series*. Mineola, NY: West Publishing, 1980.

Sitomer, Curtis J. "Should the Constitution Apply in School?" *Christian Science Monitor* (September 6, 1984).

Turner, Mary Jane, and Parisi, Lynn. *Law in the Classroom: Activities and Resources, Revised*. Boulder, CO: Social Science Education Consortium, in Cooperation with ERIC Clearinghouse for Social Studies/Social Science Education, 1984.

Vardin, Patricia, and Brody, Ilene, eds. *Children's Rights: Contemporary Perspectives*. Teachers College, Columbia University Press, 1978.

"DOES THE FOURTH AMENDMENT BELONG IN SCHOOL?"*

by Joseph L. Daly

***State of New Jersey v. T.L.O.*, a Juvenile**
(Docket No. 83-712)
Argued March 28, 1984
Reargued October 2, 1984

ISSUES

In *New Jersey v. T.L.O.*, the Court will decide how far the Constitution reaches into schools by focusing on two specific legal issues:

1. Does the Fourth Amendment's exclusionary rule apply to searches made by public school officials and teachers in school?
2. Did the assistant principal violate the Fourth Amendment in opening T.L.O.'s purse under the circumstances of this case?

FACTS

On March 7, 1980, Ms. Chen, a teacher at Piscataway, New Jersey, High School, walked into the school's restroom and found two students, T.L.O. and another girl, holding lit cigarettes. Because their action violated school rules, Chen took the girls to the office of the Assistant Vice Principal, Theodore Choplik. When he asked the girls if they had been smoking, T.L.O. denied it and further claimed that she did not smoke at all. [In all the case briefs and arguments, the student is identified only by the initials T.L.O. in order to keep her name out of the record because she is under 18. This protects her name and reputation from any lasting bad effects of the lawsuit.]

Choplik then asked her to come into a private office and requested her purse, which she handed to him. When he opened it, he saw a package of cigarettes and a package of rolling papers for cigarettes. The juvenile denied that these belonged to her. On the basis of experience, Choplik knew that rolling papers indicated marijuana, and when he looked further into the purse, he found marijuana, drug paraphernalia, $40 in one-dollar bills, and documentation about T.L.O.'s marijuana sales to other students.

Choplik then called T.L.O.'s mother and notified the police. Upon question-

---

*From *Preview of the United States Supreme Court Cases* by the Public Education Division of the American Bar Association. Used with permission of the ABA, 750 North Lake Shore Drive, Chicago, IL 96061.

ing at police headquarters, T.L.O. admitted selling marijuana in school. A delinquency complaint was drafted and filed that day. [A "delinquency procedure" is commonly used for those under 18 who commit offenses. Those declared "juveniles" or "delinquents" by a court will usually be sentenced to some type of supervision by the court, or sometimes placed in foster care or a juvenile detention center.] T.L.O. was subsequently tried, found guilty, and adjudicated delinquent. Later, she was sentenced to probation for one year.

T.L.O. appealed her case, first to the Superior Court of New Jersey, Appellate Division. That court also held that the evidence seized in the search of T.L.O.'s purse should be admitted. She then appealed to the Supreme Court of New Jersey, which agreed with her that the Fourth Amendment exclusionary rule applied to searches and seizures of students by school officials in public schools. It held that the evidence should not have been admitted.

BACKGROUND AND SIGNIFICANCE

1. *Did the Fourth Amendment's exclusionary rule apply to searches made by public school officials and teachers in school?*

The Court in this case is asked to weigh the Fourth Amendment's guarantee of freedom from unreasonable searches and seizures against students' rights to an institutional environment conducive to education.

Remember that the Fourth Amendment only protects against unreasonable searches and seizures by the state, or by government agents. New Jersey argues here, that school officials are not involved in law enforcement. Therefore, the state claims, excluding evidence that these officials gather from a criminal proceeding would have little meaning and, therefore, little or no deterrent impact upon their actions.

On the other side, T.L.O. views the school authorities as governmental agents whose actions should be subject to the Fourth Amendment. The fact that school authorities are state employees and act with state authority to implement state laws and regulations governing education compels the conclusion, according to T.L.O., that they are government agents rather than merely private citizens for Fourth Amendment purposes.

To further support its argument, New Jersey hopes to persuade the Court that the school authorities stand *in loco parentis* (Or "in place of the parent"). When parents entrust their children to the public schools, they have a right to expect that the schools will, to the best of their ability, stand in the place of the parent and protect the students from harmful influences while educating them. To do this, it is essential that school officials have broad supervisory and disciplinary power—just as parents have. Because the parent could search a child without regard to the Fourth Amendment, so should a school official.

T.L.O. argues, however, that because of modern compulsory education laws, the premise that the parent specifically delegates the authority to the teacher is unfounded. Most lower courts have found that teachers act as agents of the government, not of the parents, and as such, are subject to the Fourth Amendment.

2. *Did the assistant principal in this case violate the Fourth Amendment?*

The state of New Jersey agrees that students do not shed their Fourth Amendment rights when they enter a school. New Jersey wants the Court to recognize that students have Fourth Amendment protections in the school, but the word "reasonable" should be interpreted less strictly for school officials than for police.

T.L.O. argues that a student has a legal right to expect privacy while in school and that that expectation is substantial. She points out that, in a case decided last term, *Hudson v. Palmer*, 104 S. Ct. 3194 (1984), the Court decided that a prisoner has no legal right to expect privacy in a jail cell. The Court must adopt a standard which would give students more Fourth Amendment rights than prison inmates. T.L.O. also argues that Fourth Amendment rights and expectations by students must be conscientiously protected by the courts to help the public school system achieve its primary goal—educating students.

The state argues that courts must set stricter guidelines for school officials because school systems have become "the hotbed of crime and violence." T.L.O. disagrees. She cites statistics from the National Institute of Education, "Violent Schools—Safe Schools: The Safe School Study Report to the Congress," 2 (1978), ERIC #ED-175-112 (The Safe School Report), which concluded that only eight percent of the nation's schools were experiencing a serious crime problem. In fact, some researchers feel that four percent is a more accurate estimate. So, T.L.O. argues, it would indeed be irrational to strip the vast majority of students of all but a minimal expectation of privacy to attempt to solve the problems of a relative few.

ARGUMENTS

For New Jersey

1. The Fourth Amendment exclusionary rule should not be applied to searches conducted by public school officials in school.

For T.L.O.

1. As the decision below rested on adequate and independent state grounds, the Court should dismiss the writ of *certiorari* as improvidently granted.
2. The Fourth Amendment exclusionary rule is constitutionally mandated when the state attempts to use evidence illegally seized from a student by public school personnel.

AMICUS ARGUMENTS

[In briefs filed by the *amici* (friends of the court), additional arguments are raised on both sides of the case.]

For the National School Boards Association in Support of New Jersey

1. School searches are necessary to maintain order, discipline, and safety.

2. The Fourth Amendment was not intended to apply in the school setting.
3. Criminal justice standards are not transferrable to the special setting of the school.
4. Student lockers are not protected by the Fourth Amendment.
5. Alternatives exist to the Fourth Amendment to protect students' constitutional rights.

For the New Jersey School Boards Association in Support of New Jersey

1. The exclusionary rule does not apply to searches conducted by school officials in good faith.

For the American Civil Liberties Union and the American Civil Liberties Union of New Jersey in Support of T.L.O.

1. Juveniles do not shed their Fourth Amendment right to be free from unreasonable searches at the schoolhouse gate.
2. Juveniles do not abandon their expectations of privacy by attending school.
3. The necessity of the exclusionary rule is not less vital in the education system than in similar nonlaw enforcement contexts.
4. The benevolent concept of *in loco parentis* cannot be applied to deny juveniles the essential protections of the Fourth Amendment.

(3-21) THE CONSTITUTION QUIZ

Objectives:
- To assess the basic knowledge of the U.S. Constitution
- To stimulate interest in the Constitution and the rights in the criminal justice system
- To compare the individual's knowledge of the Constitution with that found in a national survey

Grade Level: 7–12

Time Required: 40–60 minutes

Materials Needed: Copies of "The Constitution Quiz"

Description:

1. "The Constitution Quiz" is based on a research study funded by the Hearst Corporation in 1986.* After the class has completed the survey, you may compare their results with those from the survey of adults.
2. You might duplicate the quiz and assign students to survey adults in their community to see if their results are similar to those from the Hearst Corporation study.

---

*This quiz was based on a survey of 1,004 adults sponsored by the Hearst Corporation.

Name ______________________ Date ______________________

THE CONSTITUTION QUIZ

Directions: *Indicate whether each of the following statements is true or false.*

T F

____ ____ **1.** The Constitution establishes English as the national language and requires its use in schools and government.

____ ____ **2.** Public schools may require students to pledge allegiance to the flag.

____ ____ **3.** The Constitution created a Federal Government and defined its powers.

____ ____ **4.** The Constitution was drafted to declare independence from England.

____ ____ **5.** Public schools are permitted to require moments of silence for prayer.

____ ____ **6.** A person accused of a serious crime who cannot afford a lawyer must be provided with one.

____ ____ **7.** The President of the United States can suspend the Constitution in time of war or national emergency.

____ ____ **8.** The President acting alone cannot conclude treaties with foreign nations.

____ ____ **9.** The Constitution allows the states to impose the death penalty.

____ ____ **10.** Nothing in the Constitution prohibits states from legalizing the sale of marijuana within their borders.

Directions: *Fill in the blanks with the appropriate answers.*

11. What was the landmark decision in which the Supreme Court ruled that suspects must be told their rights before questioning by police? ______________________

12. The first ten amendments to the Constitution is known as ______________________

13. Who is the Chief Justice of the U.S. Supreme Court? ______________________

Adapted from the Hearst Corporation Constitution Survey, 1986. Used with permission.

POSSIBLE RESOURCE PERSONS

ACLU representative
Amnesty International spokesperson
Auditor
Bailiff
Board of Education president
Board of elections representative
City council representative
City planner
Civil engineer
Clerk of courts
Congressional representative
County commissioner
County records
Criminologist
Drug enforcement officer
Environmental Protection agent
Ex-convict
FBI agent
Immigration office representative
Internal Revenue Service agent
Judge
Juvenile court judge
Law professor
Lawyer
League of Women Voters representative
Lobbyist
Mayor
Naturalized citizen
Police chief
Political party chairperson
Prison warden
Probation officer
Public defender
Public utility commission spokesperson
School superintendent
Sheriff
Senator

Small claims court referee
Social Security administrator
State highway patrol officer
Tax assessor
Traffic court judge
Zoning office representative

FIELD TRIP IDEAS

Archives
Board of Education meeting
City council meeting
County commissioner's session
Court house
Environmental Protection Agency
Federal Reserve branch
Historical museum
Jail
Naturalization ceremony
Public debates
Public hearing
Regulatory commission
State capitol
State legislative session
State supreme court
Traffic commission
Traffic court
Trial

ORGANIZATIONS WORTH WRITING

American Civil Liberties Union
132 West 43rd Street
New York, NY 10036

American Political Science Association
1527 New Hampshire Avenue, NW
Washington, DC 20036

Associated Press
50 Rockefeller Plaza
New York, NY 10020

Center for Law and Education
Gutman Library, 3rd Floor
Six Appian Way
Cambridge, MA 02138

Center for War/Peace Studies
218 East 18th Street
New York, NY 10003

Citizenship Development Program
Mershon Center
Ohio State University
199 West 10th Avenue
Columbus, OH 43201

Constitutional Rights Foundation
1510 Cotner Avenue
Los Angeles, CA 90025

Federal Trade Commission
Pennsylvania Avenue at
6th Street, NW
Washington, DC 20580

Law in a Free Society
606 Wilshire Boulevard, Suite 600
Santa Monica, CA 90401

League of Women Voters of the
United States
1730 M Street, NW
Washington, DC 20036

National Assessment for
Educational Progress
CN 6710
Princeton, NJ 08541

National Association for the
Advancement of Colored People
1790 Broadway
New York, NY 10019

National Center for Law-Focused
Education
Law in American Society
Foundation
33 North LaSalle Street, Suite 1700
Chicago, IL 60602

National Institute for Citizen
Education in the Law
25 E Street, NW
Washington, DC 20001

National Organization for Women
Chicago Chapter
West Jackson Boulevard
Chicago, IL 60604

National Organization on Legal
Problems in Education
5401 Southwest Seventh Avenue
Topeka, KS 66606

Robert A. Taft Institute of
Government
420 Lexington Avenue
New York, NY 10017

SANE
711 G Street, SE
Washington, DC 20003

Tax Foundation, Inc.
1 Thomas Circle, NW
Suite 500
Washington, DC 20005

Ward's Modern Learning Aids
Division
5100 West Henrietta Road
P.O. Box 92912
Rochester, NY 14692-9012

Chapter 4

CONSUMER ECONOMICS

One thing of which we may be certain is that all students will receive money and all will spend money at some point during their lives. One of the most important skills we can teach our students is the ability to make wise consumer choices.

The broad variety of learning activities in this chapter are designed to make consumer education readily applicable to students' daily lives. Projects such as "Peanut Butter Distribution" and "Buy Your Desk" expose students to the basic forces of a consumer-driven economy. "Generic Foods: A Taste Test Comparison," "Let's Go Shopping," and "Planning a Dream Vacation" develop skills in wise consumer spending. Other learning activities, such as "Smoker's Interview," "What Do Employers Want?," and "Purchasing Status" explore the motivations and influences that affect decisions in a capitalist economy.

(4-1) GENERIC FOODS: A TASTE TEST COMPARISON

Objectives:
- To make objective comparisons between two commodities
- To practice rational decision making
- To understand the concept of value in food purchasing

Grade Level: 7–12

Time Required: 40–60 minutes in class

Materials Needed: At least 6 pairs of food items, one generic and one name brand of each; copies of the "Generic Foods Taste Comparison" worksheet

Description:

1. Obtain at least 6 name brand food items and their generic equivalents. Items might include corn chips, crackers, chocolate chips, peanut butter, tomato juice, vanilla wafers, or jelly.
2. Arrange the pairs of foods at several taste-testing stations around the room. Place the foods in containers labeled only A or B. Randomly vary the assignment of letters to the generic and name brand items.
3. As students circulate to each station, they should taste each item and complete the "Generic Foods Taste Comparison" worksheet.
4. Post the votes of all students on the board, determining which item of each pair was believed to be the generic product. Give the price and size of each product and have the class calculate the per unit price for each item. Post these on the board next to their votes.
5. Process the activity with the following questions:
   a. On which items was it most difficult to differentiate between the generic and the name brand product?
   b. Are there genuine differences between the name brand product and its generic equivalent?
   c. Which items represent the best value?
   d. Which generic products were judged clearly inferior to the name brand?
   e. Why do more people not buy generic products?
   f. What role does advertising play in developing our preferences?

Optional Activities:

1. Complete the taste comparison activity as above but also including store brand products.
2. Invite a pharmacist to class to discuss generic medications.
3. Have students visit several local supermarkets and list all the generic products they find available.

Name ______________________ Date ______________________

GENERIC FOODS TASTE COMPARISON

Rate each item on a scale of 1 (least desirable) to 10 (most desirable).
Circle the letter of the product you believe to be the generic item.

Item	Taste Rating (1–10)		Comments
	A	B	
1. ________			
2. ________			
3. ________			
4. ________			
5. ________			
6. ________			

(4-2) BUY YOUR DESK: THE COMPETITIVE MARKETPLACE

Objectives:
- To recognize how the laws of supply and demand operate in the competitive marketplace
- To discover how the value of any service or good is determined

Grade Level: 7–12

Time Required: Trial period lasts from 1–16 weeks

Materials Needed: Ample supply of "Funny Money"

Description:

1. Explain that students will be paid in "Funny Money" bills for class attendance and performance. You might suggest the following "wages" or design your own:

a. Each class attended (on time)	$ 5
b. Each class attended (tardy)	$ 2
c. Daily homework completed	$ 5
d. Quizzes:	
Grade of A	$20
Grade of B	$10
Grade of C	$ 5
Grade of D	$ 1
e. Exams:	
Grade of A	$50
Grade of B	$40
Grade of C	$30
Grade of D	$10
f. Special Projects	$5–75

   The class may wish to negotiate a price for other activities, such as classroom duties or service projects.

2. Tell the class what goods or services may be purchased with their "Funny Money."

   Hold an auction each week for their desk. Students may bid for their favorite seat. You might even add a few cushioned chairs to spur the bidding. The least desirable seats (probably the front center) will go the cheapest.

Students who come to class without their books, paper, or pencils may rent one from the teacher or from other students.

Occasionally present special products or privileges for competitive bidding. Many merchants are quite cooperative in supplying sample products such as posters, sports passes, movie tickets, fast food coupons, and so on. The value of all items should be determined by competitive bidding since that is the main point of the lesson.

FUNNY MONEY
50
50
Official Seal
FIFTY
BUCKS
50
50
WISE CONSUMER DOLLARS

FUNNY MONEY
5
5
Official Seal
FIVE
BUCKS
5
5
WISE CONSUMER DOLLARS

FUNNY MONEY
10
10
Official Seal
TEN
BUCKS
10
10
WISE CONSUMER DOLLARS

FUNNY MONEY
1
1
Official Seal
A
BUCK
1
1
WISE CONSUMER DOLLARS

(4-3) PLANNING A DREAM VACATION: COMPARISON SHOPPING

Objectives:
- To do comparison shopping of various modes of travel
- To plan a vacation itinerary
- To work as a team

Grade Level: 10–12

Time Required: Three weeks to gather data; 2 hours in class

Materials Needed: Copies of "Dream Vacation Planning Guide"

Description:

1. Introduce the lesson by suggesting that the class is going to plan a trip. They may choose a destination that is anywhere in the United States. Divide the class into groups of 5 or 6, each selecting a different destination for study. The plans should include a low-budget option as well as a first-class itinerary for the same destination.
2. The plans for each destination will include all the information identified on the "Dream Vacation Planning Guide." Each group will divide the tasks to be accomplished.
3. On the due date, each group will report the results of their search, specifying how they will travel, where they will stay, and what they will see or do while there. Encourage the group to dress up their presentation with travel posters, charts, and maps.

Optional Activities:

1. Invite a travel agent to class to discuss how to plan a trip and the services they provide.
2. Have students write to the chamber of commerce or travel bureau about their dream vacation destination, requesting information on local sites of interest and a list of local lodgings.

DREAM VACATION PLANNING GUIDE

Use the following steps to guide your group in planning your dream vacation:

1. Identify a destination. Your trip will last 10 days. Develop a low-budget plan and a first-class, luxury trip to the same destination.
2. You must find accurate costs of this trip, including transportation, lodgings, meals, and special events admissions. In planning your dream vacation, accurate cost estimates of various modes of travel should be obtained through local bus companies, auto clubs, travel agents, or airlines. Develop a chart comparing the alternative modes of travel and the costs and time required by each.
3. Research your destination by writing for travel brochures, lodging costs, and other literature that will help you plan your trip. Do not settle for one set of costs provided by a travel agent; obtain a range of possibilities from original resources.
4. Plan a daily itinerary for the full 10 days, including where you will stay, eat, and what you will visit or do. Again, plan a low-budget and a luxury itinerary.
5. Gather materials for your class presentation. Try to include maps, posters, travel brochures, cost comparison charts, and any other material to make your presentation appealing and interesting. On the due date, you will present your planned trip to the rest of the class.

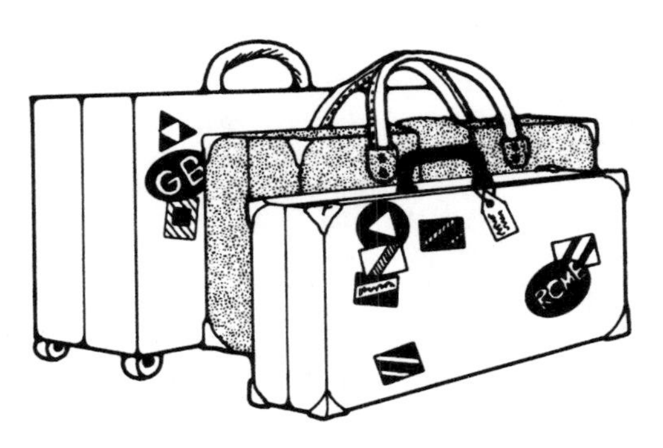

(4-4) PEANUT BUTTER DISTRIBUTION

Objectives:
- To gain an appreciation for the variety of occupations required to produce and distribute a product
- To recognize the complex interdependence of our economic and labor resources

Grade Level: 7–9

Time Required: 30–45 minutes

Materials Needed: A jar of peanut butter

Description:

1. Hold up a jar of peanut butter. Explain that the purpose of this lesson is to identify all the workers who play a role in the production and distribution of a jar of peanut butter.
2. As the class brainstorms the occupations involved, write each occupation on a note card that can be taped to the chalkboard or pinned on a bulletin board. Then attempt to arrange the cards in the sequence in which they are involved in the production and distribution process.
3. Here are some helpful hints: Read the ingredients label to the class. Point out the label, the jar, and the lid. These should be separate sequences in your flow chart. You will need to suggest how far back the process should go. Beginning with the raw peanut would be a logical starting point, but point out the myriad of jobs represented before that stage (for example, fertilizer, farm implements, and fuel producers and distributors).
4. The following are some discussion questions:
   a. How do these layers of workers affect the cost of a product?
   b. What is the effect of a labor stoppage at any level of the process?
   c. How might the distribution process be made more efficient?
   d. What is the effect of having so many diverse occupations involved in a manufacturing and distribution process? And how does this affect the quality of a product?

Optional Activities:

1. Have a few volunteers design a bulletin board display from the flow chart generated in class. They might illustrate it with pictures of the different occupations involved.

2. Assign each student to develop a similar production and distribution flow chart for different products. You might have them write to a manufacturer or distributor of the assigned product for specific information. The completed flow charts can be posted for others to view.
3. Invite a representative from a local distributor to discuss the distribution network for that product.

(4-5) FACT VERSUS OPINION IN TELEVISION ADS

Objective:
- To differentiate factual statements from opinions
- To explore the objectivity of television advertisements

Grade Level: 7–12

Time Required: 30 minutes in class; 1–3 nights allowed for homework preparation

Materials Needed: Tape recorders or cassettes

Description:

1. To prepare this assignment, students are to select one television commercial and prepare a verbatim written transcript. They will need to record the commercial to aid in preparing the written transcript. All factual statements should be underlined. Opinions should be circled.
2. On the due date, break the class into groups of 3. Have them share their homework, verifying that facts and opinions have been appropriately designated. Any items that the groups cannot agree on should be presented to the entire class for discussion.

(4-6) LET'S GO SHOPPING: UNIT PRICING

Objectives:
- To be able to compare items on a per unit basis
- To become aware of the costs of familiar products and food items

Grade Level: 7–12

Time Required: 40–60 minutes in class; 2–3 nights for homework preparation

Materials Needed: Copies of "Let's Go Shopping" activity sheet

Description:

1. Assign each student a different product. They are to visit a grocery store and make a list of the prices and sizes of all brands of that product. Remind them to note the exact size in a specific unit of measure (ounces, units, inches, and so on) for each item. This information should be recorded on the "Let's Go Shopping" activity sheet.
   You can develop your own shopping list, but include everyday items such as the following:

Toilet paper	Catsup	Ice cream
Bleach	Dish detergent	Popcorn
Yogurt	Cornflakes	Flour
Toothpaste	Paper napkins	Sugar

2. Break the class into groups of 4. Have each student identify one size of her or his product that is available in 2 or more brands (for example, 20 ounces of sliced yellow cling peaches). The student should also tell the rest of the group the price of each brand. The group then computes the per unit price for each brand of that product. The group should continue to do the same with one size from each person's list.

3. Have each group present their calculated per unit prices to the rest of the class. As each item is presented, you might have the rest of the class guess the price of that item. (Many students have little idea how much grocery items cost.)

4. Post the per unit calculations on a bulletin board for a few days. For follow-up homework, have the students calculate the per unit prices for the rest of the sizes on their lists.

Name ______________________ Date ______________________

LET'S GO SHOPPING

Product ____

Store ____

For each brand, list all the sizes available. Be sure to specify the exact unit of measure (ounces, pounds, number of sheets, and so on). List the price of each item. Per unit prices will be calculated in class.

Brand	Size	Price	Per Unit Price

(4-7) SMOKER'S INTERVIEW

Objectives:
- To develop interviewing data-gathering skills
- To draw conclusions from data
- To gain insight into the factors facilitating cigarette smoking

Grade Level: 7–12

Time Required: 40–50 minutes in class; one week for completion of interviews

Materials Needed: Copies of "Smoker's Interview Guide"

Description:

1. Facilitate a discussion on why people smoke. Consider whether the reasons for starting differ from the reasons for continuing.
2. Suggest that the class gather objective data to test their hypotheses. Distribute the "Smoker's Interview Guide" and discuss the questions on it. Each student is assigned to interview five smokers. Announce the due date for all interviews.
3. On the due date, have the students discuss their findings in groups of 3. Instruct them to look for commonalities. They should also develop a graph indicating the total number of times each reason was given for smoking.
4. On a large piece of newsprint, have a volunteer construct a frequency graph of smokers' motivations. This may be completed outside of class.
5. Process the experience as a large group with the following questions:
   a. How do the reasons offered by people for starting to smoke differ from the reasons that they continue?
   b. Did the reasons offered by teenage smokers differ from those suggested by older smokers?
   c. How honest do you think people were in indicating their true feelings about their smoking behavior?
   d. What role do you think cigarette advertising plays in promoting smoking behavior?
   e. Should all cigarette smoking be banned?
   f. What are the indirect costs of cigarette smoking on the rest of society?
   g. Some employers refuse to hire smokers because they are greater health risks. Is this unfair discrimination?

Optional Activities:

1. Conduct similar interviews with users of smokeless tobacco.
2. Distribute small cocktail straws to the students. Instruct them to hold their noses, place the straws in their mouths, and breathe through them for thirty seconds. Announce that that is comparable to having emphysema.
3. Invite a speaker from the American Cancer Society to discuss the latest research on the effects of smoking. You might also contact representatives from the American Tobacco Institute for their perspective. Encourage the students to evaluate the information objectively.

Name ______________________ Date ______________________

SMOKER'S INTERVIEW GUIDE

1. Sex: M F Age__________
2. How long have you smoked cigarettes?__________
3. Approximately how many do you smoke in a day?__________
4. At what age did you begin smoking?__________
5. What do you think motivated you to begin smoking?

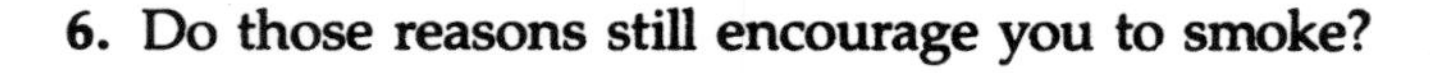

6. Do those reasons still encourage you to smoke?

7. What else do you get out of smoking?

8. Do you believe the warning labels printed on cigarette packs?

9. What do you see as the disadvantages of smoking?

10. Please try to estimate how much you have spent on cigarettes since you first began smoking. $_____

11. Have you ever tried to stop?

12. If so, what makes stopping difficult?

13. In what ways do you believe smokers are being treated unfairly today?

(4-8) WHAT DO EMPLOYERS WANT?

Objectives:
- To practice interviewing skills
- To gain insights into the criteria employers use in selecting employees
- To develop generalizations from collected data
- To gain experience in talking with prospective employers in a "safe" climate

Grade Level: 10–12

Time Required: 1–2 weeks for interviews to be completed; 40–60 minutes for class analysis of data

Materials Needed: Copies of "Employer Interview Guide" handout

Description:

1. Begin the lesson allowing 10 minutes for small groups (3–5 students) to brainstorm the characteristics employers look for in selecting employees. Have the groups list their chosen characteristics on newsprint and post them in front of the room.
2. Inform the class that they will have an opportunity to test their hunches by interviewing employers on the traits they use in selecting employees. Distribute copies of the "Employer Interview Guide."
3. Each student should select one employer to interview, using the questions suggested on the "Employer Interview Guide" and any others they would like to add. Set a deadline for the completion of the assignment.
4. On the due date, have the students share their findings in groups of 4–5 students. They should look for those characteristics that were mentioned most frequently.
5. When the groups report back to the entire class, you may have someone develop a frequency table on the board to assess how often each characteristic is mentioned. The following questions might be helpful in stimulating discussion:
   a. Do employers from different businesses look for different things? (Clerical, sales, skilled trades, professional)
   b. What role do grades seem to play in employer decisions?
   c. What role does an applicant's interpersonal skills seem to play in hiring decisions? How are they judged?
   d. How important is appearance?
   e. What things discourage an employer from selecting an applicant?

Optional Activities:

1. Invite a panel of area employers representing various fields to come to class to discuss what they look for in prospective employees. Have the class prepare questions that may aid their own job-seeking efforts.
2. Invite an employment counselor to class to discuss how students might make themselves more attractive to employers.
3. Have students role-play employment interviews, alternating being employer, applicant, and observer.

Name ______________________________ Date ______________________________

EMPLOYER INTERVIEW GUIDE

Employer Interviewed______________________________

Title______________________________

1. How many people does your organization currently employ?

2. How are most of your job openings advertised?

3. Who is involved in employee selection?

4. What is the most important thing you look for in a potential employee?

5. What other qualifications do you value?

6. What importance is placed on grades?

7. What things are most likely to disqualify an applicant?

8. What advice would you offer to students to make themselves more attractive to employers?

(4-9) PURCHASING STATUS

Objectives:
- To recognize how status seeking influences consumer decisions
- To identify the commodities that contribute to status in one's peer group

Grade Level: 10–12

Time Required: 40–60 minutes

Materials Required: Copies of "Status Survey" handout

Description:

1. Suggest that we spend money to fulfill our needs and desires. Some are survival needs, such as food and shelter. Others fulfill higher-level social needs, such as attaining prestige, influence, or peer approval.
2. Propose that commodities that provide status in one group may not in another. You might include a couple of humorous examples, such as blue jeans, and a Madonna sweatshirt may be very "in" with high school students but would likely result in a loss of status for a stockbroker on Wall Street.
3. Have the class complete "Status Survey" handout either in class or as homework.
4. Break the class into groups of 4–5 to discuss their results. Suggest that they attempt to identify commonalities.
5. As a total group, proceed with the following questions:
   a. Which items were most frequently rated as high in status value? Which were lowest?
   b. What high-status purchases were not included on the survey?
   c. Which high-status purchases would have been rated lower a year ago?
   d. Which items would have been rated higher a year ago?
   e. How can some purchases meet both basic survival needs and status needs as well? (Designer clothing is a good example.)
   f. Cite examples of how advertisers play on our need for status in marketing their goods.
   g. How would you alter your spending habits if status and peer approval were not important to you?
   h. What businesses would probably collapse if status and peer approval were universally shunned?

Optional Activities:

1. Suggest that the students have their parents complete the "Status Survey" handout for comparison with their choices. Have someone compile the results for extra credit. After they are presented to the class, submit the study to the school newspaper for publication.
2. Have students bring several advertisements appealing to their need for status or approval. You might videotape a couple of such examples from television. Analyze the latent messages of the commercials.

STATUS SURVEY

Rate each of the following purchases as to the amount of status it would hold among your group of friends:

	Very Much Out	Somewhat Out	Neutral	Somewhat In	Very Much In
1. Blue jeans	______	______	______	______	______
2. Harvard sweatshirt	______	______	______	______	______
3. Blue nail polish	______	______	______	______	______
4. Reebok shoes	______	______	______	______	______
5. Cowboy hat	______	______	______	______	______
6. Godiva chocolates	______	______	______	______	______
7. Trip to Europe	______	______	______	______	______
8. Wing-tip shoes	______	______	______	______	______
9. Leather jacket	______	______	______	______	______
10. Tickets to a ballet	______	______	______	______	______
11. Tickets to a Bruce Springsteen concert	______	______	______	______	______
12. Leather basketball	______	______	______	______	______
13. Computer	______	______	______	______	______
14. Your own Volkswagen	______	______	______	______	______
15. Your own Volvo	______	______	______	______	______
16. Gold necklace	______	______	______	______	______
17. Leather briefcase	______	______	______	______	______
18. Hair permanent	______	______	______	______	______
19. Cologne	______	______	______	______	______
20. Compact disk player	______	______	______	______	______
21. Your own telephone	______	______	______	______	______
22. Country club membership	______	______	______	______	______

______ Male ______ Female

(4-10) MONEY AND YOUR VALUES

Objectives:
- To explore the psychological and social roles money plays in our lives
- To discover the personal meaning of wealth

Grade Level: 10–12

Time Required: 1–2 hours

Materials Needed: Copies of "Money and You" handout

Description:

1. Distribute copies of the "Money and You" handout. Direct the students to circle the number in front of the quotations that most closely represent their beliefs about money and wealth.
2. You may choose either to proceed to step 3 or to process their answers as an entire class or in smaller groups.
3. Instruct the class to assume that each of them just inherited a million dollars. They are to record what they would do with the money. After a few minutes, solicit their responses, recording them on the board.
4. In small groups, have the class discuss: "What values are represented by the items listed on the board?" and "What psychological and social needs are being met through their expenditures of money?"
5. Have the groups report to the total class on their discussions. Facilitate further discussion with the following questions:
   a. How are the values implied in the quotations you checked on the "Money and You" handout represented in how you would spend your million dollars?
   b. How would a million dollars change your life? How would you spend your time?
   c. How do you account for the apparent unhappiness of many lottery winners?
   d. What does money really buy? (Possible answers: time, status, power)
   e. How is wealth portrayed on television?
   f. Why are television game shows that give away large sums of money so popular?
   g. What do you suppose Picasso meant when he said, "I'd like to be a poor man with lots of money"?
   h. How important is money in your definition of success?

MONEY AND YOU

Which of the following statements most closely reflects your thoughts about money and wealth?

1. "All things, divine and human—virtue, fame, honor—are slaves to the beauty of riches."

   Horace

2. "A man who possesses wealth, possesses power, but it is a power to do evil as well as good."

   Azel Stevens Roe

3. "The Americans have little faith. They rely on the power of the dollar."

   Ralph Waldo Emerson

4. "Possessions, outward success, publicity, luxury—to me these have always been compatible. I believe that simple and unassuming manner of life is best for everyone, best both for body and the mind."

   Albert Einstein

5. "Wealth is not of necessity a curse, nor poverty a blessing."

   Roswell Dwight Hitchcock

6. "The love of money is the root of all evil."

   New Testament: I Timothy 6:10

7. "Make all you can, save all you can, give all you can."

   John Wesley

8. "It is preoccupation with possession more than anything else, that prevents men from living freely and nobly."

   Bertrand Russell

9. "I've been rich and I've been poor, and believe me rich is better."

   Joe Louis

POSSIBLE RESOURCE PERSONS

Advertising agency representative
Agricultural extension agent
Attorney
Auditor
Banker
Better Business Bureau spokesperson
Building inspector
Business and trade organization representative
Career counselor
Chamber of commerce representative
Congressional representative
Consumer fraud investigator
Contractor
Credit bureau representative
Distributor
Economist
Employment agency representative
Engineer
Entrepreneur
Environmental control officer
Farmer
Financial planner
Funeral director
Grocer
Insurance agent
Investment advisor
Manufacturer
Nutritionist
Real estate agent
Safety inspector
School business agent or treasurer
Stockbroker
Tax return preparer
Transportation official
Union official
Union organizer
Utilities spokesperson

Weights and standards auditor
Welfare official

FIELD TRIP IDEAS

Civil lawsuit trial
Auction
Bank
Better Business Bureau office
Career fair
Factories
Farm
Federal Reserve district office
Food distributor
Food processing plant
Newspaper office and printer
Grain elevator
Grocery
Stockbrokerage firm
Stock market exchange
Television studio
Utility
Waste disposal plant

ORGANIZATIONS WORTH WRITING

American Bankers Association
Banking Education Committee
1120 Connecticut Avenue, NW
Washington, DC 20036

American Cancer Society
90 Park Avenue
New York, NY 10016

American Council of Life Insurance
Education Division
1850 K Street, NW
Washington, DC 20006

American Council on Consumer Interests
238 Stanley Hall
University of Missouri
Columbia, MS 65201

American Economic Association
1313 21st Avenue South
Nashville, TN 37212

American Federation of Labor and Congress of Industrial Organizations
AFL-CIO Building
815 16th Street, NW
Washington, DC 20006

American Home Economics Association
2010 Massachusetts Avenue, NW
Washington, DC 20036

American Institute of Banking
1120 Connecticut Avenue, NW
Washington, DC 20036

American Iron and Steel Institute
Public Relations Department
1000 16th Street, NW
Washington, DC 20036

American Petroleum Institute
1220 L Street, NW
Washington, DC 20005

American Stock Exchange
Public Affairs Division
86 Trinity Place
New York, NY 10006

Betty Crocker
General Mills, Inc.
Department 360
400 2nd Avenue South
Minneapolis, MN 55440

Board of Governors of the Federal Reserve System
20th Street and Constitution Avenue, NW
Washington, DC 20551

Bureau of Labor Statistics
Associate Commissioner
Office of Publications
U.S. Department of Labor
200 Constitution Avenue, NW
Washington, DC 20210

Bureau of the U.S. Budget
Assistant Director for Public Affairs
Office of Management and Budget
Executive Office Building
Washington, DC 20503

Chamber of Commerce of the United States
1615 H Street, NW
Washington, DC 20062

Changing Times
Education Service, Suite G-84
1729 H Street, NW
Washington, DC 20006

Chase Manhattan Bank
1 Chase Manhattan Plaza
New York, NY 10015

Citizens' Advisory Committee on Environmental Quality
722 Jackson Place, NW
Washington, DC 20006

Consumer Affairs Office
U.S. Department of Agriculture
14th Street and Independence Avenue
Washington, DC 20250

Consumer Product Safety Commission
1111 18th Street, NW
Washington, DC 20207

Consumers Union
256 Washington Street
Mount Vernon, NY 10553

Cost of Living Council
P.O. Box 7075
Congress Heights Station
Washington, DC 20032

Council of Better Business Bureaus, Inc.
1515 Wilson Boulevard
Arlington, VA 22209

Credit Union National Association
Box 431
Madison, WI 53701

Dow Jones and Company, Inc.
11501 Columbia Pike
Silver Springs, MD 20910

Dow Jones and Company, Inc.
44 Broad Street
New York, NY 10006
Dun and Bradstreet, Inc.
1290 Avenue of the Americas
New York, NY 10019

Family Service Association of
America
44 East 23rd Street
New York, NY 10010

Federal Reserve System
Public Services
Division of Administration
20th Street and Constitution
Avenue, NW
Washington, DC 20551

Firestone Tire and Rubber
Company
Director of Consumer Affairs
1200 Firestone Parkway
Akron, OH 44317

Food and Drug Administration
5600 Fishers Lane
Rockville, MD 20857

Forecast for Home Economics
902 Sylvan Avenue
Englewood Cliffs, NJ 07632

General Mills
Department 435
400 Second Avenue South
Minneapolis, MN 55440

Good Housekeeping
Bulletin Service
959 Eighth Street
New York, NY 10019

Grocery Manufacturers of America
205 East 42nd Street
New York, NY 10017

Home Economics Education
Association
National Education Association
1201 16th Street, NW
Washington, DC 20036

Home Economics Instructional
Media Center
Texas Tech University
P.O. Box 4067
Lubbock, TX 79409

Institute of Life Insurance
488 Madison Avenue
New York, NY 10032

Insurance Information Institute
110 Williams Street
New York, NY 10038

Joint Council on Economic
Education
1212 Avenue of the Americas
New York, NY 10036

Economics
Two Park Avenue
New York, NY 10016

Kraft Foods
P.O. Box 956
Dayton, OH 45401

Major Appliance Consumer Action
Panel
20 North Wacker Drive
Chicago, IL 60606

Media and Consumer Foundation,
Inc.
P.O. Box 850
Norwalk, CT 06852

Metropolitan Life Insurance Co.
Health and Welfare Division
1 Madison Avenue
New York, NY

National Center for Research in
Vocational Education
Ohio State University
1960 Kenny Road
Columbus, OH 43210

National Dairy Council
6300 River Road
Rosemont, IL 60656

National Foundation for Consumer
Credit, Inc.
Federal Bar Building West
1819 H Street, NW
Washington, DC 20006

National Funeral Directors
Association
135 West Wells Street
Milwaukee, WI 53203

National Safety Council
School and College Department
444 North Michigan Avenue
Chicago, IL 60611

New York State Council on
Economic Education
135 Western Avenue
Albany, NY 12203

New York Stock Exchange
20 Broad Street
New York, NY 10003

Nutrition Foundation, Inc.
99 Park Avenue
New York, NY 10016

Ohio Office of Consumer's Counsel
137 East State Street
Columbus, OH 43215

J. C. Penney Co., Inc.
Educational and Consumer
Relations
1301 Avenue of the Americas
New York, NY 10019

Prudential Insurance Company
Public Relations Department
Box 36
Newark, NJ 07101

Sears, Roebuck and Co.
Consumer Information Service
Department 703, Public Relations
303 East Ohio Street
Skokie, IL 60076

U.S. Department of Commerce
14th Street and Constitution
Avenue, NW
Washington, DC 20236

Wall Street Journal
200 Burnett Road
Chicopee, MA 01021

Chapter 5

SOCIOLOGY

All the world is indeed a stage in the study of sociology. The daily lives of students provide an ever-present laboratory for the study of sociology. The groups to which students belong—families, gangs, churches, clubs, classes, cliques, and teams—provide myriad opportunities to apply and experience the content and skill of sociology.

Most activities in this chapter teach sociological concepts and also provide practice in skills of data collection and observation. Questionnaires are included for studying leisure time, parent-teen problems, school norms, and attitudes toward school. Direct interviewing skills are strengthened through the study of school vandalism, changing social norms as seen by senior citizens, and "How Good Are Your Questions?" and "Job Satisfaction Interviews." Observational techniques are employed in studying school vandalism, cartoon violence and discrimination, and violating a social norm.

Many suggestions are given for distributing the results of these projects. The results of these experiments, surveys, and interviews may be of interest to other students, parents, and the community. The opportunities for even greater learning can be enhanced by sharing the outcome with others.

(5-1) GLASSES AND BRACES: EXPERIENCING DISCRIMINATION

Objectives:
- To appreciate the personal and social effects of unfair discrimination
- To identify common biases that students may hold

Grade Level: 7–12

Time Required: 1–5 class periods

Materials Needed: None

Description:

1. Announce that the class will be operating under new rules. (You may choose not to tell the class how long these rules are going to be in effect.) Develop a list of rules and privileges that favor students who wear braces or glasses. Make it clear that sunglasses do not qualify. Students who wear braces have special status above those who wear glasses. You might adapt some of the following:
   a. No one else may sit down until all persons wearing braces or glasses have taken their seats. Students with braces get first choice.
   b. You might set up a preferred lounge area with comfortable chairs and refreshments for the use of these students wearing braces.
   c. When called on by the teacher, anyone wearing glasses may choose to pass. Students with braces may pass and select another student to answer the question.
2. During the experience, continue teaching regularly scheduled class content while assuring that the new rules are enforced. The experiment may continue from 1 to 5 days.
3. At the end of the project, facilitate a class discussion focusing on the reactions and feeling of all 3 groups. You may include the following questions:
   a. How did it feel to be granted privileged status?
   b. What did it feel like to be discriminated against?
   c. How does this experience differ from discrimination against a minority?
   d. How did the behaviors of each group begin to change?
   e. Did any students who usually wear contacts begin to wear their glasses?
   f. How did you begin to see those of the other group differently?
   g. If these rules became permanent norms, what might be the consequences?
4. Break the class into groups to brainstorm the question "What groups of people unfairly receive privileged status in our world today?" Allow 5 minutes for the groups to list as many examples as possible. Discuss the examples brainstormed.

Optional Activities:

1. Focus a classroom discussion on the differences between racial discrimination against a minority and apartheid as practiced against a majority in

South Africa. You might choose to have students do research on the topic first.

2. Invite a speaker from the National Association for the Advancement of Colored People or the B'nai B'rith, or other civil rights advocacy group.

(5-2) CHANGING SOCIAL NORMS: SENIOR CITIZEN INTERVIEW

Objectives:
- To identify specific social norms that have changed in the past 80 years
- To practice interview data-gathering skills
- To better understand the social values and expectations of previous generations

Grade Level: 7–12

Time Required: 40–60 minutes in class; 2 weeks allowed for interviews.

Materials Needed: Copies of the "Changing Social Norms Interview Guide"

Description:

1. Facilitate a discussion comparing life as a teenager today with what it might have been like in 1900. Encourage consideration of the social norms governing education, sexual behavior, interpersonal relationships, religion, career choice, recreation, work, family responsibilities, and sex roles. Have 2 volunteers record the 2 lists on sheets of newsprint. Also consider how these norms were enforced and the penalties for violating them.
2. Distribute copies of the "Changing Social Norms Interview Guide." Clarify any questions about the form. The class may choose to add questions.
3. Students have 2 weeks to interview senior citizens about their adolescent years. The interviewees should be at least 60; ideally some will be in their 80s or older.
4. On the due date, break the students into groups based on the ages of their interviewees (that is, 60s, 70s, 80s) to discuss the results of their interviews.
5. Each group should record their common findings on a sheet of newsprint.
6. Each group will present their findings to the rest of the class and post their newsprint on the wall.
7. Invite the class to contrast their interview results with their personal experiences today.

Optional Activities:

1. Lower the age limit to include interviews with adults from 20 on up. This would provide more data about trends.
2. Obtain the cooperation of a local nursing home. The class might visit the nursing home and interview volunteer residents. Most would welcome such interest.
3. Have a few volunteers draft the class's findings into an article for publication in the school or local newspaper.

Name ______________________ Date of Interview ______________________

CHANGING SOCIAL NORMS INTERVIEW GUIDE

Age of Interviewee ____________ Sex: M F

1. Where did you live as a teenager?

2. What was a typical school day like? What was expected of you? What behaviors got students into trouble? What punishments were used?

3. What did you do for recreation? Of which activities did parents disapprove?

4. What were relationships with parents like? What kinds of things got them angry at you? What won their praise?

5. What kinds of teenagers were most popular? What won peer approval? Which behaviors would bring disapproval from your friends?

6. What were the career expectations held of you? By whom? How were they communicated?

7. Describe social etiquette when you were growing up. How do you think manners differed from today?

8. Describe dating behavior and relationships with the opposite sex. Where did you go on dates? What were seen as acceptable courtship behaviors?

9. How was teenage pregnancy viewed?

10. What responsibilities did you have? What happened if you didn't meet them?

(5-3) WHAT WOULD YOU DO?

Objectives:
- To develop insights into the conflicting roles of parents
- To create empathy for another person's perspective

Grade Level: 7–12

Time Required: 30–50 minutes

Materials Needed: Copies of "What Would You Do?" handout

Description:

1. Some degree of parent-child conflict is inevitable. This structured activity invites students to consider the role demands of being a parent. It encourages students to weigh the societal responsibilities of parenthood against the immediate demands of the child.
2. Introduce the topic with a discussion on the problems of being a parent. Potential questions for exploration include the following:
   a. Why might people choose to be parents?
   b. What do adults gain from being parents?
   c. What does it cost them?
   d. What are the most difficult aspects of being a parent?
   e. What responsibilities do parents have to society? To their children?
   f. What are their greatest concerns about being parents?
3. Distribute the "What Would You Do?" handout. Allow approximately 15 minutes for students to respond individually to the situations. It might also be assigned as homework.
4. Discuss their responses as a large group or in small groups. Challenge them to relate their answers to the earlier class discussion on parental responsibilities.

Optional Activities:

1. Assign the class to interview their parents (or someone else's) to discover how their parents would respond to the situations depicted on the "What Would You Do?" handout.
2. Invite a panel of parents to discuss the challenges and rewards of parenthood. You may want to invite parents who do not have children in your class.

Name ______________________ Date ______________________

WHAT WOULD YOU DO?

How would you handle each of the following situations if you were the parent?

1. Despite being reminded in the morning, 11-year-old Sammy missed a dentist appointment because he stopped to play tag after school.

____

____

____

2. Ann, a high school senior, returned home at 2:00 A.M. in a highly intoxicated state.

____

____

____

3. Yvonne was caught shoplifting a blouse. She received a stern warning but was released without charges.

____

____

____

4. While her parents were out, Caroline and her friend Beth, both 15, drove her parents' car around the neighborhood. Her parents returned just as the girls were pulling into the driveway.

____

____

____

5. Brenda's parents have strong suspicions that she is sexually active. She is 13, although most of the boys who have been calling are two or three years older.

____

____

____

6. One night, Troy's parents discovered him crawling out the window at 3:00 A.M. He is 14 years old.

___

___

___

7. Virtually every time they get in the car, Danny and Denise, 6-year-old twins, begin fighting.

___

___

___

8. While playing with matches, 8-year-old Carlos accidentally caught the garage on fire. It was extinguished by his father with minimal damage.

___

___

___

9. Lois frequently sneaks a flashlight to bed to read comic books until three or four in the morning. She then refuses to get up in the morning to get ready for school.

___

___

___

10. Nine-year-old Mike has been increasingly using obscenities in front of everyone, including his grandparents.

___

___

___

11. Cindy received all As and Bs until the eighth grade. This year, she has been getting mostly Cs and Ds. Her only explanation has been that the teachers do not like her.

___

___

___

(5-4) WHAT ARE THEIR VALUES?

Objectives:
- To identify values from exhibited behaviors
- To recognize how values are communicated through daily actions

Grade Level: 10–12

Time Required: 30–50 minutes

Materials Needed: Copies of "What Are Their Values?" handout

Description:

1. This activity is a valuable follow-up activity to discussions of values and value systems. The focus is on how our daily actions reveal our basic values.
2. Break the class into groups of 3 or 4 and distribute copies of the "What Are Their Values?" handout. Instruct the groups to brainstorm the values they believe underlie the behavior depicted in the first vignette. After 4 or 5 minutes, stop process the groups' answers to the first vignette to see that the task is understood.
3. You may let the groups complete the rest of the handout and then process their responses, or you may choose to stop for discussion after each vignette.
4. The class might suggest behaviors from other cultures or subcultures for analysis. Stress that their responses are merely hypotheses that might need verification. Explore how such verification might be obtained.

Name ______________________________ Date ______________________________

WHAT ARE THEIR VALUES?

Hypothesize what values might underlie each of the following behaviors:

1. Manuel buys a savings bond for each of his four children on their birthdays.

____

____

2. Mr. Malinowski jogs three miles every morning before going to work.

____

____

3. Jean took a part-time job after school to buy a car.

____

____

4. Allen plays basketball every chance he gets.

____

____

5. Haitian voodoo doctors brush a patient's body with a live chicken to cleanse it of bad spirits and impurities.

____

____

6. When three black families moved into the neighborhood, Mr. Jones put his house up for sale.

____

____

7. Many Amish parents have gone to jail rather than send their children to public school.

8. Upon losing their fortunes during the stock market crash of 1929, some people committed suicide by jumping from their windows.

9. Susan refuses to marry a man she loves and stays home to tend her invalid father.

10. Ellen cries when she is not selected by the college of her choice.

11. When Tim's friends teased him for not smoking, he accepted a cigarette.

(5-5) WHERE DOES YOUR LEISURE TIME GO?

Objectives:
- To help students recognize how they spend their leisure time
- To make decisions through group consensus

Grade Level: 7–12

Time Required: 30–50 minutes

Materials Needed: Copies of "Leisure Time Activities" checksheet and "Adult Participation in Leisure-Time Activities"

Description:

1. Allow the students to complete the "Leisure Time Activities" checksheet indicating each of the activities in which they regularly participate.
2. Have each student predict which leisure activities have the highest adult participation. These rankings should be done in the column titled "Your Ranking of Adult Participation."
3. In groups of 4 or 5, they are to rank the top 10 activities in which the greatest number of adults participate. The groups are to discuss their individual rankings and attempt to agree based on group consensus. Voting is prohibited.
4. Present the correct rankings as listed in the adult participation table. Have students count the number of top 10 ranked activities they included in their rankings.
5. Collect the final group rankings and list them on the board. It adds to the drama to give each group a name, such as "Fruits," "Nuts," "Turkeys," and "Buzzards." Determine which group had the greatest number of the top 10 activities listed.
6. Discuss the process groups used to arrive at their decisions. What factors helped or hindered the decision-making process.

Optional Activities:

1. Have the students survey their parents to collect data on adult participation in these leisure-time activities. Compare those results with their own and the rankings from the national study.
2. The class may elect to collect data from a larger sample of students of varying ages for comparison. The results could be submitted to the school or local newspaper for publication.

ADULT PARTICIPATION IN LEISURE-TIME ACTIVITIES

Type of Activity	Number (millions)	Percent[1]	Type of Activity	Number (millions)	Percent[1]
Flower gardening	40	47	Basketball	11	13
Swimming	35	41	Hunting	11	13
Vegetable gardening	34	40	Golf	10	12
Bicycling	28	33	Ping-Pong/table tennis	10	12
Fishing	26	30	Baseball	9	11
Camping	20	23	Tennis	9	11
Jogging	19	22	Canoeing/rowing	9	10
Bowling	18	21	Roller skating	8	9
Aerobics	17	20	Horseback riding	7	8
Weight training	16	19	Target shooting	7	8
Billiard, pool	15	18	Skiing	6	7
Softball	15	18	Waterskiing	6	7
Calisthenics	13	15	Raquetball	5	6
Motor boating	12	14	Sailing	5	6
Volleyball	12	14	Touch football/flag	5	6

[1]Percent of U.S. adults 18 years and over.
Source: National Gardening Association, Burlington, VT, unpublished data. Based on data from the Gallup Organization, Princeton, NJ. Used with permission.

Name ______________________ Date ______________________

LEISURE-TIME ACTIVITIES

1. In the first column, rank the top 10 activities in which you regularly participate: 1 = most frequent, and so on.
2. In the second column, predict the rank of the 10 activities you think have the greatest number of adult participants in the United States: 1 = most participants, and so on.
3. In the third column, list your group rankings of the top 10 activities in adult participation.

Your Top 10 Leisure Activities	Type of Activity	Your Ranking of Adult Participation	Group Ranking of Adult Participation
______	Weight training	______	______
______	Baseball	______	______
______	Touch football/flag	______	______
______	Bowling	______	______
______	Sailing	______	______
______	Ping-Pong/table tennis	______	______
______	Aerobics	______	______
______	Hunting	______	______
______	Basketball	______	______
______	Waterskiing	______	______
______	Skiing	______	______
______	Camping	______	______
______	Tennis	______	______
______	Fishing	______	______
______	Volleyball	______	______
______	Target shooting	______	______
______	Horseback riding	______	______
______	Motor boating	______	______
______	Bicycling	______	______
______	Vegetable gardening	______	______
______	Roller skating	______	______
______	Canoeing/rowing	______	______
______	Calisthenics	______	______
______	Softball	______	______
______	Swimming	______	______
______	Flower gardening	______	______
______	Billiard, pool	______	______

(5-6) TODAY'S HEROES AND HEROINES

Objectives:
- To identify the contemporary people who are admired by youth today
- To enhance survey data collection skills

Grade Level: 7–12

Time Required: 40–60 minutes in class; 3 days for data collection

Materials Needed: None

Description:

1. Ask students to list (anonymously on a sheet of paper) the 3 living people they most admire.
2. Collect the nominations, and have several students develop a frequency chart on the chalkboard to determine which people are most often listed.
3. Suggest that the class develop their data into a survey to poll a sample of their school to determine who the heroes and heroines are.
4. In developing your survey, list females and males separately, including only those who were nominated at least twice in the initial classroom survey.
5. Have the class plan the format and distribution of the survey. They might have respondents rank their top 3 choices or rate each nominee on a scale of 1 to 5. The survey form might also ask for the respondents' sex, grade level, and other possible demographic information to provide for comparisons. The class should determine how the survey will be distributed and collected. It might be feasible to enlist the cooperation of several teachers for distribution during their classes.
6. After the data are collected, have groups of students tally the results, using frequency counts to determine what people are rated most highly by the various groups of students.
7. Discuss the survey results with the class. Use the following questions to process the experience:
   a. What conclusions can you draw from your data?
   b. Why do you think the people rated highly are so admired?
   c. What values do these results seem to reflect?
   d. Were there any surprises?
   e. What limitations are there in your study?

f. What other questions would you have liked to have asked?

g. How might these results compare with those from your parents? Elementary age children?

Optional Activities:

1. Have the class extend the survey to poll adults, perhaps their parents or faculty members. It may be possible to survey a group of elementary students.
2. Save the results of this survey to allow comparisons with the results of surveys from future classes.

(5-7) ATTITUDES TOWARD SCHOOL

Objectives:

- To consider one's personal values and attitudes toward school
- To practice data collection through a questionnaire
- To present data in a meaningful form

Grade Level: 7–12

Time Required: 40–60 minutes in class; 2 days for homework

Materials Needed: Copies of "Attitudes Toward School Survey"

Description:

1. Distribute copies of the "Attitudes Toward School Survey" for completion in class. Tabulate the results on the board and facilitate a discussion of the results.
2. Assign each student to have 3 students not in this class complete copies of the survey. On the due date, have the class tabulate the results. Discuss.
3. Present the survey results to the school newspaper staff for a possible article.

ATTITUDES TOWARD SCHOOL SURVEY

Directions: On a 5-point scale, indicate the degree to which you agree or disagree with each of the following statements.

1 = Strongly disagree
2 = Mildly disagree
3 = Undecided
4 = Mildly agree
5 = Strongly agree

______ **1.** For the most part, school has been a pleasant experience.
______ **2.** Most of my teachers seem to care about me as a person.
______ **3.** My teachers demand too much work from me.
______ **4.** Getting a good education is important to me.
______ **5.** The main purpose of education is to help me find a good job.
______ **6.** I work harder in school than do most students.
______ **7.** I do only enough work in school to get by.
______ **8.** School has encouraged me to think for myself.
______ **9.** I look forward to going to most of my classes.
______ **10.** I should spend more time studying.
______ **11.** If my teachers demanded more, I would probably work harder.
______ **12.** I feel that I could discuss personal problems with most of my teachers.
______ **13.** I am reluctant to participate in most class discussions.
______ **14.** I sometimes cheat on tests.
______ **15.** My teachers seem to enjoy teaching.
______ **16.** I would consider teaching as a career.
______ **17.** Most students are apathetic toward school.
______ **18.** School is boring.
______ **19.** I am more concerned with getting good grades than with how much I learn.
______ **20.** School is a very lonely experience.
______ **21.** I try to please my teachers.
______ **22.** My school is a safe place.
______ **23.** Compulsory school attendance should be abolished.
______ **24.** Discipline in our school should be tighter.
______ **25.** School encourages me to be creative.

(5-8) SURVEY OF PARENT-TEEN PROBLEMS

Objectives:
- To practice objective data-gathering techniques
- To identify the conflicts most frequently encountered between parents and their adolescent children

Grade Level: 10–12

Time Required: 40–60 minutes in class; 1 week for data collection

Materials Needed: Copies of "Parent-Teen Survey"

Description:

1. The class should complete the "Parent-Teen Survey." Instruct the students not to put their names on the survey because it will be collected.
2. Facilitate a general discussion of the students' responses to the survey.
3. Suggest that it might be interesting to compare their answers with those of their parents. Ask the class to predict how their parents would respond to the survey.
4. Help the class develop a small study to collect survey data from parents and perhaps additional students. They might each be responsible for finding two or three parents to complete the survey.
5. Allow one week for all data to be collected. Students can tabulate the results with frequency counts and percentages. This can be done by groups in class or out of class by a few volunteers.
6. If possible, have the table of results typed and duplicated. Facilitate a discussion on the results, including questions such as the following:
   a. How accurate were your predictions of how parents would respond?
   b. What surprises occurred in the data?
   c. How representative are these results of the opinions of parents in your community?
   d. How might this sample be biased?
   e. What further research might you like to do in this area?

Optional Activities:

1. The results of your survey might be submitted to a local or school newspaper for publication.
2. A panel of parents might be invited to class to discuss their reactions to the survey questions.

PARENT-TEEN SURVEY

Directions: On a 5-point scale, indicate the degree to which you agree or disagree with each of the following statements:

Statement	1 Strongly Disagree	2 Mildly Disagree	3 Undecided	4 Mildly Agree	5 Strongly Agree
1. Teenagers should be permitted to select their own clothes.	______	______	______	______	______
2. Parents should monitor their teen's homework.	______	______	______	______	______
3. High school students should have to keep their parents informed of where they will be.	______	______	______	______	______
4. Teens are entitled to an allowance.	______	______	______	______	______
5. Parents should not enter their teenager's room without permission.	______	______	______	______	______
6. Parents should establish curfews for their adolescents.	______	______	______	______	______
7. Parents have a responsibility to influence their children's religious and moral values.	______	______	______	______	______
8. It is important for teens and parents to spend time together.	______	______	______	______	______
9. It is essential that parents and teens be able to discuss sexuality together.	______	______	______	______	______
10. Parents owe their children a college education.	______	______	______	______	______
11. Every teenager should have assigned chores at home.	______	______	______	______	______
12. Teens should be free to choose whether or not to attend church or synagogue.	______	______	______	______	______
13. Parents should have no direct role in choosing a teenager's friends.	______	______	______	______	______

(5-9) SATURDAY MORNING CARTOONS: STUDYING TELEVISION VIOLENCE

Objectives:
- To apply the principles of scientific observation and data gathering
- To identify the amount of violence to which children are exposed on television

Grade Level: 10–12

Time Required: 40–60 minutes in class; 2–3 hours homework preparation

Materials Needed: Copies of "Television Violence Observation Form"; local TV guide for Saturday morning

Description:

1. Mention that charges have often been made that television exposes children to too many violent acts. Explain that this project will enable the class to collect data to test that hypothesis objectively.
2. Distribute the "Television Violence Observation Form" to the class. Explain how the students should make frequency marks in each category each time that a violent act is observed.
3. As an option, you might videotape a 5–10 minute segment of a Saturday morning cartoon. As the cartoon is shown, students should record on their forms the instances of violent acts. Have the class compare their observations to see how consistent they are. Discuss the concept of reliability in observations. Have the class discuss how they can increase the reliability of their observations so that there is minimal discrepancy between the scores of two observers watching the same cartoon.
4. Assign 4 groups to each watch one hour of Saturday morning cartoons (one group is assigned 8:00–9:00 A.M., another 9:00–10:00 A.M., and so on). To emphasize the scientific method, randomly assign students to time slots. Have the students in each group randomly divide the group into the number of television channels airing cartoons during that time slot. All observations should be made the following Saturday, with all data due Monday.
5. On the due date, have teams of students collate the data, producing frequency counts for each category. Their data should allow students to answer the following questions:
   a. What was the most violent hour of Saturday morning television in total number of violent acts?

b. What was the most violent cartoon observed?
c. On the average, how many violent acts occur in one hour of Saturday morning cartoons?
d. Which channel presented the most violent morning of television?
e. How many violent acts would children be exposed to in a year if they watched four hours of cartoons every Saturday?
f. What are the limitations in generalizing from this little study?

Optional Activities:

1. The class might extend the study to prime-time television. Choose one night of the week for all observations, or collect data from the top ten rated television programs.
2. Have students go to the library to collect articles on the effects of television violence. (Although the results are inconclusive, several scientific studies have attempted to link television violence with violent behavior.)
3. Invite the director of programming from a local television station to visit the class to discuss how television programming is selected. Have the students prepare questions before the visit.

TELEVISION VIOLENCE OBSERVATION FORM

Name of Observer ______________________ Date ______________________

Cartoon(s) Observed ____

Beginning Time ______________________ Ending Time ______________________

Television Channel ______________________

Directions: Record each separate instance of violence with a tally mark in the most appropriate category. Count each act only once.

Action	Frequency Tally	Total
Hitting with hands		
Pushing, shoving		
Shooting, knifing		
Bombing, smashing another person		
Destroying property		
Other		

Total violent acts: ______________________

(5-10) VIOLATING A SOCIAL NORM

Objectives:
- To experience the effects of violating an established social norm
- To observe the response of others to deviation from expected social behavior

Grade Level: 10–12

Time Required: 30–60 minutes in class; allow 2–5 days for completion of assignment

Materials Needed: Copies of "Norm Violation Reaction Sheet"

Description:

1. Ask the students to identify a social norm or expectation that they could violate to study the reactions of others. Require that it be a harmless and legal behavior that is atypical for that person. Examples of such norm-violating actions might include the following:
   a. Give away flowers at a shopping center.
   b. Wear formal attire to school or an informal social event.
   c. Ask a teacher for more homework.
   d. Stand facing the rear in an elevator.
   e. Stand up in class each time you are called on by a teacher.
   f. Begin singing or playing a musical instrument on a street corner.
2. Distribute the "Norm Violation Reaction Sheet" to be completed by the students after their "experiment" in violating social norms.
3. On the due date, invite students to share the responses they received and how they felt when violating a social norm.

Name ______________________________ Date ______________________________

NORM VIOLATION REACTION SHEET

Describe the setting and the norm being violated: ______________________________

____

____

____

How did people respond to your behavior? ______________________________

____

____

____

Why do you think people reacted as they did? ______________________________

____

____

____

What do you think would be the consequence of continuing the behavior? ______________________________

____

____

____

How did you feel while deviating from the established norm? ______________________________

____

____

____

____

____

____

(5-11) CASE STUDY OF SCHOOL VANDALISM

Objectives:
- To study the occurrence of vandalism in your school
- To develop the skills of data collection

Grade Level: 10–12

Time Required: 1–2 hours in class; one week out of class

Materials Needed: Copies of "Vandalism Interview Guidelines"

Description:

1. Have the class brainstorm the evidence of vandalism they have seen in schools. Someone should record the list on the board or on newsprint.
2. Randomly assign the class to teams to investigate a section of the building to collect data on vandalism in your school. As an in-class excursion or as an assignment, have the teams of students tour the building, recording all incidences of vandalism. Encourage them to quantify their findings as much as possible. Teams could be assigned to interview the custodians, principal, counselors, and fellow students. The questions on the "Vandalism Interview Guidelines" handout can be used to structure the interviews.
3. Have the teams report their findings to the class. Process the experience with the following questions:
   a. How much of a problem is vandalism in our school?
   b. What are the most frequent indicators of vandalism?
   c. Why do you think vandalism occurs?
   d. What are the consequences of vandalism? To students? To the community?
   e. What actions might decrease the amount of vandalism in our schools?
4. You might invite the principal or superintendent to visit the class to respond to students' questions about vandalism. Ask the administrators to bring figures on the costs of vandalism for your building and for the entire school district.

VANDALISM INTERVIEW GUIDELINES

For school administrators:

- How much of a problem is vandalism in our school?
- What are the most prevalent forms of vandalism here?
- How much of the school budget does vandalistic destruction consume?
- Why do you think students vandalize school property?
- Has vandalism increased or decreased?
- What happens to students caught vandalizing school property?

For custodians:

- What kinds of vandalism do you see around our building?
- Which forms of vandalism are frequent?
- How much of your time must you spend on vandalistic destruction?
- Has vandalism increased or decreased since you started working here?

For counselors:

- What motivates students to vandalize school property?
- What effect do you think it has on other students?
- How should students who are caught vandalizing schools be handled?
- What efforts might decrease school vandalism?

For other students:

- How much of a problem is vandalism at our school?
- What kinds of vandalism are most frequent?
- Why do people vandalize school property?
- What are the effects of school vandalism?
- How should people who vandalize schools be handled?
- What actions might decrease school vandalism?

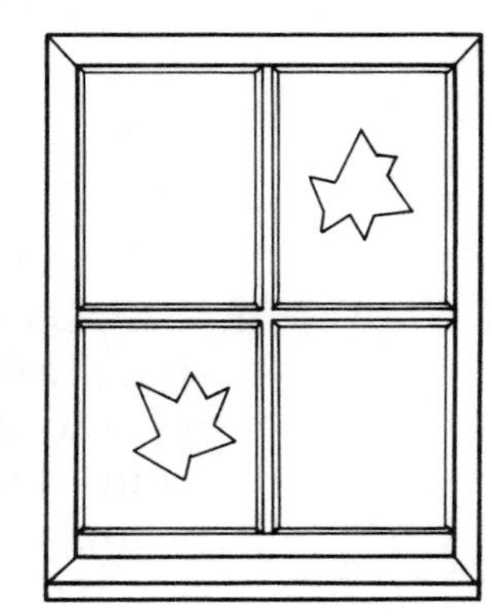

(5-12) INS AND OUTS: STUDYING SCHOOL NORMS

Objectives:
- To identify the social norms and folkways sanctioned in your school
- To practice data gathering to support a conclusion

Grade Level: 10–12

Time Required: 40–60 minutes

Materials Needed: Copies of past and current yearbooks or school newspapers

Description:

1. Present a brief discussion on social folkways and norms. Introduce this lesson by writing "In" and "Out" above two columns on the chalkboard.
2. Ask the class what behaviors must students who wish to be "in" at your school exhibit? How should they dress? Talk? How do they spend their time and money? Do the same for the "out" column.
3. Ask what fads or "in" behaviors existed last year at this school that are now "out"? Discuss the idea of how socially sanctioned behaviors can change over time.
4. Distribute copies of school yearbooks or newspapers from previous years. It is ideal to have samples dating back as far as possible. Have small groups of students search these publications for evidence of what was "in" and "out" during that year. They should list on newsprint the fads and norms, along with the evidence that supports their conclusions, for presentation to the rest of the class.
5. After groups have shared the results of their investigations, have the class discuss the following questions:
   a. How are students today most obviously different from those of previous years?
   b. What customs or norms have continued unchanged at our school?
   c. Which new fads or folkways that currently exist do you think will last longest?
   d. Which "in" behaviors are most likely to be "out" next year?
   e. Who influences what is "in" or "out" at your school?

(5-13) HOW GOOD ARE YOUR QUESTIONS?

Objectives:
- To use questions effectively in face-to-face interviewing
- To demonstrate appropriate use of open-ended, close-ended, and clarifying questions

Grade Level: 10–12

Time Required: 40–60 minutes

Materials Needed: None

Description:

1. Demonstrate the 3 types of questions by asking a volunteer 3 close-ended questions; a second student, three open-ended questions; and a third, three clarifying questions. Briefly, the characteristics of the three types of questions are as follows:
   a. *Close-ended questions* can usually be answered with one word, demand little thought, often require only rote recall; useful for gathering specific pieces of information or seeking a commitment.
      What is your name?
      Are you from Ohio?
      Who is the quarterback?
      Will you serve on the planning committee?
      Where is the Thames River?
      When are you leaving?
   b. *Open-ended questions* are more thought-provoking and may seek opinions or demand creativity, and elicit longer answers; usually begin with "how," "why," or "what."
      How can we improve school spirit?
      Why do you want to go to college?
      What preparations need to be made for the dance?
      How do I get there from here?
      Why do you like your job?
   c. *Clarifying questions* can be either open-ended or close-ended, although generally open-ended are preferable to minimize prolonged silences, especially in conversations. The clarifying question probes the information available. The questions are linked, staying with a particular topic, rather than hopping from one area to the next. A dialogue is created between the questioner and answerer.

A: What do you like most about this school?

B: Well, I think it is the friendly atmosphere we have here.

A: What tells you it is friendly?

B: People are willing to talk to you, even if they don't know you real well. It's not like you have to be in their clique. It's not like my old school.

A: What was it like there?

B: It was the pits. I always felt left out of things... like I didn't belong.

2. Have the group form pairs. One person is to begin by asking three close-ended questions of her partner. The questions should be about three different topics. Then the pair reverses roles. Allow 3–5 minutes.
3. The pairs do the same thing with three different open-ended questions. This usually requires 5–6 minutes. Repeat the process with clarifying questions. Emphasize that this time they must stay with the same topic, with each question probing further the previous answer. Allow 6–8 minutes.
4. Process the experience with the following questions:
   a. Which type of questions did you find most difficult to ask? Easiest?
   b. Which were most enjoyable to answer?
   c. How did you feel differently asking each of the sets of questions? Answering?
   d. Which would be most useful in starting a conversation?
   e. What must you do before you can ask a clarifying question? (Answer: Listen)

Optional Activities:

1. Have the class form groups of 4. One person is selected as the focus person. The task of the other 3 is to interview the focus person. You might assign a general topic for the interview, such as future ambitions, or hobbies, or allow an open interview. Emphasize that the focus person always has the right to pass. The interviewers may not enter the conversation except to ask questions. The assignment is to keep the focus person talking for 10 minutes. Rotate the focus persons until all have been interviewed. As an alternative, you can invite the class to interview you.
2. As an action assignment, ask the class to practice asking clarifying questions every chance they get for the next day or two. Challenge them to meet one new person by using clarifying questions. At the next class, facilitate a discussion of their experiences.

(5-14) JOB SATISFACTION INTERVIEWS

Objectives:
- To conduct and analyze personal interviews
- To consider the factors contributing to job satisfaction

Grade Level: 10–12

Time Required: 30 minutes to describe assignment; 1 or 2 weeks to conduct interviews; 40–50 minutes to discuss results

Materials Needed: Copies of "Job Satisfaction Interview Form"

Description:

1. Lead a class discussion on what factors they believe make a job satisfying.
2. Distribute copies of "Job Satisfaction Interview Form." After reviewing the form, the class may decide to add additional questions.
3. Assign each student to interview three working adults. Emphasize that no names should be mentioned to preserve the confidentiality of the respondents. Set a deadline for all interviews to be completed.
4. On the day the interviews are due, break the class into groups of 3 to discuss their interviews. Ask them to identify any trends that emerge and to draw conclusions about what factors seem to contribute most to job satisfaction. Allow 20–30 minutes for group discussions and 2–3 minutes for each group to report their conclusions to the class.

JOB SATISFACTION INTERVIEW FORM

Interviewer ______________________________

Date of Interview ______________________________

---

1. Occupation ______________________________
2. How long have you been engaged in this occupation? ______________________________
3. How long have you worked at your current place of employment? ______________________________
4. Describe a typical day at work. ______________________________

____

____

____

____

5. What do you enjoy most about your work? ______________________________

____

____

6. What do you enjoy the least about your work? ______________________________

____

____

7. If a 1 represents complete dissatisfaction and a 9 represents total satisfaction, please rate each of the following in terms of how satisfied you are with your current job:

Rating

____ The hours

____ The pay

____ Fringe benefits

____ The physical work conditions

____ Your coworkers

____ Your supervisor(s)

____ Possibility for future advancement

____ Personal fulfillment

WORK

POSSIBLE RESOURCE PERSONS

Advertising agency spokesperson
Anthropologist
Archeologist
Big Brothers or Big Sisters representatives
Career counselor
Child abuse officers
City planner
Civil rights worker
College students
Criminologist
Detective
Divorce lawyer
Employment office director
Feminist
Gerontologist
Handicapped services spokesperson
Immigrant
Juvenile court judge
Labor negotiator
Legislators
Marriage counselor
Minority advocates
News editor
Parents
Planned Parenthood representative
Pollster
Prison warden
School superintendent
Social policy expert
Social psychologist
Social workers
Sociologist
Sociology professors
Substance abuse counselor
Suicide prevention agency personnel
Television programming director

Theologian
Welfare department representatives

FIELD TRIP IDEAS

Day care center
Group meetings
Nursing home
Police department
Prison, jail
Public hearing
Senior citizen center
Shelter for the homeless
Social agency
Welfare department

ORGANIZATIONS WORTH WRITING

Al-Anon Family Groups
Headquarters, Inc.
One Park Avenue
New York, NY 10016

American Association of Retired
Persons
1909 K Street NW
Washington, DC 20049

American Educational Publishers
Institute
One Park Avenue
New York, NY 10016

American Humane Association
9725 East Hampden
Denver, CO 80281

American Institute of Family
Relations
5287 Sunset Boulevard
Los Angeles, CA 90027

American Social Health Association
260 Sheridan Avenue, Suite 307
Palo Alto, CA 94306

American Sociological Association
1722 N Street, NW
Washington, DC 20036

American Vocational Association
120 Engineering Center
Athens, GA 30602

B'Nai B'Rith International
1640 Rhode Island Avenue, NW
Washington, DC 20036

Association for Supervision and
Curriculum Development
225 North Washington Street
Alexandria, VA 23314

Bureau of the Census
Social and Economics Statistic
Administration
U.S. Department of Commerce
14th Street and Constitution
Avenue, NW
Washington, DC 20233

Council of Anthropology and Education
American Anthropological Association
1703 New Hampshire Avenue, NW
Washington, DC 20009

Education Development Center, Inc.
55 Chapel Street
Newton, MA 02160

Regional Office
Food and Drug Administration
1141 Central Parkway
Cincinnati, OH 45202

Foundation for Change, Inc.
1619 Broadway, Room 802
New York, NY 10019

International Planned Parenthood Federation
18–20 Lower Regent Street
London SW1Y 4PW, England

National Education Association
1201 16th Street, NW
Washington, DC 20036

Population Institute
110 Maryland Avenue, NE
Washington, DC 20002

Public Affairs Committee
381 Park Avenue South
New York, NY 10016

Public Education Religion Studies Center
Wright State University
Dayton, OH 45431

U.S. Department of Labor
Bureau of Labor Statistics
300 South Wacker Drive
Chicago, IL 60606

Zero Population Growth, Inc.
1346 Connecticut Avenue, NW
Washington, DC 20036

Chapter 6

PSYCHOLOGY

There is an inherent high interest in the topics covered in psychology because they directly relate to the personal life issues of every student. It should be difficult to make psychology dull.

For virtually every topic covered in psychology classes, it is possible to involve students in experiments, observations, questionnaires, interviews, role plays, and simulations. In this chapter, these and other teaching strategies are used to explore learning, memory, helping skills, goal setting, mental health, behavior change, and creativity.

(6-1) THE BODY CONTINUUM

Objectives:
- To use the continuum to measure the degree a trait exists
- To examine personal time usage habits and attitudes

Grades: 7–12

Time Required: 10 minutes

Materials Needed: None

Description:

1. Ask the class to stand against one wall. (They may need to move furniture so that there is plenty of room.)
2. Demonstrate that a continuum is a line drawn between two polarities along

which people can indicate where they fall on some issue. For example, you might draw a line on the chalkboard and write the words "hot" and "cold" at either end. Then place a checkmark along the continuum to indicate how hot or cold you feel at that moment.

3. Tell the class that the wall behind them represents a continuum and that they may indicate where they fall on a variety of issues related to time usage by moving their bodies along the wall.
4. Read the following issues, assigning one polarity to the left end of the wall and the other to the right end. Have them move their bodies after each issue is presented.

Issue: Procrastination

Do it now ———————————————— Don't do today what you can do tomorrow

Issue: Promptness

10 minutes early ———————————————— Better late than never

Issue: Neatness of your room

Clean, clean, clean ———————————————— Clutter, clutter

Issue: TV viewing

Never watch it ———————————————— Have developed square eyes

Issue: Success in life

It's all luck ———————————————— It's all hard work

(6-2) WHAT IF . . . ?

Objectives:
- To project potential consequences
- To practice creative imagination
- To develop logical hypotheses

Grade Level: 7–12

Time Required: Variable

Materials Needed: None

Description:

The following "Thought Stimulators" can be used in a variety of ways. They can be discussed in either large or small groups. Each group could be assigned a different topic and report their conclusions back to the class. Students can write on the same or different stimulator statements for homework.

How would the world be different if...

...we all spoke one language?
...printing had not yet been invented?
...people never laughed?
...everyone always had a headache?
...school was in session 50 weeks a year?
...males were not allowed to work or vote?
...no one could keep a secret?
...we could read each other's minds?
...no one had to work for a living?
...everyone had an IQ of 100? 160?
...grades were abolished?
...all parents had only one child?
...everyone was a twin?
...peer approval was not important?
...most people were left-handed?
...we didn't have music?
...no one ever lied?
...there was no electricity on Saturdays?
...we didn't daydream?
...we couldn't tell fact from opinion?
...everyone was nonassertive?
...redheads could foretell the future?
...driver's licenses were no longer required?
...schools all eliminated athletic competition?
...we selected careers by spinning a wheel?
...compulsory school attendance was ended?
...students hired the faculty?
...everyone used wheelchairs?

... we never needed to sleep?
... all work paid the same?
... people did not have long-term memory?
... we could transplant brains?
... knowledge came in pills?
... we had no sense of taste?

(6-3) UNUSUAL USES: STIMULATING CREATIVITY

Objectives:
- To apply the skills of brainstorming
- To develop a receptive attitude toward creativity

Grade Level: 7–12

Time Required: 20–30 minutes

Materials Needed: Props for brainstorming, such as chalkboard, eraser, nylon hose, golf ball, Styrofoam cup, plastic milk carton, or used tire

Description:

1. Introduce the traditional rules of brainstorming:
   a. Delay all evaluation.
   b. Suggest as many ideas as possible.
   c. Build on the ideas of others.
   d. Zany, half-baked ideas are welcome.
2. Break the class into groups of 4 or 5.
3. Explain that each group is to apply the principles of brainstorming in generating as many possible uses of an object you will present. Emphasize that they should list each idea without evaluating it. Newsprint and markers are optional for posting the lists. Hold up a common object such as a chalkboard eraser, umbrella, or volleyball. Announce a 5-minute time limit for generating the possible uses of their object.
4. Have each group report 2 or 3 of their ideas. If you let the first group give all of their ideas, the other groups may not have much to add.
5. You may wish to repeat the process with another object.

Optional Activities:

1. Assign or have the students suggest a problem they would like to confront. It might be a problem facing the school or one confronted by most adolescents. Possible topics for brainstorming are as follows:
   a. How to meet people
   b. Ways to earn money
   c. How to improve relations with parents
   d. How to improve school spirit
   e. Ways to make the school more attractive
2. Select an everyday item that might be improved. Assign the groups to brainstorm possible improvements in the suggested item. Possible products for improvement might include the following:

Bathtub	Library	Closets
Desk	Shoes	Chair
Telephone booth	Mailbox	Automobile
Picnic basket	Classroom	Watch
Television	Pen	Lawnmower
Flashlight	Purse	Hammer
Examinations	Refrigerator	Alarm clock

Helpful Resources:

Osborn, Alex. *Applied Imagination*. New York: Scribner's Sons, 1963.

Parnes, Sidney J., Noller, Ruth B., and Biondi, Angelo M. *Guide to Creative Action*. New York: Scribner's Sons, 1977.

Rawlinson, J. Geoffrey. *Creative Thinking and Brainstorming*. New York: Wiley, 1981.

(6-4) UNFINISHED PICTURES: INVITING CREATIVITY

Objectives:
- To explore the meaning of creativity
- To stimulate creative perception in students
- To recognize that different people may approach the same task uniquely yet creatively

Grade Level: 7–12

Time Required: 20–40 minutes

Materials Needed: Copies of "Unfinished Pictures" activity sheet

Description:

1. Distribute a copy of the "Unfinished Pictures" activity sheet to each student. Direct the class to draw a separate picture in each box incorporating the lines provided.
2. Allow approximately 15 minutes to complete the drawings. To share the results, you might select any of the following activities:
   a. Have students pass their drawings to the next student. After a few seconds, have them rotate those drawings to the next student. Continue passing the drawings until all students have received their own drawings. Discuss with the group the variety of perceptions that led to their creative drawings.
   b. Have students tape or pin their drawings to the wall. Then allow the students to circulate around the room to view each other's drawings. You might have several students describe the mental process they pursued in creating their drawings.
   c. Have students nominate the drawings they found most interesting, unique, or bizarre. Discuss their criteria for their selections.

UNFINISHED PICTURES

(6-5) PEANUTS, PEANUTS: USING YOUR SENSES

Objectives:
- To recognize the importance of sensory experiences in gathering information
- To combine senses to make discriminations
- To recognize that things that appear similar also have differences

Grade Level: 7–12

Time Required: 15 minutes

Materials Needed: Bag of peanuts in their shells

Description:

1. Let students pick a peanut from the bag.
2. Allow 3 minutes for the students to learn everything they can about their peanuts without breaking them open. Encourage them to use all of their senses.
3. Break the class into 2 or more groups for the following activity. Have the students in each group place their peanuts in a pile in the middle of a desk and mix them up.
4. Instruct the participants to retrieve their "personal" peanut from the pile.
5. Process the experience with the following questions:
   a. What things helped you identify your peanut?
   b. What senses did you use?
   c. What made the task more difficult?
   d. What does this experience teach us about dealing with other people?

(6-6) PHOTOGRAPHIC MEMORY TEST

Objective:
- To test short-term memory and eidetic imagery (photographic memory) ability

Grade Level: 7–12

Time Required: 5 minutes for 2 days

Materials Needed: Copies of "Photographic Memory Test"; blank paper

Description:

1. Distribute copies of the "Photographic Memory Test" face down. Students are not to look at them until signaled.
2. Give students 15 seconds to study the test, remembering as many of the objects as possible.
3. When time is called, instruct the class to place the test out of view and list the objects on blank sheets of paper.
4. After two minutes, allow students to score the number of the 25 objects successfully recalled.
5. Have a few students record the group data on the board.
6. The following day, ask students again to list all the objects they can recall. Score and graph the results of this trial. Discuss the results with the class.

PHOTOGRAPHIC MEMORY TEST

(6-7) SIMILARITIES AND DIFFERENCES

Objectives:
- To appreciate the shared experiences and attributes that bind human beings together
- To recognize and appreciate the differences that create individuality
- To practice interpersonal communication skills

Grade Level: 7–12

Time Required: 40–50 minutes

Materials Needed: None

Description:

1. Have the class form pairs. It is better if close friends do not work together.
2. For the first 10 minutes, they are to list as many mutual traits, interests, and experiences as they can discover. "In what ways are you alike?"
3. The second 10 minutes should be used to identify and list all the differences. "In what ways are you different?"
4. Have each pair combine with another pair, forming groups of four. Invite these groups to discuss their findings, especially looking for how the lists of the 2 pairs compare.
5. After a 10–12 minute discussion, form a large group to process the insights gained.

(6-8) POSSIBLE EXPLANATIONS: DEVELOPING ALTERNATIVE HYPOTHESES

Objectives:
- To generate alternative causal explanations for events
- To develop an attitude of open-mindedness

Grade Level: 7–12

Time Required: 30–60 minutes

Materials Needed: Copies of "Alternative Explanations" worksheet

Description:

1. Begin with a brief discussion of the concept that the true reasons for people's behaviors may not be readily apparent. Several alternative explanations may be possible.
2. Either provide each student with a copy of the "Alternative Explanations" worksheet or make a separate overhead transparency for each of the vignettes.
3. Have the entire group consider the first vignette. As students contribute possible alternative explanations for the person's behavior, record them on the chalkboard or newsprint. Record all hypotheses, even the nonsensical ones. Keep probing for additional alternative explanations until you have 15 or 20.
4. Have the students consider the second vignette in groups of 3 or 4. Urge them to brainstorm in their groups all the possible explanations for the person's behavior. After 5 to 10 minutes, solicit the alternative explanations from the class. When discussing these, stress the importance of open-mindedness since we cannot know for certain which explanation is true. Indeed, the behavior may be the combined result of several causes.
5. Continue the small-group brainstorming process with the remaining vignettes, allowing approximately 5 minutes for each. You may choose to stop the group after each vignette for discussions, or wait until all are completed.

Optional Activities:

1. Have the class suggest their own behavior vignettes that they would like to brainstorm. Ask the group to brainstorm alternative explanations for these.
2. Assign the class to identify 3 specific behaviors of others they observe. These may be actions of friends, parents, teachers, or other persons. They are to brainstorm in writing alternative explanations for these behaviors. Suggest that the students indicate with asterisks those they believe most likely to be the causes of the observed behaviors.

Name ______________________ Date ______________________

ALTERNATIVE EXPLANATIONS

Propose as many alternative explanations as possible for the behaviors of the persons in each vignette.

1. Mr. Davis is seated at a table in a new restaurant. He puts down his menu and leaves the restaurant without ordering. Why did he leave?

   ____

   ____

   ____

2. As Denise enters the biology classroom, she says hello to Matt. Matt turns and walks away without responding. Why might Matt have responded as he did?

   ____

   ____

   ____

3. When Laurie receives yesterday's math test from the teacher, she smiles and kisses the paper. Her score on the test was 72. Why did she react that way?

   ____

   ____

   ____

4. Mike and David are walking down the hall together. Kevin approaches from behind and knocks the books out of David's hands. How many explanations can you think of for Kevin's behavior?

   ____

   ____

   ____

5. As Susie and Carol are talking about the prom, Margie begins to cry and runs from the room. Why might she behave that way?

   ____

   ____

   ____

6. When Brett answers the telephone, the caller identifies herself as Ms. Bell, Brett's science teacher. Ms. Bell asks to speak with one of Brett's parents. Why did Ms. Bell call?

   ____

   ____

   ____

(6-9) INTERVIEWING MENTALLY HEALTHY PEOPLE

Objectives:
- To identify the personal characteristics of mental health
- To practice interviewing skills

Grade Level: 7–12

Time Required: 45–60 minutes in class; outside preparation, 30–90 minutes

Materials Needed: One copy of the "Mental Health Interview Form" for each student

Description:

1. This is an appropriate activity to follow up a discussion on the traits of mentally healthy people, such as Maslow's research on self-actualized persons. Ask students to think of the two or three persons they know personally whom they believe to be mentally very healthy. Using the "Mental Health Interview Form" as a guideline, the students are assigned to interview one (or, as an option, two) of these perceived mentally healthy persons.
2. Stress that the interview form is to be used to structure the interview, but that they are encouraged to ask clarifying questions throughout the interview. The interviews should be at least 15 minutes long. It is suggested that the deadline for the assignment be at least a week to allow sufficient time to schedule the face-to-face interviews.
3. After the interview, students should record and analyze their interviews. You might suggest that they attempt to apply the criteria of mental health previously discussed in class to their interviewees, noting areas of congruence.
4. On the date the assignment is due, process the experience in a group discussion. Possible questions for consideration might include the following:
   a. How accurate were your initial perceptions of this person's mental health?
   b. In what ways did your subject conform to the criteria of mental health discussed previously in class? Which criteria did they not meet?
   c. What were the ages of your subjects? Do you think age influences the mental health of an individual? (The average age of Maslow's self-actualized subjects was 55.)

d. How comfortable did your subjects appear in discussing their own strengths and weaknesses?
e. What did you admire most about this person?
f. How did this person view happiness?
g. What personal insights did you gain from talking with this person?
h. What values does this person try to live by?

Helpful Resources:

Johnson, David W. *Reaching Out.* 3rd ed. Englewood Cliffs, NJ: Prentice-Hall, 1986.

Maslow, Abraham. *Motivation and Personality.* 2nd ed. New York: Harper and Row, 1970.

Name ______________________ Date ______________________

MENTAL HEALTH INTERVIEW FORM

Use the following questions to structure the interview, but ask clarifying questions:

1. What things do you enjoy most in life? ______________________

2. What things upset or annoy you? ______________________

3. What principles do you try to follow in interacting with other people? ______________________

4. What goals would you yet like to accomplish? ______________________

5. What does happiness mean to you? ______________________

6. What do you think are your greatest strengths? ______________________

7. What would you most like to change about yourself? ______________________

8. What advice would you give others for living a happy, fulfilling life? ______________________

(6-10) BECOMING A SKILLED LISTENER

Objectives:
- To accurately reflect the feelings of another person
- To understand and demonstrate the concept of empathy in interpersonal communication

Grade Level: 10–12

Time Required: 40–60 minutes

Materials Needed: Copies of "Empathic Listening" activity sheet and "Feelings Vocabulary" handout

Description:

The empathic response is a valuable active listening technique. It can be a preferred alternative to giving advice and excessive questioning in helping another person deal with grief, conflict, frustration, and stress.

1. Break the group into triads. Students in each triad should identify themselves as A, B, or C, each person in the triad having a different letter.
2. Distribute copies of the "Empathic Listening" activity sheet to each student.
3. Give the following directions to the class:

> "In a moment I will call a letter; for example, Person A. That means that Person A is to be the listener. Your task is to respond to the first written quotation using an empathic response. For training purposes, we will all begin with the same format. Respond to the written quotation with three words. And to show you what a nice person I am, I'm going to give you the first two!
>
> "Respond with 'You feel_____.' [Write on the board or transparency.] Fill in the blank with the single word that you believe most accurately describes how the speaker is feeling at the time he or she made the comment in the quotation.
>
> "The task of the other two triad members [B and C in this example] is to give person A feedback on whether there are other words that might more accurately reflect how the speaker felt at the time the quotation was made. This will take only about a minute or two, and then we will discuss your answers.
>
> "Let's try the first one, Person A."

4. After approximately a minute, interrupt the group and ask for the feeling words they chose. After soliciting a variety of words, ask the group, "Which one is right?"

"The answer, of course, is that all of them or none of them might be correct. That is the reason we use this skill. You can never know for certain how another human being feels. We can guess or project how we might feel in that situation but never know for sure. That is why it is important to check out our perceptions.

"We are developing an essential counseling ingredient called 'empathy.' Empathy is the ability to communicate to another human being that 'I'm trying to understand what it is like to be you.' Note that it is not enough that you understand how the other person feels; you must communicate that understanding."

5. Direct Person B to respond to statement number 2 on the "Empathic Listening" activity sheet. After another minute, solicit feedback on the feeling words generated.

   Emphasize that the empathic response is offered as a tentative observation. It should end with a period, not a question mark. Ask the group how they would respond to "Do you feel frustrated?" The options are "yes" or "no" and then silence. The intention is to invite the other person to talk. Stress that if the empathic response is correct, the speaker will generally respond "yes" and then voluntarily elaborate. If the response was inaccurate, the speaker will usually respond with "Well, no, not exactly frustrated, but rather . . . " and provide clarification. Either way, the listener gains, although the objective is to be accurate as frequently as possible.

6. Continue to the third statement with Person C. This quotation illustrates how people frequently ask questions not with the intention of gaining information but rather to express emotions they feel too vulnerable to express directly. What feelings are behind the speaker's question? It may be helpful to solicit examples of questions used to express emotions. Ask what possible feelings might be behind the questions.

   Other examples and possible feelings are as follows:

"Do we have to do this?"	Boredom, resentment, irritation
"Why did you do that?"	Anger, disappointment, frustration
"Haven't you finished yet?"	Annoyance, impatience
"Do you really like her?	Jealousy, frustration
"How can you be so cruel?"	Hurt, rage, rejection

7. While the triads are working on the fourth quotation, place copies of the "Feelings Vocabulary" handout beneath their desks. Discuss the importance of validating positive feelings as well as negative ones. Direct students to use the vocabulary list to discover 3 more feeling words that might be appropriate for quotation number 4.

8. After practicing the basic empathic response on a few additional quotations, introduce the following format:

   "You feel ______ about ______ ."

   This more advanced form of the empathic response includes not only the feeling but also the source of that feeling.

   Next, stress that students must learn to phrase the empathic response in a variety of ways, lest it begin to sound awkward. Give some examples and solicit others.

The following are examples of alternative phrasing of the empathic response:

"You are upset with your brother."

"You seem rather down today."

"I hear a lot of anger."

"It sounds like you're rather frustrated with school."

"It's exciting yet a bit scary to be leaving for college."

9. Allow students to practice with the remaining quotations on the "Empathic Listening" activity sheet. Emphasize the importance of practicing the skill until it becomes reflexive.

Optional Activities:

1. Play videotaped segments of any soap opera. Stop the dialogue occasionally, asking the class to respond to the character with empathic responses. You can have them respond in triads as in the above exercise.
2. Encourage students to practice using the empathic response whenever possible in their daily lives. After several days, invite them to share their experiences and the results of that practice.

Helpful Resources:

Aspy, David, and Roebuck, Flora. *Kids Don't Learn from Teachers They Don't Like.* Amherst, MA: Human Resource Development Press, 1977.

Carkhuff, Robert R. *The Art of Helping.* Amherst, MA: Human Resource Development Press, 1983.

Egan, Gerard. *The Skilled Helper.* Monterey, CA: Brooks/Cole Publishing, 1986.

Name ______________________ Date ______________________

EMPATHIC LISTENING

Visualize another student verbalizing each of the following statements to you. Use an appropriate empathic response to reflect the student's feeling.

1. "I've about had it with school. I feel like throwing in the towel."

   You feel ____ .

2. "I want kids to be my friends. But it seems the harder I try, the less they seem to like me."

   You feel ____ .

3. "I don't see why we have to take math. What good is it going to do me in the real world anyway?"

   You feel ____ .

4. "Wow! I finally aced a history test. I really studied and it paid off."

   You feel ____ .

5. "I don't understand why you didn't invite me to your party. I thought we were supposed to be friends."

   You feel ____ .

6. "My mom and dad are getting a divorce. I don't know what will happen to me. I guess they just don't care about us kids anymore."

   You feel ____________________ about ____________________ .

7. "I'm on pins and needles thinking about tomorrow's game. I hardly slept a wink last night."

   You feel ____________________ about ____________________ .

8. "Just get off my case. I don't need your help!"

   You feel ____________________ about ____________________ .

9. "If you're not a jock or a brain, nobody cares about you in this school."

   You feel ____________________ about ____________________ .

FEELINGS VOCABULARY

Positive Feelings			Negative Feelings				
able	fine	merry	afraid	disconcerted	frustrated	melancholy	somber
active	firm	mighty	agitated	disenchanted	furious	miffed	sore
adequate	forceful	motherly	aggravated	disgruntled	gloomy	miserable	sorrowful
alive	formidable	opinionated	alarmed	disgusted	glum	mistrustful	sorry
ambitious	fortunate	overjoyed	angry	dismayed	grieved	mixed up	spiteful
amused	fulfilled	overwhelming	anguished	disoriented	hateful	moody	startled
anxious	gay	peaceful	annoyed	displeased	helpless	mournful	stunned
assertive	gentle	pleasant	anxious	distracted	hopeless	negative	terrible
aware	glad	pleased	apathetic	distraught	horrified	nervous	terrified
blissful	gleeful	positive	appalled	distressed	hostile	out of it	timid
bold	glorious	powerful	apprehensive	distrustful	hurt	outraged	tormented
brave	good	productive	bad	disturbed	ill	painful	trapped
bubbly	great	proud	baffled	doubtful	inadequate	panicky	troubled
calm	happy	reliable	befuddled	down	incapable	perplexed	turned off
capable	healthy	relieved	bewildered	downcast	incensed	petrified	uncomfortable
cheerful	impregnable	resistant	bored	downhearted	indignant	pitiful	uneasy
compassionate	independent	satisfied	bothered	downtrodden	ineffective	powerless	unfit
confident	indestructible	spirited	burdened	embarrassed	inflamed	provoked	unhappy
consistent	intense	secure	burned up	emotional	infuriated	puny	unloved
content	invisible	strong	confounded	exasperated	intimidated	puzzled	unpleasant
courageous	jolly	super	confused	exhausted	irate	quiet	unsure
delighted	joyful	surprised	critical	fearful	irked	rattled	unwanted
determined	joyous	thankful	cross	fed up	irritated	remorseful	upset
ecstatic	jubilant	thrilled	crushed	flabbergasted	jumpy	revengeful	useless
elated	lighthearted	tickled	cutting	flustered	left out	run down	vulnerable
enduring	loud	tranquil	deflated	foggy	leery	sad	weak
energetic	loved	up	dejected	forgetful	lonely	self-pitying	worn out
enthralled	loving	uplifted	despairing	fragile	lost	silly	worried
everlasting	lucky	vibrant	despondent	frail	low	shaky	
excited	marvelous	wonderful	depressed	frantic	mad	shy	
exuberant	memorable	zealous	disappointed	frightened	mean	sober	

(6-11) GOAL-SETTING CARD SORT

Objectives:
- To recognize the value of setting long-range goals
- To identify goals students would like to accomplish during their lifetimes
- To break long-term goals into shorter-term objectives and actions

Grade Level: 10–12

Time Required: Variable

Materials Needed: One set of "Goal Cards" for each student (duplicate the cards on the heaviest paper stock available; cut along the dotted lines to form individual cards, and place a rubber band around each deck of cards); copies of "Personal Goal Profile" and "My Goals This Week" handouts

Description:

1. Distribute a deck of "Goal Cards" to each student.
2. Read the following directions:

   "Each person should have a deck of cards. Please do not chew on them since I need them back. Take the rubber band off of the deck and sort your deck into 3 piles. On the left, place the cards containing goals in which you have no interest. On the right, place those cards containing goals you might like to accomplish sometime between now and the time you turn 95. In the middle pile, place those cards for which you are undecided. You will end up with three piles: No, Maybe, and Yes."
3. After all students have sorted their cards into 3 piles, ask them to count the number in their right-hand or Yes pile. If they have more than 10 cards in the pile, direct them to resort that pile into 2 piles: those goals they are red-hot about and those that are only lukewarm. Continue re-sorting until they have their decks down to the top 10 goals.
4. Have the students rank order their top 10 "Goal Cards" in order (1, most important; 10, least important).
5. Ask the class to write their goals in order on a blank sheet of paper. Invite them to carry their lists with them for the next month or to post them at home where they will see their lists each day. (It may be desirable to describe the research on mental rehearsal and subconscious motivation.)

Optional Activities:

1. Have students construct collages that depict their desired goals. Respect their right to personal privacy and do not force students to show their collages or lists to other students. Encourage them to hang their goal posters in their rooms at home.
2. Distribute copies of the "Personal Goal Profile" to the students. Have them select one goal to use in completing the profile. The intent is to encourage long-range planning of the resources and subgoals necessary to accomplish a life goal. You might encourage them to share their plans in small groups.
3. On the chalkboard, write the date it will be exactly 10 years from today. Tell the students to imagine it is that date. They are to write a brief essay based on their fantasies on what their life will be like. No one else need see their writings. Questions they should ponder include the following:
   a. Where will you be living?
   b. How will you be spending your time?
   c. What will your relationships be like?
   d. What will your life-style be like?
   e. What kind of income do you expect?
   f. Which people will be important to you?

   From their dream essay, students can begin to identify goals they would like to pursue. They might compare these goals with the results of the card sort activity. Are they congruent?
4. Distribute copies of "My Goals This Week." Encourage the students to develop short-term goals to be completed within the coming week. These short-term goals should move them toward completion of their longer-range goals. Students may wish to pair up with another student for mutual support and to report progress toward their weekly goals. The activity may be repeated for several weeks in succession.

Helpful Resources:

Campbell, David. *If You Don't Know Where You're Going, You'll Probably End Up Somewhere Else.* Allen, TX: Argus Communications, 1974.

Lee, Wayne. *Formulating and Reaching Goals.* Champaign, IL: Research Press, 1978.

Morrisey, George. *Getting Your Act Together: Goal Setting for Fun, Health and Profit.* New York: Wiley, 1980.

GOAL CARDS

EARN A COLLEGE DEGREE	TRAVEL TO INTERESTING PLACES
GET MARRIED	OWN MY OWN BUSINESS
HAVE CHILDREN	MOVE TO A DIFFERENT CLIMATE
IMPROVE THE RELATIONSHIPS WITH MY FAMILY	BECOME PROFICIENT AT A MUSICAL INSTRUMENT

GOAL CARDS

HAVE GOOD HEALTH	BUY A HOUSE
BECOME FINANCIALLY SECURE	HELP OTHERS LESS FORTUNATE THAN I
* * WILD CARD * * WRITE YOUR OWN GOAL	BE ELECTED TO PUBLIC OFFICE
MAKE NEW FRIENDS	BE AN ACTIVE MEMBER OF MY RELIGIOUS COMMUNITY

GOAL CARDS

BE IN A PLAY	CLIMB A MOUNTAIN
WRITE A BOOK	LEARN TO FLY AN AIRPLANE
EXCEL IN A SPORT	BE MORE ASSERTIVE
LIVE A LONG LIFE	LOSE WEIGHT

GOAL CARDS

HAVE LOTS OF LEISURE TIME	OBTAIN JOB SECURITY
BUY AN EXPENSIVE CAR	BECOME LESS SHY
BE IN A MOVIE	BECOME AN EXPERT IN SOME AREA OR FIELD
HAVE MONEY TO INVEST	LOOK ATTRACTIVE

Name ______________________ Date ______________________

PERSONAL GOAL PROFILE

1. Goal:

2. By what date would you like to accomplish this goal?

3. How will you objectively determine whether you have attained your goal?

4. Why do you want to achieve this goal?

5. How will your life be any different if you do not reach your goal?

6. What will it cost to reach your goal?

a. Financially?

b. In time?

c. Other resources?

7. What shorter-term objectives will you need to accomplish to achieve your long-term goal?

8. What things can you do in the next week that will contribute toward your goal?

9. What strengths do you have that will assist you in attaining your goal?

10. What obstacles must you overcome in reaching your goal?

a. Internal?

b. External?

11. How can you best meet these challenges?

My Goals This Week

- ______________________________
  ____
- ______________________________
  ____
- ______________________________
  ____
- ______________________________
  ____
- ______________________________
  ____
- ______________________________
  ____

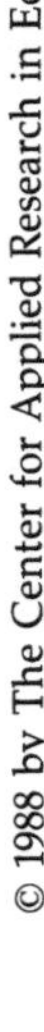

(6-12) EXPECTATIONS

Objectives:
- To identify the self-expectations possessed by each student
- To recognize how the expectations of others influence our behaviors

Grade Level: 10–12

Time Required: 20 minutes

Materials Needed: Copy of "Expectations Worksheet" for each student

Description:

1. Distribute copies of the "Expectations Worksheet" to the class. Introduce the idea that we all develop expectations of ourselves that influence our behaviors. Often these expectations arise from the expectations that others have of us. In turn, both our own and others' expectations may influence our behaviors.
2. Invite the students to write in the circle several expectations they hold of themselves. These might take the form of goals such as "to attend college" or traits like "to be honest."
3. The students should identify the people in their lives who hold expectations of them. Instruct the participants to label those others on the lines at the top of the squares. Rather than specific names, they might choose role categories such as "parents," "friends," "teachers," "relatives," or "neighbors." After the boxes are labeled, invite the students to list in the circles the expectations those people have of that student.
4. On the chalkboard or previously prepared poster, list the following sentence stems:

   "I learned . . . "

   "I discovered . . . "

   "I recognized . . . "

   "I was surprised . . . "

   "I suspect . . . "

   "I wonder . . . "

   Invite the participants to complete one or two of the sentence stems based on the insights gained from this exercise. Volunteers may choose to share their insights either with the total group or in small groups. Do not force students to reveal their personal insights. Their personal privacy must be respected.

Expectations Worksheet

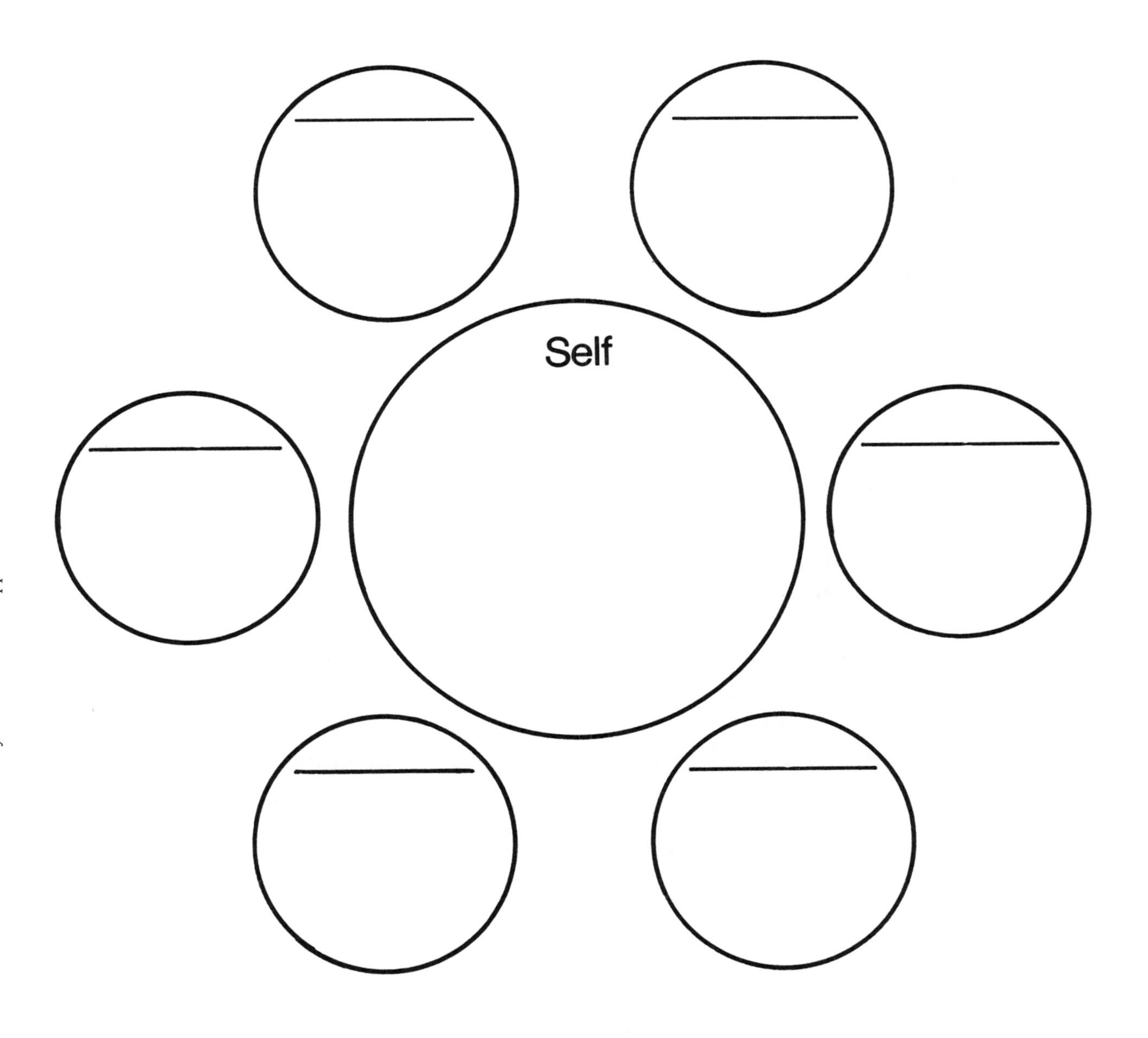

(6-13) NONVERBAL ATTENDING

Objectives:
- To recognize the influence of nonverbal posture on the communication process
- To develop nonverbal attending behaviors that invite effective communication

Grade Level: 10–12

Time Required: 15 minutes

Materials Needed: None

Description:

1. Ask the class to describe a good listener. Focus on the nonverbal messages sent by the effective listener. Researchers on counseling effectiveness have suggested that five specific nonverbal cues relate to helping effectiveness:
   a. Feet flat on the floor
   b. Moderate eye contact
   c. Shoulders squared with speaker
   d. Leaning forward
   e. Open, relaxed posture (arms not folded, lack of fidgeting, and so on)
2. Ask the students to form pairs. One person is designated as the speaker, the other the listener. The speaker is instructed to talk on any topic for one full minute without stopping. The listener is directed to begin with good nonverbal attending behaviors. After 30 seconds, flick the light switch once. This is the cue to the listener to change from good nonverbal attending to poor nonverbal attending.
3. After one minute, stop the conversations. Since turnabout is fair play, reverse the roles.
4. After the second minute, stop the conversations. Ask the students how they felt when their listeners shifted their body postures. Emphasize that even in an artificial situation, feelings like frustration, anger, rejection, or loneliness are experienced.
5. Suggest that students practice effective nonverbal attending as an action assignment for the next day or two. The next day, break the class into small groups to discuss their experiences.

(6-14) PERSONAL REINFORCEMENT SURVEY

Objectives:
- To identify the reinforcers that influence students' behavior
- To recognize that what is rewarding to one person may not be to another

Grade Level: 10–12

Time Required: 30 minutes; may be assigned as homework

Materials Needed: Copies of "Personal Reinforcement Survey"

Description:

1. This activity can be used during a discussion of behavioral psychology and how positive and negative consequences shape our behaviors.
2. Distribute copies of "Personal Reinforcement Survey." Assign students to complete the survey anonymously, either in class or as homework.
3. If time permits, a group of students might be assigned to collect and tabulate the results for presentation to the class. The students should submit the surveys anonymously to protect their privacy.
4. After presentation of the results, lead a discussion on the role of reinforcement in influencing behaviors. Stress the individual differences in the reinforcement preferences, noting that there are few universal reinforcers.

PERSONAL REINFORCEMENT SURVEY

Directions: Using the following scale, indicate your degree of preference for each of the items listed. How much do you like each item?

1 Dislike Very Much	2 Dislike Somewhat	3 Undecided	4 Like Somewhat	5 Like Very Much

Value	*Item*	*Value*	*Item*
_____	**1.** New clothes	_____	**21.** Walking
_____	**2.** Records, tapes	_____	**22.** Bicycling
_____	**3.** Movies	_____	**23.** Visiting museums
_____	**4.** Rock music	_____	**24.** Cats
_____	**5.** Classical music	_____	**25.** Dogs
_____	**6.** Bluegrass music	_____	**26.** Swimming
_____	**7.** Jazz	_____	**27.** Playing basketball
_____	**8.** Parties	_____	**28.** Watching basketball
_____	**9.** Meeting new people	_____	**29.** Playing volleyball
_____	**10.** Flowers	_____	**30.** Watching volleyball
_____	**11.** Driving a car	_____	**31.** Playing football
_____	**12.** Books	_____	**32.** Watching football
_____	**13.** Magazines	_____	**33.** Playing tennis
_____	**14.** Being invited to someone's house	_____	**34.** Watching tennis
_____	**15.** Going out to dinner	_____	**35.** Playing hockey
_____	**16.** Receiving letters	_____	**36.** Watching hockey
_____	**17.** Using a computer	_____	**37.** Playing baseball
_____	**18.** Reading	_____	**38.** Watching baseball
_____	**19.** Cooking	_____	**39.** Horseback riding
_____	**20.** Dancing	_____	**40.** Photography

1 Dislike Very Much	2 Dislike Somewhat	3 Undecided	4 Like Somewhat	5 Like Very Much

Value *Item*

_____ **41.** Swimming

_____ **42.** Playing cards

_____ **43.** Eating

_____ **44.** Broccoli

_____ **45.** Candy

_____ **46.** Desserts

_____ **47.** Milk shakes

_____ **48.** Soft drinks

_____ **49.** Diet colas

_____ **50.** Pizza

_____ **51.** Hamburgers

_____ **52.** Chocolate

_____ **53.** Compliments

_____ **54.** Smiles

_____ **55.** Praise

_____ **56.** Kisses

_____ **57.** Talking with friends

_____ **58.** Learning a new skill

_____ **59.** Attending school

Value *Item*

_____ **60.** Helping others

_____ **61.** Sleeping late

_____ **62.** Staying out late

_____ **63.** Video games

_____ **64.** Watching people

_____ **65.** Flirting

_____ **66.** Meditating

_____ **67.** Praying

_____ **68.** Attending church

_____ **69.** Talking on the telephone

_____ **70.** Dating

(6-15) CONTRACTING FOR BEHAVIOR CHANGE

Objectives:
- To apply the principles of behavior modification in increasing or decreasing a personal behavior
- To write and implement a self-change contract

Grade Level: 10–12

Materials Needed: Copies of "Personal Behavior Change Checklist," "Guidelines for Effective Self-Contracts," and the sample contracts

Time Required: 30–50 minutes in class; completion deadline, 4–6 weeks

Description:

1. This assignment must follow a study of the basic principles of behavior modification: positive reinforcement, shaping, intermittent reinforcement, punishment, and extinction. The "Personal Behavior Change Checklist" may be completed by students to identify potential behaviors for a self-change contract.
2. Distribute and discuss the "Guidelines for Effective Self-Contract" handout and the sample self-contract. Reinforce and clarify the components of a successful self-contract. Review various forms for monitoring and graphing progress.
3. Assign students to write a self-contract that meets the criteria specified in the handout. This can be done in class, with students critiquing each other's self-contract, or as homework.
4. Announce how the assignment will be graded. It is recommended that one grade be given for submission of an approved contract and that bonus credit be given for its successful completion.
5. Require that contracts receive teacher approval before implementation. Assure that students are setting reasonable targets for behavior change, neither too high nor too low.
6. Set a deadline for completion of the project, optimally 4 to 6 weeks. On the due date, you might have a celebration for those who successfully completed their contracts.

Helpful Resources:

Goodwin, Dwight L., and Coates, Thomas J. *Helping Students Help Themselves.* Englewood Cliffs, NJ: Prentice-Hall, 1976.

Homme, Lloyd. *How to Use Contingency Contracting in the Classroom.* Champaign, IL: Research Press, 1972.

Thoresen, Carl E., and Mahoney, Michael J. *Behavioral Self-Control.* New York: Holt Rinehart and Winston, 1974.

Watson, David L., and Tharp, Roland G. *Self-Directed Behavior: Self-Modification for Personal Adjustment.* Monterey, CA: Brooks/Cole Publishing, 1977.

PERSONAL BEHAVIOR CHANGE CHECKLIST

Directions: Check those behaviors you would like to change. No one else need see your checklist. You might use the results to develop a goal plan for personal improvement.

I would like to:

______ **1.** Stop biting my fingernails.

______ **2.** Decrease arguing with others.

______ **3.** Eat less.

______ **4.** Waste less time.

______ **5.** Stop smoking.

______ **6.** Use less profanity.

______ **7.** Stop using drugs.

______ **8.** Reduce my consumption of alcoholic beverages.

______ **9.** Stop being late.

______ **10.** Procrastinate less.

______ **11.** Stop having headaches.

______ **12.** Worry less.

______ **13.** Be less shy.

______ **14.** Accept criticism better.

______ **15.** Be able to speak in front of a group.

______ **16.** Be more assertive.

______ **17.** Relax more.

______ **18.** Carry on conversations better.

______ **19.** Study more.

______ **20.** Be less anxious about dating.

______ **21.** Make decisions better.

______ **22.** Exercise more.

______ **23.** Watch less television.

______ **24.** Be in better physical condition.

______ **25.** Be better organized.

______ **26.** Manage my money better.

______ **27.** Be more helpful to others.

______ **28.** Daydream less.

______ **29.** Resist peer pressure better.

______ **30.** Be less fearful of leaving home.

______ **31.** Express my affection to others.

______ **32.** Express anger more effectively.

______ **33.** Stop putting myself down.

______ **34.** Walk more.

______ **35.** Practice a musical instrument more.

______ **36.** Stop throwing tantrums.

______ **37.** Smile more.

______ **38.** Stop screaming.

______ **39.** Cry less.

______ **40.** Keep my room cleaner.

______ **41.** Be more punctual.

______ **42.** Get up earlier.

______ **43.** Go to bed earlier.

______ **44.** Help more with household chores.

______ **45.** Talk with parents more.

______ **46.** Give more compliments.

______ **47.** Other ____.

GUIDELINES FOR EFFECTIVE SELF-CONTRACTS

1. Select a specific behavior you would like to increase or decrease.

2. Identify an objective and measurable means of monitoring your progress (for example, calories eaten, minutes of practice, miles run, pages read).

3. State positively the goal and the deadline (for example, to lose 8 pounds within 6 weeks, to practice the guitar an average of 30 minutes per night for the next 5 weeks).

4. Break your main goal into weekly objectives. It is best to start with small changes and gradually increase or decrease to reach your long-term goal.

5. Identify a major reward for the successful completion of your goal. It must be something you really value and will not receive unless you complete your contract. You might negotiate with your parents or others for a privilege or object you desire. Smaller rewards for meeting each week's target behavior are also desirable.

6. It may increase your motivation to identify a punishment or penalty for failure to meet your contract (for example, loss of a privilege, doing someone else's chores, donating money to a cause you detest).

7. Devise a graph for monitoring your daily progress. It may be helpful to get a relative or friend involved in verifying your progress.

8. Submit your contract in writing for your teacher's approval before implementing it.

SAMPLE BEHAVIOR CHANGE CONTRACT

Name: Janet E. Davis   Date: September 15, 1989

Goal:

To increase my average daily piano practice time from 5 minutes to 35 minutes by December 1, 1989.

Subgoals:

To increase weekly average practice by 5 minutes each week.

Reward:

Each week my subgoal is met, I will be allowed to stay out an hour later on weekend nights. If my final goal is achieved, my parents agree to have a telephone installed in my room.

Penalty:

Any week I fail to meet the subgoal, I agree to wash the dishes all weekend.

Signed ______________________________

____

Behavior Sample Contract

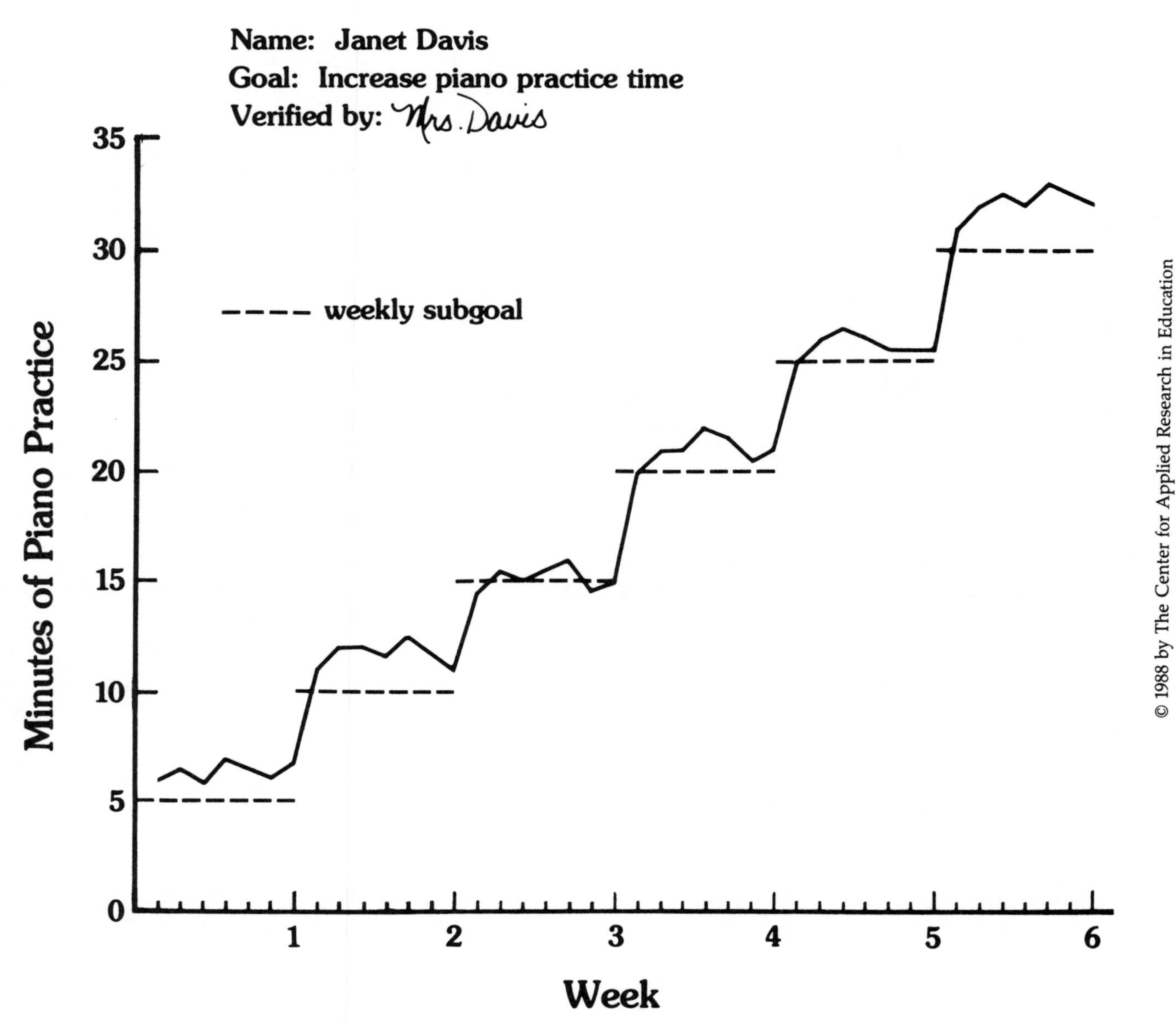

(6-16) POSITIVE AND NEGATIVE SELF-TEST

Objectives:
- To recognize how beliefs influence feelings
- To discover how irrational beliefs sometimes create self-defeating feelings
- To substitute more rational beliefs for irrational ones in self-talk

Grade Level: 10–12

Time Required: 30–45 minutes

Materials Needed: Copies of "Action-Beliefs-Consequent Feelings" transparency and "Self-Talk Analysis" handout

Description:

1. If you are not already familiar with the concepts of cognitive behavioral psychology or Albert Ellis' Rational Emotive Therapy, it is advisable to review one of the resources listed below.
2. On the chalkboard or a poster, reveal Epictetus' quotation, "Men feel disturbed not by things, but by the views they take of them." Facilitate a discussion of the quotation's meaning. Emphasize that events in life do not themselves create stresses, but rather it is our interpretation of those events as expressed in our self-talk.
3. Display the "Actions-Beliefs-Consequent Feelings" overhead transparency. Briefly explain Ellis' A-B-C theory that actions stimulate certain beliefs, which in turn evoke consequent feelings.
4. Write on the board three headings: "Actions," "Beliefs," and "Consequent Feelings." Work through an example such as "not getting hired for a job." Beneath the "Actions" heading, write "not hired." Ask the class what feelings such a person might experience. Write these on the board beneath the "Consequent Feelings" heading. Continue to probe for possible feelings. Likely responses will include "angry, frustrated, hurt, disappointed, and relieved." Emphasize that not everyone who does not get hired feels the same way, thus something else must account for the feelings.

   For each feeling listed, ask the class what persons experiencing that feeling must be saying to themselves. Under the "Belief" heading, write the belief expressed in the self-talk next to the corresponding feeling. For example:

Action	Belief	Consequent Feelings
Not hired for a job	"I'll never get a job."	Depression
	"I was discriminated against."	Anger
	"I almost had to go to work."	Relief
	"I guess I just didn't have enough experience."	Disappointment

5. Distribute copies of the "Self-Talk Analysis" handout. Break the class into groups of 3 or 4. Assign them to analyze the first example on the handout, looking for alternative positive and negative self-talk statements or beliefs. Allow 5 minutes to complete the first example; then discuss it as a large group. You may choose to stop for discussion after each of the remaining examples or let them finish all the rest and then compare the results.
6. Next, introduce the idea of irrational versus rational beliefs. Ellis has proposed a number of general irrational beliefs that create self-defeating feelings. These include the following:

   "I must have the love and approval of everyone."

   "I must be completely competent in everything I do to be a worthwhile person."

   "It is catastrophic and awful when things do not go as I wish."

   Discuss why these beliefs must be ultimately self-defeating and therefore irrational.
7. Discuss the errors of thinking we sometimes fall prey to when creating negative self-talk. Such traps as mind reading, fortune-telling, and predicting catastrophes should be discussed.

Optional Activities:

1. Have students keep a 3-day log of stress events that occur in their lives. Have them enter the action, beliefs or self-talk, and consequent feelings for each event. They should describe how to dispute the self-defeating negative beliefs.
2. For several days, take 5 minutes to have the class apply the A-B-C theory to a different event, exposing and disputing the irrational beliefs that emerge.

Helpful Resources:

Bard, James A. *Rational Emotive Therapy in Practice.* Champaign, IL: Research Press, 1980.

Ellis, Albert. *Humanistic Psychotherapy.* New York, NY: McGraw-Hill, 1974.

Walen, S. D., Ginseppe, R., and Wessler, R. L. *A Practitioner's Guide to Rational-Emotive Therapy.* New York: Oxford University Press, 1980.

Action ⇒ Beliefs ⇒ Consequent Feelings

SELF-TALK ANALYSIS

After each vignette, suggest alternative self-talk statements the person might generate.

1. Bill tries out for the basketball team but does not make the team.

2. Alice's parents have told her they are getting a divorce.

3. Michelle forgot to bring her geometry homework to school and received an F for the day.

4. Dan has asked three girls to the prom, but each has turned him down. Two said they already had dates; the third gave no reason.

5. Sally has discovered that she is pregnant.

6. Jimmy wants a moped for his birthday, but his parents refuse to buy him one.

(6-17) INTERPERSONAL COMMUNICATION ROADBLOCKS

Objectives:
- To identify the roadblocks to effective interpersonal communication
- To increase motivation for improving interpersonal communication skills

Grade Level: 10–12

Time Required: 45–60 minutes

Materials Needed: None

Description:

1. Have the entire class brainstorm roadblocks to effective interpersonal communication. Post the potential roadblocks on the chalkboard or on newsprint.
2. Break into groups of 2 or 3. Assign each group a different communication roadblock. Allow 10 minutes for the groups to develop a brief dialogue to present an example of the assigned communication roadblock. (As an alternative, prepared transcripts can be distributed to the students.)
3. Each demonstration is followed by a discussion of what happened and how that roadblock can be minimized.

Optional Activities:

1. Students can be assigned to observe the interpersonal communications of themselves, others, or television characters. Instances of communication roadblocks can be reported either in writing or at a future class discussion.
2. Combine several of the communication roadblock dialogues into a presentation on "Roadblocks to Effective Communication" with suggestions for improving interpersonal communication. This program can be presented to other classes, elementary or junior high students, or to parent or community groups.

Helpful Films:

Communicating Effectively, Barr Films, 1976
Communicating Non-Defensively, McGraw-Hill Films, 1982
The Power of Listening, CRM Films, 1978
You're Not Listening, Barr Films, 1978

(6-18) POKER: ON THE IMPORTANCE OF HAVING OPTIONS

Objective: • To recognize that the probability of finding an effective solution increases with the number of options

Grade Level: 11–12

Time Required: 5 minutes

Materials Needed: One poker deck of playing cards

Description:

1. Ask how many students know the rules of poker. (You may choose to substitute any other similar card game.) Select one student to volunteer for a friendly game.
2. Deal the cards, 1 to the student, 2 to you, until the student has 5 cards and you have 10. As you deal, you can announce the progress of the hand ("one pair," "possible straight," and so on.)
3. Obviously, with 10 cards, you should have the winning hand. If not, continue giving yourself cards until you can beat the opponent's hand.
4. Ask the class why you never lose. Discuss the analogy to finding options in dealing with life's problems. The more ideas we have, the greater the probability of coming up with a good idea.

(6-19) APPLIED BEHAVIOR MODIFICATION

Objectives:
- To apply the principles of shaping and intermittent reinforcement in modifying a person's behavior
- To increase awareness of the emotional reactions of both teacher and learner

Grade Level: 10–12

Time Required: 30–40 minutes

Materials Needed: Paper cups; bag of shelled corn; set of "Teaching Tasks" cards

Description:

1. This activity is an excellent follow-up to study of the principles of behavior modification or operant conditioning. It requires the student to demonstrate mastery of shaping and intermittent reinforcement.
2. Have the group divide into pairs. One person will begin as the trainer, the other as the student.
3. Give each pair 2 paper cups, one filled with kernels of corn, the other empty.
4. Explain that the purpose of the activity is for the trainers to teach their students a new behavior. Emphasize that the only way the trainers may communicate with their students is by dropping a kernel of corn into the empty cup. Participants may not talk or nonverbally cue their partners. They are working as a team and want to master the assigned "Teaching Task" as quickly as possible.
5. Give a "Teaching Task" card to each trainer and instruct the pairs to begin. Once a pair has mastered the assigned task, have them reverse roles with a new "Teaching Task" card.
6. After each pair has had a chance to reverse roles at least once, discuss the activity with the following questions:
   a. What things made learning the new behavior difficult?
   b. What made teaching the behavior difficult?
   c. In what ways is this activity similar to changing behaviors of others in the real world? (for example, potty training an infant, training an animal, coaching a sport, teaching high school students)
   d. Why did some trainers experience partial success in teaching the new behavior, only to have their students regress?

e. How did you feel when you could not succeed in teaching a task to your student? How did the unsuccessful student feel? How does that translate to our daily lives?

Teaching Task Cards

Type each of the following onto separate 3″ x 5″ index cards:

PUT HEAD ON THE DESK
STAND ON ONE LEG FOR TEN SECONDS
CUP HANDS OVER EARS
FLAP ARMS LIKE WINGS
PUT LEFT HAND OVER RIGHT EYE
STAND AND TURN A COUNTERCLOCKWISE CIRCLE
PLACE A BOOK ON THE FLOOR
WALK OVER AND TOUCH THE TEACHER ON THE SHOULDER
SQUAT AND WADDLE LIKE A DUCK
TAKE OFF LEFT SHOE
ROLL UP RIGHT SHIRT SLEEVE
PUT BOTH HANDS ON TOP OF HEAD
TAKE OFF WATCH
STAND AND HOP LIKE A BUNNY
TAKE OFF GLASSES AND PLACE ON THE DESK
OPEN ANY BOOK TO PAGE 25

(6-20) FREUDIAN PSYCHOLOGY CROSSWORD PUZZLE

Objective: • To review Freudian psychology terms and ideas

Grade Level: 7–12

Time Required: One period

Materials Needed: Copies of "Freudian Psychology Crossword Puzzle"

Description:

Distribute copies of the crossword puzzle for students to complete individually or in pairs in the classroom.

Name ______________________ Date ______________________

FREUDIAN PSYCHOLOGY CROSSWORD PUZZLE

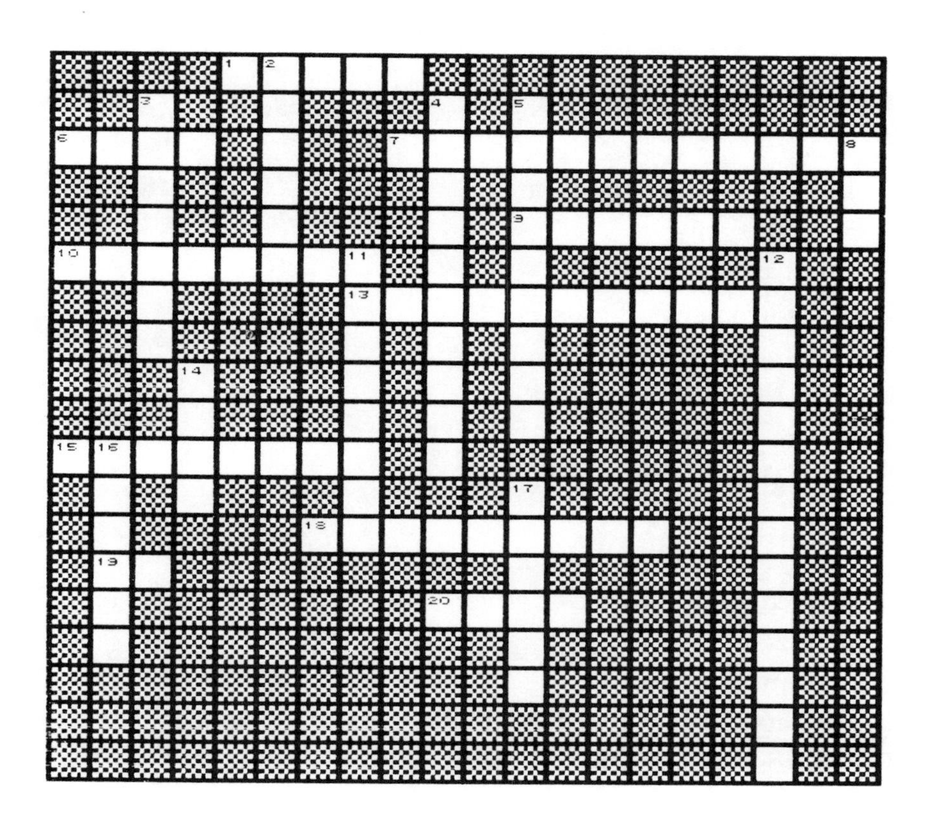

ACROSS

1. Alfred ____
6. "____ association"
7. Part of client-analyst relationship
9. "Slip of the ____"
10. Artifically induced trance-like state
13. Pushed from awareness
15. Goal of the "id"
18. In present awareness
19. Pleasure-seeking part of personality
20. Freud disciple, Carl ____

DOWN

2. Sleeping scenes
3. ____ complex
4. Techniques for evaluating personality
5. Life and death ____
8. Rational part of personality
11. Includes conscience
12. Freud's method of treatment
14. First stage of psychosexual development
16. Source of instinctual energy
17. Home of Freud

POSSIBLE RESOURCE PERSONS

Alcoholics Anonymous representative
Animal trainer
Biofeedback trainer
Corporate human resource development manager
Counselor
Crisis intervention counselor
Former students
Hypnotist
Law enforcement officials
Lawyers
Marriage therapist
Members of the clergy
Neurologist
Nurses
Nursing home administrator
Parapsychologist
Pediatrician
Peer counselor
Police department official for lie detector demonstration
Psychiatrist
Psychometrician
Psychologist
Psychology professors
Social workers
Telephone crisis center director

FIELD TRIP IDEAS

Behavior change clinic
Community mental health center
Court
Day care center
Drug rehabilitation center
Elementary school
Hospital
Jails or prison

Mental hospital
Nursing home
Supervised workshops for mentally retarded
University research laboratory
Vocational rehabilitation center
Zoo

ORGANIZATIONS WORTH WRITING

American Guidance Service, Inc.
Publishers Building
Circle Pines, MN 55014

American Medical Association
535 North Dearborn Street
Chicago, IL 60610

American Psychological Association
1200 17th Street, NW
Washington, DC 20036

Association for Childhood Education International (ACEI)
3615 Wisconsin Avenue, NW
Washington, DC 20016

BRS/LVE, Inc.
9381-D Davis Avenue
Laurel, MD 20707

Mental Health Materials Center, Inc.
419 Park Avenue South
New York, NY 10016

National Association for Mental Health
10 Columbus Circle, Suite 1300
New York, NY 10019

National Institutes of Mental Health

Narcotic Addiction and Drug Abuse Information
5454 Wisconsin Avenue
Chevy Chase, MD 20015

U.S. Department of Health and Human Services
Office of Youth Development
Room K21D
200 Independence Avenue, SW
Washington, DC 20201

University Associates, Inc
8517 Production Avenue
San Diego, CA 92121

Chapter 7

GEOGRAPHY

The study of geography promotes an understanding of the relationships between people and their environment. Its objectives are to help students understand the world in which they live, and to recognize the interdependence of individuals, groups, and nations. Activities in this section are grouped according to spatial distribution, spatial relationships, and spatial interaction on our earth. At a time of potential global conflict, resource depletion, and environmental crises, geographical information may be incomplete in equipping students to live in today's world. Teaching strategies may need to include activities that allow students to clarify their values about preserving our earth. These strategies need to include practices that permit students to define and redefine their value judgments that can affect not only our world but also the world of future travelers.

(7-1) INTRODUCTION: THE WORLD OF ________

Objective:
- To acquaint students with the many worlds and the geographical influences on their lives

Grade Level: 7–12

Time Required: 15–30 minutes

Materials Needed: Copies of "The World of ________" activity sheet; pencils

Directions:

1. Have students complete copies of "The World of ___________" worksheet. They should put their names in the center circle and add their information in all the other blanks (city, addresses, and so on).
2. Discuss the activity with the following questions:
   a. How are these geographical areas alike? different? (climate, land form, population)
   b How do they influence each other?
   c. What can I control? Not control?
   d. Which of these worlds is most likely to change in the future? How?
   e. Which of these worlds is most important to me?

Street

Hemisphere

City

The World of

Name

Continent

State

Country

Region

County

(7-2) IN THE BEGINNING...

Objective: • To have students experience the difficulty of mapping a sphere

Grade Level: 7–9

Time Required: 30 minutes

Materials Needed: Some type of unmarked sphere (styrofoam balls, rubber balls, orange, and so on) for each student; markers, pen, pins; string

Description:

1. This activity demonstrates the necessity of recognizing imaginary lines, that is, equator, prime meridian,latitude, longitude as a prerequisite to map literacy.
   a. Locate the "top" of your ball (discuss difficulty of locating "top" and the need to give "top" a label—North Pole).
   b. Locate the "bottom"—label it South Pole.
   c. Draw a horizontal line midway between "top" and "bottom." Call the line the equator. Land north of the equator is know as the northern hemisphere—land below the equator is the southern hemisphere.
2. Determine if class lives in the northern or southern hemisphere.
   a. Draw 4 horizontal lines between the equator and the North Pole. Because a circle (sphere) contains 360°, we will use that measure.
   b. Label the equator 0, the first line north of the equator 20°, second line 40°, third line 60°, fourth line 80°.
3. Now repeat the process south of the equator. Draw 4 lines and label the lines 20°, 40°, 60°, 80°. We call these lines parallels or latitude. Look on a map and determine the approximate latitude of your community.
4. Draw a line from the North Pole to the South Pole. Call this line Prime Meridian. Label it 0°. (Because of England's interest in mapmaking and political power, the Prime Meridian goes through Greenwich, England.) Draw lines parallel to the Prime Meridian, and label them until you reach 180° (1/2 of sphere). Label that line the International Date Line. (As one crosses the International Date Line moving westward, the calendar is set forward one day.) Number lines eastward the same way from the Prime Meridian. (As one moves eastward across the International Date Line, the calendar is set back one day). We call these lines Longitude.

5. Find the approximate longitude of your community. Mark it on your sphere.

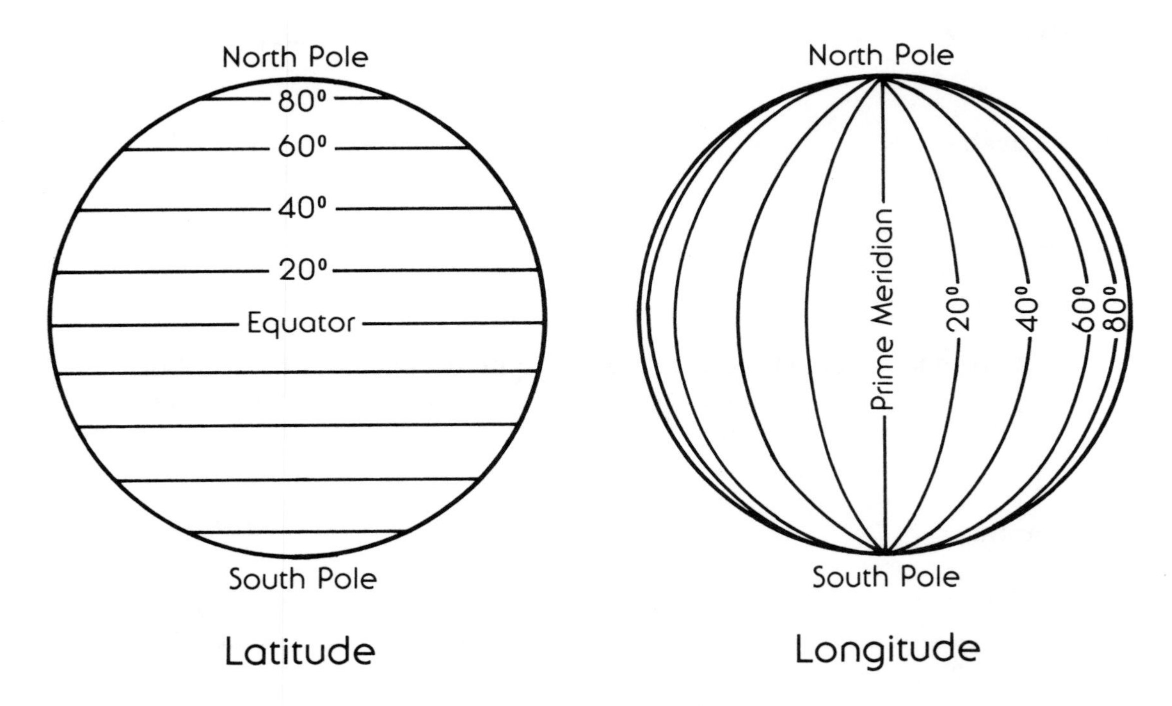

(7-3) INSIDE-OUT

Objective: • To have students realize the inconvenience of carrying a globe and the limitations of its scale for everyday use and to understand the importance of maps and the difficulty of using a "flat" object to represent a globe.

Grade Level: 7–9

Time Required: 30 minutes

Materials Needed: Sphere from activity 7–2, "In the Beginning . . . "; paper, pencil, copies of grid

Description:

1. If an orange is used for this lesson, place the orange so it will lie flat, or draw on paper a representation of the sphere used.
2. Explain that places that do not lie directly on major latitude and longitude

lines can be located exactly in terms of degrees, minutes, and seconds. Each degree of a circle contains 60 minutes, and each minute 60 seconds. Thus, Washington, D.C., is exactly 38 degrees 53 minutes and 23 seconds north of the equator. It is also exactly 77 degrees no minutes and 33 seconds west of the prime meridian. Its exact location on the surface of the earth can therefore be given as:

Latitude 38° 53′ 22″ N
Longitude 77° 00′ 33″ W

3. Find the exact latitude and longitude of your community.
4. Distribute copies of the grid.
5. Granted the grid does not exactly match the earth sphere. Maps are a projection. And while they cannot tell all the truth, they do tell one part of the truth. All modern maps are based on this standard grid. The map must include a title (what it is a map of), the scale (what distance each square represents), and symbols (pictures to represent markers such as cities, trees, lakes, and so on), legend (key that explains symbols), and a compass rose (shows N, S, E, W).

Optional Activity:

Have each student make a map of your school. Be sure to include the following: title, legend, scale, and compass rose.

Name ______________________ Date ______________________

GRID

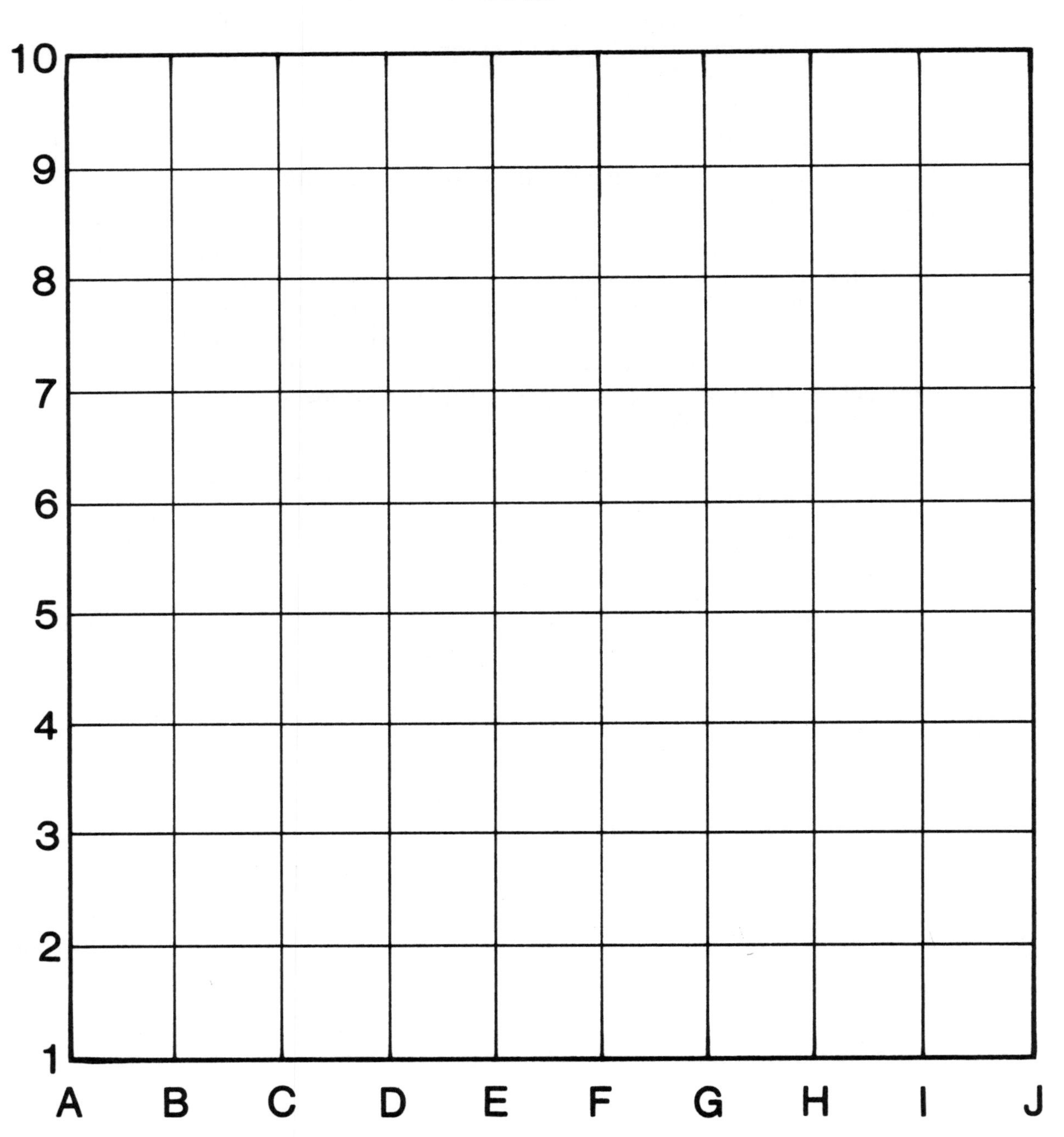

(7-4) HOME SWEET HOME

Objective: • To provide practice and reinforce the need for title, legend, scale, and compass rose

Grade Level: 7–9

Time Required: 30 minutes

Materials Needed: Grid paper, ruler, pencil

Description:

1. Have students draw a map of how to get to their homes from school. They should estimate a distance and then determine scale, draw symbols to represent landmarks, and include a legend and compass rose.
2. Invite the students to share their maps with one another. You may choose to display some or all on the bulletin board.

(7-5) THE MAPMAKER

Objective: • To acquaint students with the importance of maps and the various types of information they provide

Grade Level: 7–12

Time Required: 30 minutes

Materials Needed: Rulers, grid, pencil, reference books on your area (or on any in the world)

Directions:

1. Tell students they can use maps to show spatial distribution and spatial relationships.
2. Brainstorm and list on the chalkboard (or on an overhead projector) the varying kinds of spatial *distribution* a map can show, as follows:

a. land forms
—oceans
—rivers
—mountains
—deserts
—swamps
b. political divisions
—states
—counties
—cities
—ethnic
c. population
d. roadways, railroads
e. climate

3. Choose one of the above. Use a reference book and map it. Be sure to label (title) the map, give the scale, and provide a legend.
4. Discuss the value of using maps over using globes.
5. Have students locate places or information assigned by the teacher. Let the students exchange papers and check them for accuracy.

(7-6) WHAT TIME IS IT?

Objective: • To have students become aware that the earth grid is useful not only in the location of places but also in the measurement of time

Grade Level: 7–12

Time Required: 15–30 minutes

Materials Needed: Names of cities on slips of paper; copies of time grid; atlases for each student or group of students

Description:

1. Divide class into groups of 3.
2. Give each triad a slip of paper containing the name of a city. Ask them to figure out what time it is in that city. (At first, use only the names of cities listed on the grid.)

3. Add to the difficulty by using names of cities they must first locate in an atlas and then figure out what time it is.
4. Explain that when you travel to distant places, different regions have different time. The earth turns 360° of longitude in 24 hours. It thus turns through 15 degrees of longitude in 1 hour (360° ÷ 24 = 15°). Sunrise is one hour eariler in Philadelphia than in St. Louis because Philadelphia lies 15° of longitude east of St. Louis, and it takes the earth one hour to turn those 15 degrees.

TIME GRID

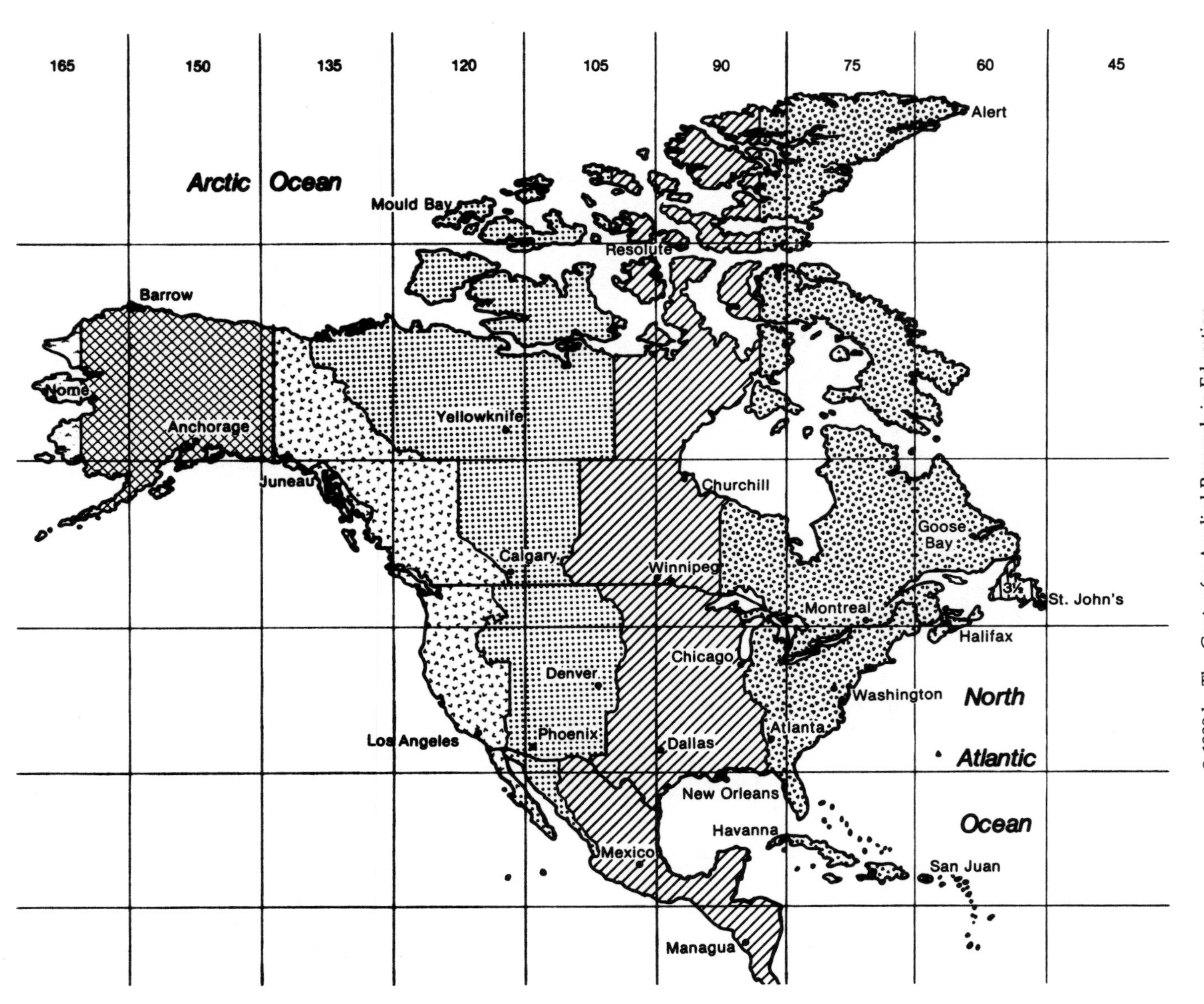

165
150
135
120
105
90
75
60
45
Alert
Arctic Ocean
Mould Bay
Resolute
Barrow
Nome
Yellowknife
Anchorage
Juneau
Churchill
Goose Bay
Calgary
Winnipeg
3½
St. John's
Montreal
Halifax
Chicago
Denver
Washington
North
Los Angeles
Phoenix
Dallas
Atlanta
Atlantic
New Orleans
Ocean
Havanna
Mexico
San Juan
Managua

(7-7) RELATIVE HUMIDITY

Objective: • To have students understand concept of relative humidity

Grade Level: 7–12

Time Required: 10 minutes

Materials Needed: Five placards that read TEMPERATURE; one placard each that reads RAIN, HAIL, SLEET, SNOW, VAPOR, AIR

Description:

1. Choose 5 students to represent TEMPERATURE. Have them attach name placards. Assign one student to be AIR. Choose 5 students to be RAIN, SLEET, HAIL, SNOW, VAPOR. AIR stands in front of class. One TEMPERATURE joins her and SNOW joins them. As TEMPERATURE is joined by more TEMPERATURE, SNOW changes to HAIL, then SLEET, then RAIN—finally VAPOR.
2. Demonstrate that as temperature increases, the air can hold more moisture. Temperature is the boss. The amount of moisture in the air is called relative humidity.

(7-8) EYEWITNESS WEATHER

Objectives:
- To have students chart the weather
- To realize that climate is a large-scale, macroconcept generalizing patterns across space and time, whereas weather is a small-scale, microconcept conveying specific information about a particular place at a particular time

Grade Level: 7–12

Time Required: 5 minutes per class for 10 weeks or longer

Materials Needed: Newspapers, notebook

Description:

1. Assign students to chart the weather of a particular location. If students have access to enough newspapers, assign 3 students to a particular geographical location and chart its weather for a semester. If not, assign the entire class to their own locality.
2. Periodically discuss weather patterns, concluding with its relationships to climate. If the class charts only its community, then near the completion of the unit, assign triads of students to chart climates of particular geographical areas that each triad chooses.

Optional Activities:

1. Invite a local meteorologist to speak to the class on weather forecasting.
2. Arrange a field trip to a local weather station to observe the instruments used in gathering weather data.

(7-9) THE SURVEYOR

Objectives:
- To develop an awareness of land uses
- To recognize the ripple effect of land use

Grade Level: 7–12

Time Required: 30–45 minutes

Materials Needed: Reference books, map grid, pencil

Description:

1. Have students survey reference books as to the major uses of land in the area.
2. Group these uses into appropriate categories such as agricultural, industrial, recreational, residential, commercial.
3. Develop symbols for each category. Then plot that data on a map.
4. Develop a legend to explain the symbols.
5. Discuss the following questions:
   a. How does each "land-use" affect other land-use in the area?
   b. What problems are created by land-use for the population?
   c. What land-use is changing? Why?

d. What proposed projects could affect land-use in the future?

e. In the United States, most cities have developed industrial areas primarily to the east of the city and the more expensive residential areas on the west. Why? (Answer: the prevailing western winds blowing smog.)

f. Who decides how land should be used? Is this the best way?

(7-10) DIVVY-UP

Objective: • To make students aware that along with spatial distribution, maps can also show spatial relationships

Grade Level: 7–12

Time Required: 40–60 minutes

Materials Needed: Rulers, grid, pencil, reference books

Description:

1. Remind students that maps can show both spatial distribution and spatial relationships.
2. Brainstorm and list on the chalkboard (or on an overhead projector) the varying kinds of spatial relationships, such as the following:
   Population density
   Per capital wealth
   Trade balance
   Manufacturing
   Farming
3. Choose one of the above. Assign students to use a reference book and map one of the forms of spatial relationship. They should label (title) the map, give the scales, and provide a legend.

(7-11) WORLD SOLITAIRE

Objectives: • To provide an introduction to geopolitics

• To become aware of interaction of natural resources, education, military strength, and culture to world power

Grade Level: 7–12

Time Required: 30–45 minutes

Materials Needed: Deck of cards for each student, paper, pencil

Description:

1. Arrange students in pairs.
2. Each student will play "World Solitaire" and apply the game to the geography of a country and its relationship to the country's place in the world community. The teacher demonstrates the card game of solitaire.

   When students cannot play any longer, they tally on a sheet of paper their 7 piles of cards that have been played. For example:

Spades	A, Q, 5, 6
Hearts	J, 10, 8, 6, 4
Diamonds	7, 4, 2
Clubs	K, J, 10, 9, 8, 7

3. Students play the games and tally their cards. (Note: Do not force students to participate if their parents disapprove of card playing.)
4. The teacher puts a transparency on the overhead (or writes on the board):
   a. 5 spades represent agricultural wealth (rich soil, mild climate with adequate rainfall, topography conducive to farming).
   b. 5 hearts represent a well-educated, skilled population.
   c. 5 diamonds represent high industrialization with energy resources, iron deposits, excellent transportation.
   d. 5 clubs represent the political system of the country that allows its population to make decisions regarding the country's policies and maintains military power to protect itself.

   Less than 5 means these items are lacking; more than 5 means these items are in abundance. Solitaire means you have it all—a perfect situation. That student wins.

5. Discuss the following questions:
   a. Did some of you receive "better cards" than others? Is that true of countries? What are some of those countries that have been "given" an advantageous lot?
   b. Did your skill in the game play any part in your winning? Does that happen to countries? (Point out that Japan has become highly industrialized without many natural resources because of the industriousness of its people.)
   c. Would it have helped if you could have traded cards with a partner? Do countries ever compensate for what they lack by trade? Name examples.

d. List the geographical "riches" of world power countries. What problems must they solve to keep their power?
e. List Third World countries whose "givens" are severely limited. What do they lack to become world powers? How can they compensate for their inadequacies?
f. Does any country have a perfect situation? Will the world always have problems? How should world disputes be solved?

(7-12) ALONE AT LAST

Objective: • To provide a lead-in to discussion of population density

Grade Level: 7–12

Time Required: 30 minutes

Materials Needed: 10 chairs spaced close together in front of class

Description:

1. Ask 4 students to come up and sit on the chairs. Give them approximately 2 minutes to sit there.
2. Ask these 4 to return to their seats. Ask 20 students to sit on the chairs. Give them 2 minutes before returning to their desks.
3. Tell them the first group represented population density in California—the second, population density in Japan. Discuss how life would be different in the first group than life for the second group as to group conflict, movement, use of land, rural versus urban, and so on.
4. What does population density tell you that a country's or a city's population does not?
5. The following chart is for your information:

Average Population Density for Selected U.S. Cities

City	Population per square mile
Oklahoma City, OK	688
Sioux Falls, SD	1,999
Cheyenne, WY	3,173
Denver, CO	4,452
Los Angeles, CA	6,384
Washington, D.C.	10,181
Chicago, IL	13,174
New York, NY	23,455

Source: Bureau of the Census (1980)

(7-13) ONE PLUS ONE = 20?

Objective: • To have students "experience" population explosion

Grade Level: 7–12

Time Required: 15 minutes

Materials Needed: Copies of the "Chart of Population Growth"

Description:

1. Illustrate population growth by having students role-play a family tree or fill in the Chart of Population Growth.
2. Pair 2 students on a line. Give them 4 "children." Have 4 of these children "marry." Only 3 have children—one couple has 5 children; one couple has 6 children; one couple has 3 children.
3. In as brief a time as 3 generations, 2 can become 20 or 35, depending on the birthrate.
4. Have students look up population statistics of the world and specific countries.
5. Discuss problems of overpopulation, underpopulation,—and restraint on birth control:

a. Cultural beliefs that wealth of family is determined by number of children
b. Religious restraints, such as belief that birth control is a sin and against the teachings of the religion
c. Lack of information about birth control
d. Lack of money to buy birth-control devices
e. Food allocation

CHART OF POPULATION GROWTH

name
marries
name

produces 4 children

name
marries
name
produces 5 children
name
name
name
name
name

name
marries
name
no children

name
marries
name
produces 6 children
name
name
name
name
name
name

name
marries
name
produces 3 children
name
name
name

(7-14) FACTS OF LIFE

Objective: • To recognize the effect geography plays on human behavior

Grade level: 7–12

Time Required: 45 minutes

Materials Needed: Copies of "Facts of Life" activity sheet, reference books

Description:

1. Break the class in groups of 3.
2. Designate each student as A, B, or C. A is leader.
3. Assign each triad the same natural element. Select one of the following:
   Annual rainfall
   Climate
   Land
   Food supply
4. Pass out copies of the "Facts of Life" worksheet for triads to complete. After allowing 15–20 minutes for each triad to fill in the three sheets, reassign the class into 3 groups. Put all As together, all Bs, all Cs.
5. Have them share the information on their sheets for approximately 15 minutes. They can add to, delete, or change comments.
6. Students should return to their original triads and discuss what they learned from the larger group for approximately 10 minutes. This activity may be repeated with different Facts of Life.

Name ______________________ Date ______________________

FACTS OF LIFE

Facts about ________

1. ______________________
2. ______________________
3. ______________________
4. ______________________
5. ______________________

Effect of ________

1. ______________________
2. ______________________
3. ______________________
4. ______________________
5. ______________________

How ________ may change

1. ______________________
2. ______________________
3. ______________________
4. ______________________
5. ______________________

Prediction of future effects of ________

1. ______________________
2. ______________________
3. ______________________
4. ______________________
5. ______________________

(7-15) I, THE JURY

Objective: • To provide a safe framework for students to examine their opinions and listen to differing viewpoints

Grade Level: 7–12

Time Required: 30–45 minutes

Materials needed: None

Description:

1. The teacher chooses a situation the students are familiar with that involves a moral geographical dilemma. The teacher presents the story as creatively and dramatically as possible to foster interest.
2. Ask students to register their decision on paper. List 3 reasons for their decision.
3. Pair each student with another who voted the *same* way. The 2 students should compare their reasons and choose the 4 most convincing ones.
4. Pair the 2 alikes who chose yes with 2 alikes who chose no. The group should list 4 reasons that each has. Regardless of viewpoint, the group narrows the list of 4 to the 2 best reasons for both sides from the 4 best reasons on both sides. Have groups of 4 identify values underlying the reason, that is, value of human dignity; group rights; and so on (probe for human values).
5. Bring group together and record values on chalkboard as students call out theirs. Classify the values through class discussion.
6. Ask students to rank the values (individually and privately—do not share).
7. Now have them vote again on the issue and give 3 reasons.
8. Process with the following questions:
   a. How many changed their minds? Why?
   b. How many did not change their minds? Why?
   c. Who did not change but had different reasons than they had originally for their choice?

(7-16) LAND OF OZ

Objective: • To apply geographic knowledge of land forms, climate, and mapping to create an imaginary country

Grade Level: 7–12

Time Required: 2 class periods

Materials Needed: Copies of grids from activity 7-3; references

Description:

1. Pass out grids.
2. Allow students to work singly, in pairs, or in triads.
3. Create the "Land of Oz." Students may rename their country if they choose.
4. After deciding on latitude and longitude, use a grid to show location and political divisions (cities, states, and so on) of your country.
5. Use other grids to show climate, land forms, population density, agriculture, and manufacturing centers.
6. Be sure each map has a title, legend, scale, and compass rose.
7. Display when completed.

(7-17) READ A MAP

Objective: • To accurately interpret the symbols and legend of a map

Grade Level: 7–12

Time Required: 20 minutes

Materials Needed: Copies of "Read a Map" activity sheet

Description:

1. Distribute copies of the activity sheet. Allow 10–15 minutes for the students to complete the answers individually.
2. The activity sheets can be collected and graded or used as review to assess skill levels.

Name ______________________________ Date ______________________________

READ A MAP

Use the map to answer the questions below. Write your answer on the line next to each statement.

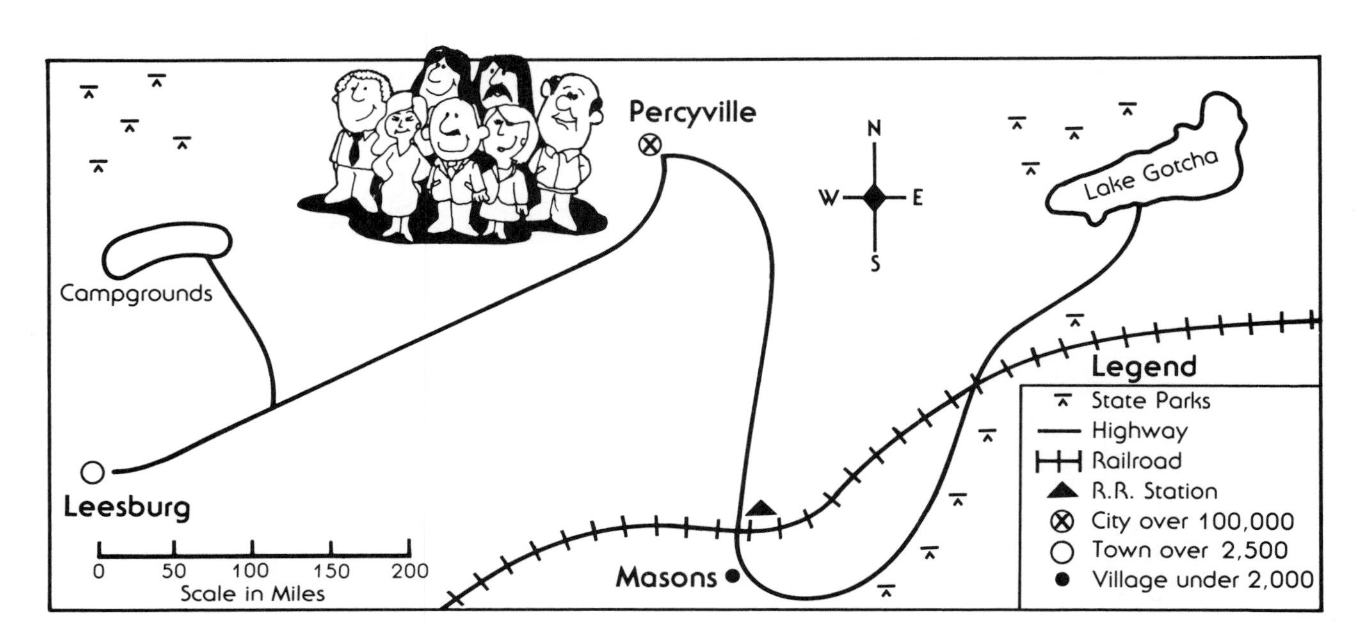

_______ **1.** Leesburg is (a) north (b) south (c) east (d) west of Masons.

_______ **2.** Percyville is a (a) city (b) town (c) village

_______ **3.** The railroad station is at (a) Leesburg (b) Masons (c) Percyville.

_______ **4.** People living in Percyville who want to ride the train must travel (a) 100 (b) 300 (c) 600 miles.

_______ **5.** The population of Masons is (a) around 15,000 (b) less than 2,000 (c) more than 100,000.

_______ **6.** Masons is (a) north (b) west (c) south of Percyville.

_______ **7.** The population of Leesburg classifies it to be a (a) city (b) town (c) village.

_______ **8.** The community closest to the railroad is (a) Masons (b) Percyville (c) Leesburg.

_______ **9.** The community farthest from the campgrounds is (a) Leesburg (b) Percyville (c) Masons.

_______ **10.** There are (a) 3 (b) 9 (c) 14 state parks located on this map.

(7-18) AFRICAN GEOGRAPHY CROSSWORD PUZZLE

Objective: • To review and reinforce facts about the geography of Africa

Grade Level: 7–12

Time Required: One period

Materials Needed: Copies of "African Geography Crossword Puzzle"

Description:

Distribute copies of the crossword puzzle and have the students complete them individually.

Name ____________________ Date ____________________

AFRICAN GEOGRAPHY CROSSWORD PUZZLE

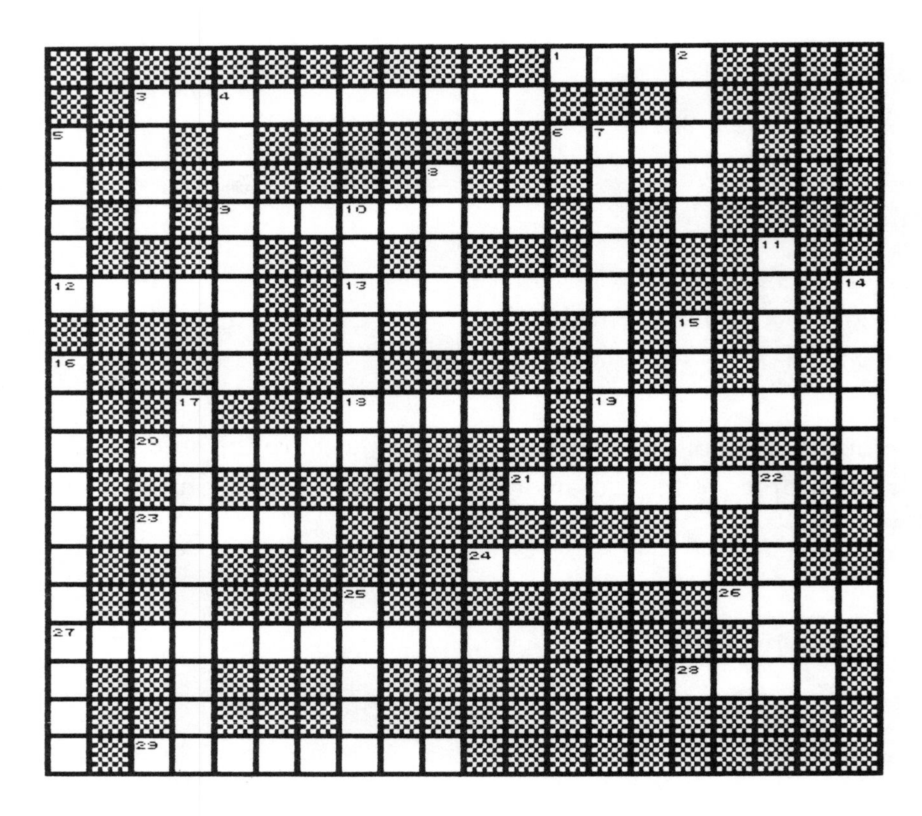

ACROSS

1. World's longest river
3. Maputo is the capital
6. Home of Nairobi
9. Site of Kalahari Desert
12. Desert north of Orange River
13. At Strait of Gibraltar
18. ______ Coast
19. Almost entirely covered by the Sahara
20. Capital is Lusaka
21. Oldest black republic in Africa
23. North Africa desert
26. Cape of Good______
27. South Africa city
28. N'Djamena is located here
29. Grasslands

DOWN

2. Site of pyramids
3. Niger River flows here
4. Formerly Rhodesia
5. Country west of Congo
7. Lake Tana site
8. Large nation in the heart of Africa
10. Easternmost country
11. Niamey is the capital
14. Africa's largest country
15. Its largest city is Lagos
16. Tanzanian volcano
17. Moroccan city
22. Luanda is the capital
25. ______ Dam

(7-19) GEOGRAPHY CROSSWORD PUZZLE

Objective: • To review and reinforce facts about geography

Grade Level: 7–12

Time Required: One period

Materials Needed: Copies of "Geography Crossword Puzzle"

Description:

Distribute copies of the crossword puzzle and have the students complete them individually.

Name ______________________ Date ______________________

GEOGRAPHY CROSSWORD PUZZLE

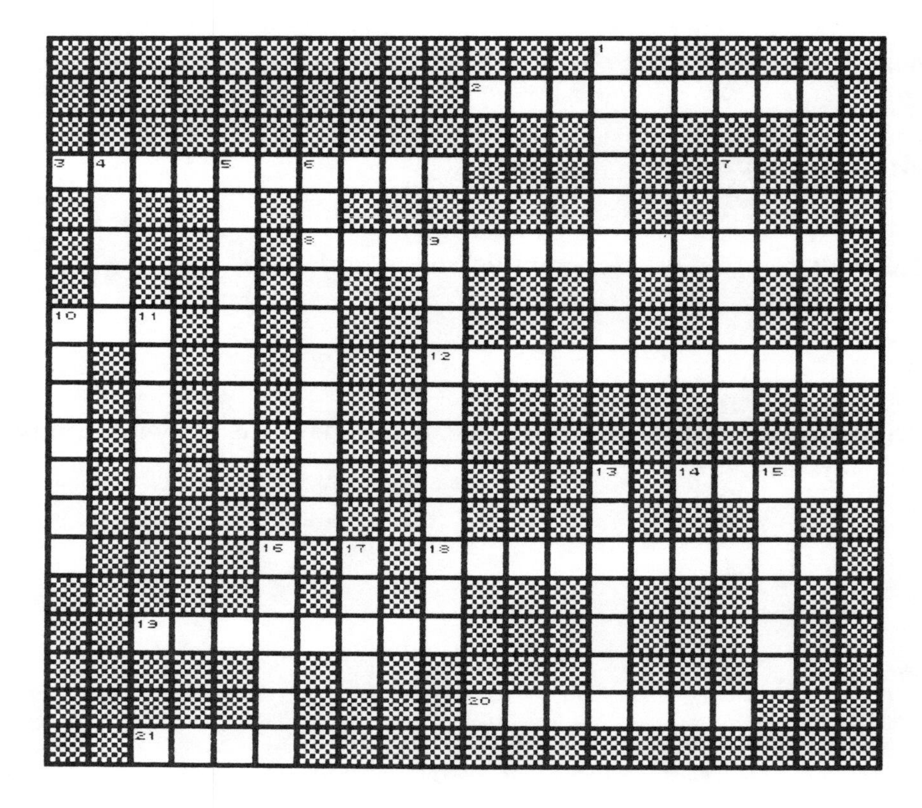

ACROSS

2. Measures atmospheric pressure
3. Inhabitants of a specific area
8. Water vapor that condenses
10. Abbreviation of South Southeast
12. Degree of hotness or coldness
14. Variation in surface level of ocean
18. Permanently frozen subsoil
19. Water vapor in the air
20. Typography of land
21. Compass______: it marks direction on a map

DOWN

1. Angular distance east or west of the prime meridian
4. Fertile spot in the desert
5. Angular distance north or south of the equator
6. Surface features of a region
7. Temperature, precipitation, and wind prevailing in a particular region
9. Art of mapmaking
10. Flat, tressless grassland
11. Third planet from the sun
13. State of atmosphere at a given time and place
15. Region barren of water
16. Vast grass-covered plain, lightly wooded
17. Pattern for making a map

ADDITIONAL PROJECTS

1. *Magazine Pictures.* Have students look through magazines and locate pictures of weather and land features. Students will write a description under each picture showing how the feature operates, helps, harms, or can be adapted.
2. *Bulletin Board.* Students in small groups are assigned a class bulletin board on the following topics:

   Life in the desert
   Volcanoes
   Earthquakes
   Farming the ocean
   Vesuvius
   Tsetse fly
   Tundra
   History of the plow
   Carbonation
   Climate
   Continental Shelf
   Deforestation and reforestation
   Time zones
   Escarpment
   Floor control
   Rain forest
   Ice Age
   International Date Line
   South Pole
   North Pole
   Meteorology
   Monsoon
   Mining
   Ocean currents
   Ozone layer
   Radiation
   Other

3. *Vacations.* Bring in vacation pictures. Look up geographical information on the site. Students may give an oral presentation on that location. Use pictures (slides are great) to tell the class the story of how that particular location developed geographically.
4. *Travel Agent.* Become a travel agent. Choose a country, a region of the United States, or the world. Create a brochure, newspaper advertisement, or TV commercial to "sell" your area to tourists.
5. *Products.* Look through magazines. Create a collage of products in the area you are studying.
6. *Models.* Have students build terrain models, shadow boxes, or dioramas to illustrate geographical principles. They might also create murals or develop a simulation game.
7. Consider the following possibilities: What if . . .

   . . . the earth had no rivers?

   . . . the earth had no deserts?

   . . . the earth had no oceans?

   . . . the earth were flat?

   . . . the earth stopped rotating?

   . . . the earth had no wind?

   . . . the earth rotated faster?

POSSIBLE RESOURCE PERSONS

Archeologist
Cartographer
City planner
Civil engineer
County extension agent
Futurist
Geography professor
Geologist
Geophysicist
Meteorologist
Mineralogist
Soil conservationist
Surveyor
Travel agent

FREE OR INEXPENSIVE MATERIALS

The following materials are sources of interesting information for geography teachers:

1. The Population Reference Bureau (PRB) will provide *Interchange* subscribers with a complimentary copy of the latest issue of *Earthwatch*, the environmental newsletter from the International Planned Parenthood Federation (IPPF). This issue reports the findings of a new study by the Food and Agriculture Organization of the United Nations on land resources and population, entitled "Land Resources for Populations of the Future." The study concluded that many Third World countries will exceed the limits of their land's carrying capacity by the year 2000 if they do not face up to their population/resources equation. It contains a table of population-supporting ratios, and maps of Africa, Asia, Central America (including the Caribbean), South America, and Southwest Asia that illustrate areas unable to support their 1975 populations even if all the cultivated land within them were used to grow nothing but food crops.

Additional copies of the special *Earthwatch* report, No. 13, 1983, are available from the Population Reference Bureau in classroom sets of twenty copies for $1 shipping and handling fee. The PRB address is 2213 M Street, NW, Washington, DC 20037 (202-785-4664).

Inquiries about back issues of *Earthwatch* should be addressed to International Planned Parenthood Federation, 18–20 Lower Regent Street, London SW1Y 4PW, England.

2. *The Global Reporter* is a new quarterly launched by the Anthropology Resource Center (ARC). It is a forum for anthropologists and other social commentators to reflect on the current world scene. The first issue (March 1983) contains stories about Brazil's Carajas project, North American evangelical missionaries in Guatemala, Barbara Chasin and Richard Franke's "Development Watch," and Robert Mathews' "Technology and Society." *The Global Reporter* is $12 per year from the ARC, Room 521, 37 Temple Place, Boston, MA 02111.

3. China in the Classroom is a resource catalog produced by the Center for Teaching About China. The 19-page catalog includes a wide variety of resources, listed according to grade level and subject. It is available at no charge from the Center for Teaching About China, 110 Maryland Avenue, NE, Washington, DC 20002.

4. *Tropical Moist Forests: The Resource, the People and the Thread* is a 67-page Earthscan paperback published in 1983. It describes in detail the loss to the world through the deforestation of rain forest, cloud forest, and swamp forest, and discusses the consequent effects on people of the forest as well as on local and global climates. Copies at $7 each may be had by writing to International Institute for Environment and Development, 10 Percy Street, London W1 PODR, England.

ORGANIZATIONS WORTH WRITING

Adirondack Mountain Club
172 Ridge Street
Glens Falls, NY 12801

Foreign Agriculture Club
Agricultural Research Service
U.S. Department of Agriculture
Room 4933
14th and Independence Avenue, NW
Washington, DC 20250

American Association for the Advancement of Slavic Studies
128 Encina Commons
Stanford University
Stanford, CA 94305

American Friends of the Middle East, Inc.
Suite 100
1717 Massachusetts Avenue, NW
Washington, DC 20036

American Geographical Society
156 Fifth Avenue, Suite 600
New York, NY 10010

Association of American Geographers
1710 16th Street, NW
Washington, DC 20009

Geography Division
Bureau of the Census
US Department of Commerce
14th Street and Constitution Avenue, NW
Washington, DC 20233

Canada Map Office
Department of Energy, Mines, and Resources Canada
615 Booth Street
Ottawa, Canada K1A 0E9

Circulation Manager
Center for Environmental Education
624 9th Street, NW
Washington, DC 20001

Chinese News Service
159 Lexington Avenue
New York, NY 10016

Geography Branch
Data Preparation Division
Bureau of the Census
Jeffersonville, IN 47232

Defense Mapping Agency
Office of Distribution Services/
DOCS
Building 56
US Naval Observatory
Washington, DC 20305

University of Georgia
Department of Social Science
Education
Geography Curriculum Project
Athens, GA 30602

Geographical Association
343 Fulwood Road
Sheffield S10 3BP, England

Hammond, Inc.
Educational Division
515 Valley Street
Maplewood, NJ 07040

International Society for
Educational Information
Kikuei Building No. 7–8
Shintomi 2-chome
Chuo-ku, Tokyo 104, Japan

Keep America Beautiful
99 Park Avenue
New York, NY 10016

National Council for Geographic
Education
Western Illinois University
Macomb, IL 61455

National Geographic Society
Educational Services
Department 86
17th and M Street, NW
Washington, DC 20036

National Wildlife Federation
1412 16th Street, NW
Washington, DC 20036

Rand McNally and Co.
8255 Central Park Avenue
Box 7600
Chicago, IL 60611

Resources for the Future, Inc.
1616 P Street NW
Washington, DC 20036

U.S. Department of Agriculture
Public Information Specialist
1 Southeastern Regional
Information Office

Consumer and Marketing Service,
USDA
1718 Peachtree Street, NW
Room 222
Atlanta, GA 30309

US Department of the Interior
Geological Survey
12201 Sunrise Valley Drive
Reston, VA 22092

Water Pollution Control Federation
Public Relations Department
2626 Pennsylvania Avenue, NW
Washington, DC 20037

World Futures Studies Federation
2424 Maile Way, Office 720
University of Hawaii
Honolulu, HI 96922

ADDITIONAL RESOURCES

Map Sources

Map Information Office U.S. Geological Survey Washington, DC 20242	(has information on all federal maps)
Superintendent of Documents Government Printing Office Washington, DC 20402	(sells federal maps published by small federal agencies, such as Weather Service, Census Bureau, and so on)
Geography and Map Division Library of Congress Washington, DC 20540	(has a reference service for its maps and sells reproductions and bibliographies)
Publications and Sales Branch National Archives and Records Service General Services Administration Washington, DC 20409	(sells photo reproduction of maps of all types plus special lists and inventories)
Distribution Division, C44 Coast and Geodetic Survey Rockville, MD 20852	(sells aeronautical and related charts and maps, mainly of foreign areas)
Commanding Officer Army Map Service ATTN: 16230 Washington, DC 20315	(sells topographic and military maps of foreign areas and strategic U.S. areas)
Bureau of the Census U.S. Department of Commerce Washington, DC 20233	(sells census maps)
Coast and Geodetic Survey Environmental Science Service Administration Rockville, MD 20852	(sells nautical and aeronautical charts of the United States and its possessions)
Forest Service U.S. Department of Agriculture Washington, DC 20250	(sells all types of maps dealing with national forests and wilderness areas)

Atlases—check for most recent edition since atlases are revised and updated frequently

Classroom Atlas—Rand McNally and Co., Chicago

Man's Domain—A Thematic Atlas of the World, McGraw-Hill Book Co., New York.

Oxford Home Atlas of the World. University Press, London and New York.

Goode's World Atlas. Rand McNally and Co., Chicago.

DATA SOURCES

American Geographical Society, Library. *Research Catalog*. 15 volumes and map supplement; G. K. Hall, Boston.

British government publications may be obtained from the sales office of Her Majesty's Stationery York House, Kingsway, London, W.C.2
(A monthly catalogue is available by subscription. H.M.S.O. also issues a series of section catalogs listing the publications of various government departments. Copies are free.)

Canada Today. Statistics of Canada, Information Canada Ottawa. Published annually.

Economic surveys of many countries may be had free by writing the following:
Barclay's Bank D.C.O. Ltd.
54 Lombard Street
London E.C.3, England

Harris, Chauncey. *Bibliographies and References for Research in Geography*, University of Chicago.

Index, *National Geographic*. National Geographic Society, Washington, DC

Statesman's Yearbook. St. Martin's Press, New York. Published annually since 1864.

United Nations Statistical Office, Department of Economic and Social Affairs, *Demographic Yearbook and Statistical Yearbook*, United Nations, New York. Published annually since 1948.

United Nations World Health Organization. *Annual Epidemiological and Vital Statistics*. United Nations, Geneva, Switzerland. Published annually since 1948.

Bureau of the Census, United States Department of Commerce. *Statistical Abstract of the United States*. Government Printing Office, Washington, DC. Published annually since 1878.

World Almanac. Newspaper Enterprise Association, New York. Published annually since 1868.

Games	Approx. Cost	Publisher
Population	$10.00	Urban Systems 1033 Massachusetts Avenue Cambridge, MA 02138
Environmental Planning	$12.60	Nova Scientific Corp. 111 Tucker Street P.O. Box 500 Burlington, NC 27215
The Dead River	$15.00	Nova Scientific Corp.
Ecology	$10.00	Urban Systems

Extinction	$12.00	Sinauer 20 Second Street Stamford, CT 06905

Additional sources of game ideas and materials:

Brain Teaser Games	Crestline Manufacturing Co. 1502 Santa Fe Street Santa Ana, CA
Simulation Games for the Social Studies Classroom	Foreign Policy Association 345 East 46th Street New York, NY 10017
	Warren Educational Supplies 980 West San Bernadino Road Corina, CA 91722

Appendix A

VISUAL MEDIA DISTRIBUTORS

ABC Video Enterprises, Inc.
American Broadcasting Co., Inc.
1330 Avenue of the Americas
New York, NY 10019

Association Films, Inc.
Sears Consumer Information
512 Burlington Avenue
LaGrange, IL 60525

Association-Sterling Films, Inc.
241 East 34th Street
New York, NY 10016

Carousel Films, Inc.
241 East 34th Street
New York, NY 10016

Churchill Films
662 North Robertson Boulevard
Los Angeles, CA 90069

Columbia Broadcasting System (CBS-TV)
4024 Radford Avenue
Studio City, CA 91604

Contemporary Films, McGraw-Hill
330 West 42nd Street
New York, NY 10036

Cornell University
Department of Communication Arts
Robert Hall
Ithaca, NY 14850

Coronet Films and Video
108 Wilmot Road
Deerfield, IL 60015

Eastman Kodak Company
Dept. 454
343 State Street
Rochester, NY 14651

Encyclopaedia Britannica Educational Corporation
425 N. Michigan Avenue
Chicago, IL 60611

Lifelong Learning
University of California Extension Media Center
2223 Fulton Street
Berkeley, CA 94720

Films Incorporated
Rental Library
8124 North Central Park Avenue
Skokie, IL 60076

Human Relations Media
175 Tompkins Avenue
Pleasantville, NY 10570

Indiana University Film Rental Order
Audio-Visual Center
Bloomington, IN 47405-5901

International Film Bureau
332 South Michigan Avenue
Chicago, IL 60604

McGraw-Hill Films
330 West 42nd Street
New York, NY 10036

Media Guild
11526 Sorrento Valley Road
Solano Beach, CA 92075

Media Library
C-5 Seashore Hall
University of Iowa
Iowa City, IA 52242

Modern Talking Picture Service, Inc.
5000 Park Street North
St. Petersburg, FL 33709

National Audio-Visual Center
Sales Branch
Eighth Street and Pennsylvania Avenue
Washington, DC 20409

Film Distribution Supervisor
Ohio State University
Department of Photography & Cinema
156 West 19th Avenue
Columbus, OH 43210

Pennsylvania State University
Audio-Visual Aids Library
University Park, PA 16802

Sunburst Communications
Room G2
39 Washington Avenue
Pleasantville, NY 10570-9971

Textfilm Department
McGraw-Hill Book Co.
330 West 42nd Street
New York, NY 10036

Time and Life Films
43 West 16th Street
New York, NY 10011

University of Southern California
Film and Video Distribution Center
School of Cinema–Television
University Park—MC 2212
Los Angeles, CA 90089-2212

Appendix B

FOREIGN EMBASSIES AND LEGATIONS

Embassy of Afghanistan
2001 24th, NW
Washington, DC 20008

Embassy of the Democratic and Popular Republic of Algeria
2118 Kalorama Road, NW
Washington, DC 20008

Embassy of the Argentine Republic
1600 New Hampshire Avenue, NW
Washington, DC 20009

Embassy of Australia
1601 Massachusetts Avenue, NW
Washington, DC 20036

Embassy of Austria
2343 Massachusetts Avenue, NW
Washington, DC 20008

Embassy of the Commonwealth of the Bahamas
Suite 865
600 New Hampshire Avenue, NW
Washington, DC 20037

Embassy of Bangladesh
2201 Wisconsin Avenue, NW
Washington, DC 20007

Embassy of Barbados
2144 Wyoming Avenue, NW
Washington, DC 20008

Embassy of Belgium
3330 Garfield Street, NW
Washington, DC 20008

Embassy of Bolivia
3014 Massachusetts Avenue, NW
Washington, DC 20008

Embassy of the Republic of Botswana
4301 Connecticut Avenue, NW
Washington, DC 20008

Brazilian Embassy
3006 Massachusetts Avenue, NW
Washington, DC 20008

Bulgarian Embassy
1621 22nd Street, NW
Washington, DC 20008

Embassy of the Socialist Republic of the Union of Burma
2300 S Street, NW
Washington, DC 20008

Burundi Embassy
2233 Wisconsin Avenue, NW
Washington, DC 20007

Embassy of the United Republic of Cameroon
2349 Massachusetts Avenue, NW
Washington, DC 20008

Embassy of Canada
1746 Massachusetts Avenue, NW
Washington, DC 20036

Embassy of the Central African Republic
1618 22nd Street, NW
Washington, DC 20008

Embassy of the Republic of Chad
2002 R Street, NW
Washington, DC 20009

Embassy of Chile
1732 Massachusetts Avenue, NW
Washington, DC 20036

Chinese Embassy
Coordination Council for North American Affairs
4301 Connecticut Avenue, NW
Washington, DC 20008

Embassy of Colombia
2118 Leroy Place, NW
Washington, DC 20008

Embassy of Costa Rica
2112 S Street, NW
Washington, DC 20008

Embassy of Cyprus
2211 R Street, NW
Washington, DC 20008

Embassy of the Czechoslovak Socialist Republic
3900 Linnean Avenue, NW
Washington, DC 20008

Embassy of Denmark
3200 Whitehaven Street, NW
Washington, DC 20008

Embassy of the Dominican Republic
1715 22nd Street, NW
Washington, DC 20008

Embassy of Ecuador
2535 15th Street, NW
Washington, DC 20009

Embassy of Egypt
2310 Decatur Place, NW
Washington, DC 20008

Embassy of El Salvador
2308 California Street, NW
Washington, DC 20008

Embassy of Ethiopia
2134 Kalorama Road, NW
Washington, DC 20008

Embassy of Finland
Chancery
3216 North Mexico Avenue, NW
Washington, DC 20016

Embassy of France
4101 Reservoir Road, NW
Washington, DC 20008

Embassy of the Republic of Gabon
2034 20th Street, NW
Washington, DC 20009

Embassy of the German Democratic Republic
1717 Massachusetts Avenue, NW
Washington, DC 20036

Embassy of the Federal Republic of Germany
4645 Reservoir Road, NW
Washington, DC 20007

Embassy of Ghana
2460 16th Street, NW
Washington, DC 20009

British Embassy
3100 Massachusetts Avenue, NW
Washington, DC 20008

Embassy of Greece
2221 Massachusetts Avenue, NW
Washington, DC 20008

Embassy of Grenada
1701 New Hampshire Avenue, NW
Washington, DC 20009

Embassy of Guatemala
2220 R Street, NW
Washington, DC 20008

Embassy of the Republic of Guinea
2112 Leroy Place, NW
Washington, DC 20008

Embassy of Guyana
2490 Tracy Place, NW
Washington, DC 20008

Haitian Embassy
2311 Massachusetts Avenue, NW
Washington, DC 20008

Embassy of Honduras
4301 Connecticut Avenue, NW
Washington, DC 20008

Embassy of Hungary
3910 Shoemaker Street, NW
Washington, DC 20008

Embassy of Iceland
2022 Connecticut Avenue, NW
Washington, DC 20008

Embassy of India
2107 Massachusetts Avenue, NW
Washington, DC 20008

Embassy of the Republic of Indonesia
2020 Massachusetts Avenue, NW
Washington, DC 20036

Embassy of Ireland
2234 Massachusetts Avenue, NW
Washington, DC 20008

Embassy of Israel
3514 International Drive, NW
Washington, DC 20008

Embassy of Italy
1601 Fuller Street, NW
Washington, DC 20009

Embassy of the Republic of Ivory Coast
2424 Massachusetts Avenue, NW
Washington, DC 20008

Embassy of Jamaica
1850 K Street, NW
Washington, DC 20006

Embassy of Japan
2520 Massachusetts Avenue, NW
Washington, DC 20008

Embassy of Jordan
3504 International Drive, NW
Washington, DC 20008

Embassy of Kenya
2249 R Street, NW
Washington, DC 20008

Embassy of Korea
2320 Massachusetts Avenue, NW
Washington, DC 20008

Embassy of the State of Kuwait
3500 International Drive, NW
Washington, DC 20008

Embassy of Lao People's Democratic Republic
2222 S Street, NW
Washington, DC 20008

Embassy of Latvia
4325 17th Street, NW
Washington, DC 20011

Embassy of Lebanon
2560 28th Street, NW
Washington, DC 20008

Embassy of the Kingdom of Lesotho
Caravel Building
Suite 300
1601 Connecticut Avenue, NW
Washington, DC 20009

Embassy of the Republic of Liberia
5201 16th Street, NW
Washington, DC 20011

Legation of Lithuania
2622 16th Street, NW
Washington, DC 20009

Embassy of Luxembourg
2200 Massachusetts Avenue, NW
Washington, DC 20008

Embassy of Madagascar
2374 Massachusetts Avenue, NW
Washington, DC 20008

Malawi Embassy
1400 20th Street, NW
Washington, DC 20036

Embassy of Malaysia
2401 Massachusetts Avenue, NW
Washington, DC 20008

Embassy of the Republic of Mali
3130 R Street, NW
Washington, DC 20008

Embassy of Malta
2017 Connecticut Avenue, NW
Washington, DC 20008

Embassy of the Islamic Republic of Mauritania
2129 Leroy Place, NW
Washington, DC 20008

Embassy of Mauritius
Suite 134
4301 Connecticut Avenue, NW
Washington, DC 20008

Embassy of Mexico
2829 16th Street, NW
Washington, DC 20009

Embassy of Morocco
1601 21st Street, NW
Washington, DC 20009

Royal Nepalese Embassy
2131 Leroy Place, NW
Washington, DC 20008

Embassy of the Netherlands
4200 Linnean Avenue, NW
Washington, DC 20008

Embassy of New Zealand
37 Observatory Circle, NW
Washington, DC 20008

Embassy of Nicaragua
1627 New Hampshire Avenue, NW
Washington, DC 20009

Embassy of the Republic of Niger
2204 R Street, NW
Washington, DC 20008

Embassy of Nigeria
2201 M Street, NW
Washington, DC 20037

Embassy of Norway
2720 34th Street, NW
Washington, DC 20008

Embassy of the Sultanate of Oman
2342 Massachusetts Avenue, NW
Washington, DC 20008

Embassy of Pakistan
2315 Massachusetts Avenue, NW
Washington, DC 20008

Embassy of Panama
2862 McGill Terrace, NW
Washington, DC 20008

Embassy of Paraguay
2400 Massachusetts Avenue, NW
Washington, DC 20008

Embassy of Peru
1700 Massachusetts Avenue, NW
Washington, DC 20036

Embassy of the Philippines
1617 Massachusetts Avenue, NW
Washington, DC 20036

Embassy of the Polish People's Republic
2640 16th Street, NW
Washington, DC 20009

Embassy of Portugal
2125 Kalorama Road, NW
Washington, DC 20008

Embassy of Qatar
600 New Hampshire Avenue, NW
Washington, DC 20037

Embassy of the Socialist Republic of Romania
1607 23rd Street, NW
Washington, DC 20008

Embassy of the Republic of Rwanda
1714 New Hampshire Avenue, NW
Washington, DC 20009

Embassy of Saudi Arabia
1520 18th Street, NW
Washington, DC 20036

Embassy of the Republic of Senegal
2112 Wyoming Avenue, NW
Washington, DC 20008

Embassy of Sierra Leone
1701 19th Street, NW
Washington, DC 20009

Embassy of the Republic of Singapore
1824 R Street, NW
Washington, DC 20009

Embassy of the Somali Democratic Republic
Suite 710
600 New Hampshire Avenue, NW
Washington, DC 20037

Embassy of the Republic of South Africa
3051 Massachusetts Avenue, NW
Washington, DC 20008

Embassy of Spain
2700 15th Street, NW
Washington, DC 20009

Embassy of Sri Lanka
2148 Wyoming Avenue, NW
Washington, DC 20008

Embassy of the Kingdom of Swaziland
4301 Connecticut Avenue, NW
Washington, DC 20008

Royal Swedish Embassy
600 New Hampshire Avenue, NW
Washington, DC 20037

Embassy of Switzerland
2900 Cathedral Avenue, NW
Washington, DC 20008

Embassy of Syria
2215 Wyoming Avenue, NW
Washington, DC 20008

Embassy of Tanzania
2139 R Street, NW
Washington, DC 20008

Royal Thai Embassy
2300 Kalorama Road, NW
Washington, DC 20008

Embassy of the Republic of Togo
2208 Massachusetts Avenue, NW
Washington, DC 20008

Embassy of Trinidad and Tobago
1708 Massachusetts Avenue, NW
Washington, DC 20036

Embassy of Tunisia
2408 Massachusetts Avenue, NW
Washington, DC 20008

Embassy of the Republic of Turkey
1606 23rd Street, NW
Washington, DC 20008

Embassy of the Republic of Uganda
5909 16th Street, NW
Washington, DC 20011

Embassy of the U.S.S.R.
1825 Phelps Place, NW
Washington, DC 20008

Embassy of the United Arab Emirates
Suite 740
600 New Hampshire Avenue, NW
Washington, DC 20037

Embassy of the Republic of Upper Volta
2340 Massachusetts Avenue, NW
Washington, DC 20008

Embassy of Uruguay
1918 F Street, NW
Washington, DC 20006

Embassy of Venezuela
2409 California Street, NW
Washington, DC 20008

Embassy of the Yemen Arab Republic
Suite 860
600 New Hampshire Avenue, NW
Washington, DC 20037

Embassy of the Socialist Federal Republic of Yugoslavia
2410 California Street, NW
Washington, DC 20008

Embassy of the Republic of Zaire
1800 New Hampshire Avenue, NW
Washington, DC 20009

Embassy of the Republic of Zambia
2419 Massachusetts Avenue, NW
Washington, DC 20008

Appendix C

Answer Keys

(1-5) PRESIDENTS CROSSWORD PUZZLE

"Presidents Crossword Puzzle"

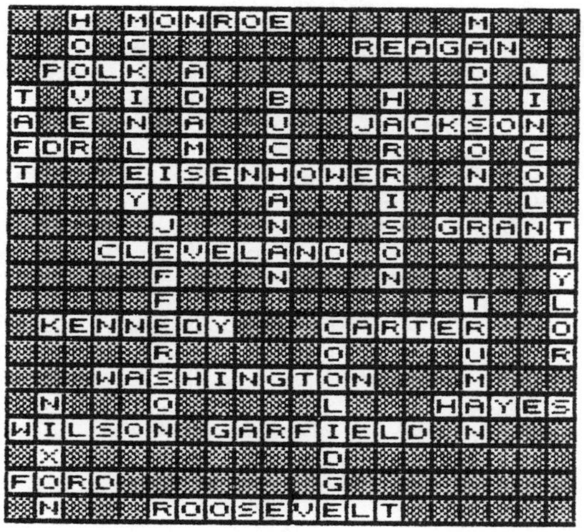

(1-14) IMMIGRATION: GRAPH INTERPRETATION

"Immigration: 1820 to 1984"

1. 1900–10
2. 1820–30, 1830–40, 1840–50, 1930–40, 1940–50
3. 4,000,000
4. 1970s
5. 3
6. 1850–60
7. 1970s

(2-3) IN THE BEGINNING—THERE WAS THE WORLD

"In the Beginning Wordsearch"

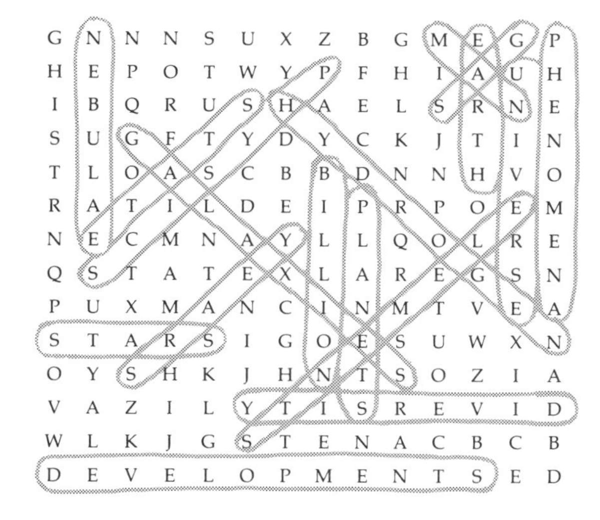

(2-7) RENAISSANCE OF LITERATURE

"Renaissance of Literature"

```
          R E B I R T H
1.            C E R V A N T E S
2.          J O N S O N
3.            D A N T E
4.      C A L V I N
5.      S P E N S E R
6.    S H A K E S P E A R E
7.  M A C H I A V E L L I
8.      B A C O N
9.      C H A U C E R
10.           P E T R A R C H
```

(2-8) PROGRAM THE COMPUTER

"'Pretend' Computer Cards"

1. The Ice Age ends. (10,000 years ago)
2. The plow is invented. (3300 B.C.)
3. Records of sales transactions are first written. (3000 B.C.)
4. The pyramids are built. (2000 B.C.)
5. Hammurabi of Babylon draws up a code of law. (1700 B.C.)
6. The Cretans build a civilization that includes such luxuries as bathrooms with copper plumbing, majestic stairways, distinctive murals, pottery, and jewelry. (1700 B.C.)
7. The Greeks capture Troy with the use of a wooden horse. (1184 B.C.)
8. The Phoenicians sail the Mediterranean. (1100–750 B.C.)
9. King Solomon, the Hebrew king, builds a temple. (950 B.C.)
10. The Greeks begin the Olympic games. (336 B.C.)
11. Rome is founded by the twins, Romulus and Remus, who according to legend have been raised by a she-wolf. (753 B.C.)
12. Nebuchadnezzar II of Babylon builds a beautiful hanging garden to remind his homesick wife of her homeland. (597 B.C.)
13. A great light illuminates the sky when Gautama Buddha is born. The ill become well. (493 B.C.)
14. Athenians practice the world's first democracy. (400 B.C.)
15. Hannibal, the Carthagenian, marches over the Alps with elephants to surprise the Italians in battle. (218 B.C.)
16. Carthage is completely destroyed, and salt is spread over the ruins. (146 B.C.)

(2-15) EARLY CIVILIZATION CROSSWORD PUZZLE

"Early Civilization Crossword Puzzle"

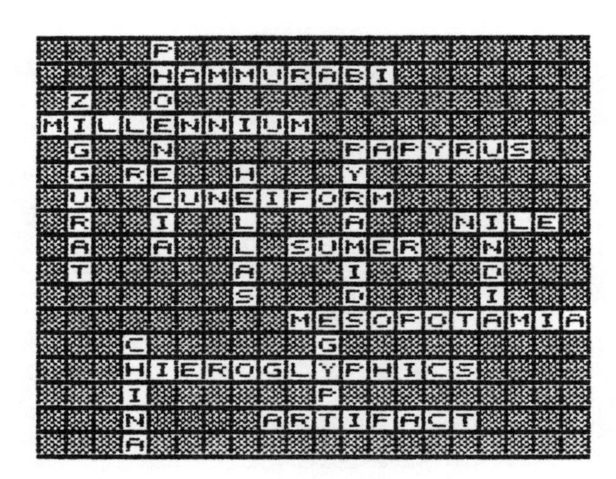

(3-1) THE JUDICIAL SYSTEM

"Judicial System"

1. Supreme Court
2. Military courts
   U.S. Court of Military Appeals
3. Highest state court
4. One of twelve U.S. courts of appeals
5. Courts of the District of Columbia
6. Supreme Court

7. Territorial courts
8. U.S. Court of Appeals
   Circuit Court of Appeals
9. U.S. Court of Appeals
   U.S. Court of Military Appeals
10. U.S. Court of International Trade

(3-11) CONSTITUTION CROSSWORD PUZZLE

"Constitution Crossword Puzzle"

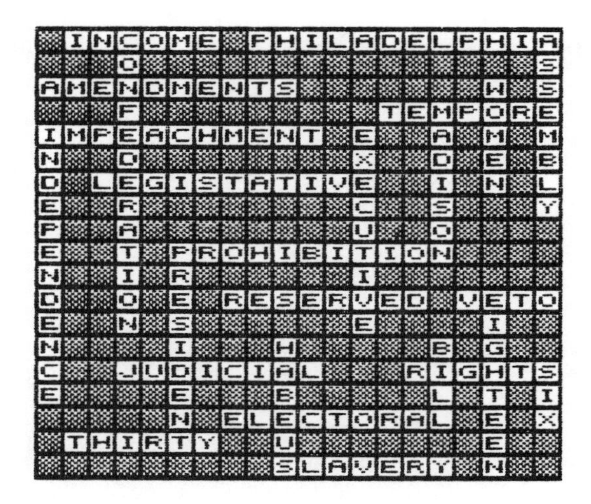

(3-13) MISTER PRESIDENT

"Mister President"

1. Theodore Roosevelt
2. Ronald Reagan
3. 15
4. 16
5. Andrew Johnson
6. Richard Nixon
7. Grover Cleveland
8. Franklin D. Roosevelt
9. Franklin D. Roosevelt
10. Millard Fillmore

(3-15) IMMIGRATION

"Immigration"

1. Europe
2. 230 million
3. Asia
4. Approximately 1¼ million
5. 1921–30
6. The Depression; the aftermath of World War I
7. 1931–40
8. 1½ million
9. 1.9 million
10. The Vietnam War and other Communist take-overs

(3-17) POPULATION

"Population Questions"

1. 1960
2. 1980
3. 20.3 million
4. The U.S. withdrawal from Vietnam and the refugees from Communist takeovers
5. 12.5 percent
6. 179.3 million
7. 10–19
8. Under 5
9. 60 and over
10. 11.1 percent

(3-21) THE CONSTITUTION QUIZ

"The Constitution Quiz"

1. False (In the Hearst survey, 64 percent believed that the Constitution did establish English as the national language.)
2. False (57 percent of the survey respondents

thought it was constitutional for schools to require students to pledge allegiance to the flag.)

3. True (54 percent answered this correctly.)
4. False (The Declaration of Independence, not the Constitution, did so. 26 percent of those surveyed answered incorrectly.)
5. False (50 percent believed that schools were permitted to require moments of silence for prayer.)
6. True (92 percent knew this one.)
7. False (49 percent believed this to be true.)
8. True (79 percent agreed.)
9. True (80 percent answered correctly.)
10. True (68 percent of those surveyed did not realize that states could legalize marijuana within their borders.)
11. Miranda (vs. Arizona) Decision (Only 45 percent could identify the decision.)
12. Bill of Rights (Only 41 percent got this one.)
13. (As of this book's publication) William Rehnquist (Warren Burger was named by 29 percent; Earl Warren, who retired in 1969, was chosen by 7 percent.)

(6-20) FREUDIAN PSYCHOLOGY CROSSWORD PUZZLE

"Freudian Psychology Crossword Puzzle"

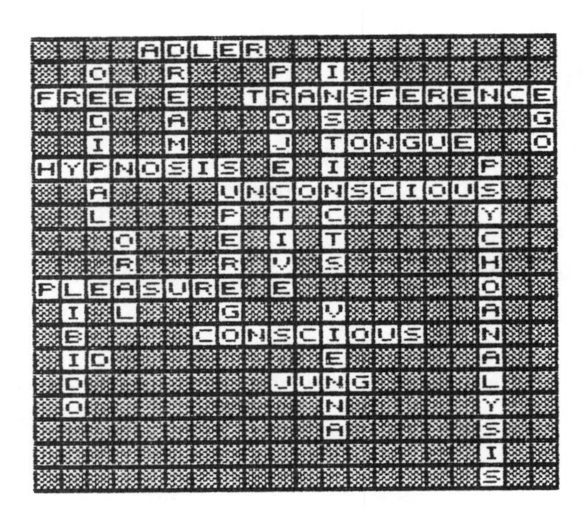

(7-17) READ A MAP

"Read a Map"

1. (d) West of Masons
2. (a) city
3. (b) Masons
4. (b) 300
5. (b) less than 2,000
6. (c) South of Percyville
7. (b) town
8. (a) Masons
9. (c) Masons
10. (c) 14

(7-18) AFRICAN GEOGRAPHY CROSSWORD PUZZLE

"African Geography Crossword Puzzle"

												N	I	L	E				
		M	O	Z	A	M	B	I	Q	U	E				G				
G		A		I								K	E	N	Y	A			
A		L		M					Z				T		P				
B		I		B	O	T	S	W	A	N	A		H		T				
O				A			O		I				I				N		
N	A	M	I	B			M	O	R	O	C	C	O				I		S
				W			A		E				P		N		G		U
K				E			L						I		I		E		D
I			C				I	V	O	R	Y		A	L	G	E	R	I	A
L		Z	A	M	B	I	A								E				N
I			S								L	I	B	E	R	I	A		
M		C	A	I	R	O									I		N		
A			B							S	A	H	A	R	A		G		
N			L				A									H	O	P	E
J	O	H	A	N	N	E	S	B	U	R	G						L		
A			N				W								C	H	A	D	
R			C				A												
O		S	A	V	A	N	N	A	S										

(7-19) GEOGRAPHY CROSSWORD PUZZLE

"Geography Crossword Puzzle"

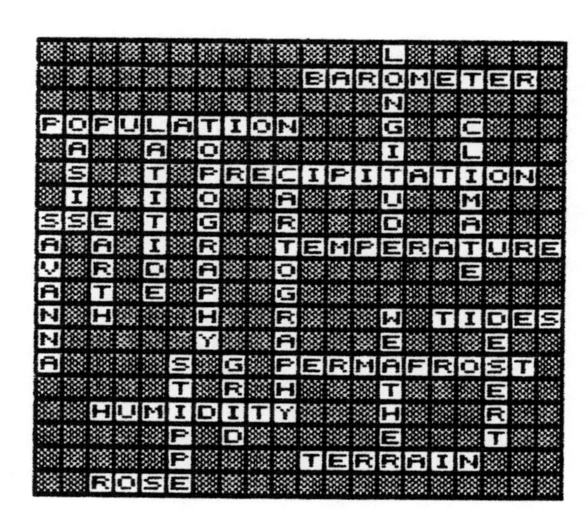